BUSINESS LAW AND PRACTICE

For 2027 exams

AF867180

Benjamin Jones

Series editors: Amy Sixsmith and David Sixsmith

REVISE SQE

First published in 2022 by Fink Publishing Ltd
This edition published in 2026

Impression number 10 9 8 7 6 5 4 3 2 1

British Library Cataloguing in Publication Data
A catalogue record for this book is available from the British Library
ISBN: 9781917183833

This book is also available in various ebook formats.
Ebook ISBN: 9781917183840

Production and typesetting by Westchester Publishing Services (UK)
Cover and text design by BMLD (bmld.uk)
Multiple-choice questions advisor: Mark Thomas
Indexing by Terence Halliday

Revise SQE
Fink Publishing Ltd
E-mail: hello@revise4law.co.uk
www.revise4law.co.uk

Notes from the publisher

1. This book reflects the SQE1 assessment specification (updated April 2026) applicable for assessments from 1 September 2026.

2. While Fink Publishing has made every attempt to ensure that advice on the qualification and its assessment is accurate, the official specification and associated assessment guidance materials are the only authoritative source of information and should always be referred to for definitive guidance. See the SRA website at https://sqe.sra.org.uk. Note that the SRA may amend their assessment guidance (including the contents of the assessment specifications) at any point.

3. Fink Publishing has robust editorial processes to ensure the accuracy of the content in this publication, and every effort is made to ensure this publication is free of errors. We are, however, only human, and occasionally errors do occur. Fink Publishing is not liable for any misunderstandings that arise as a result of errors in this publication, but it is our priority to ensure that the content is accurate. If you spot an error, please do contact us at revise4law.co.uk so we can make sure it is corrected.

Contents

Contributors iv
Introduction to Revise SQE v

Part One: Business law and practice

1 Starting a new business: types of business medium 1

2 Partnerships 18

3 Limited companies: part 1 38

4 Limited companies: part 2 63

5 Financing a business, financial records and accounting requirements 89

6 Termination and insolvency 121

Part Two: Taxation of a business and its stakeholders

7 Trading profits and VAT 144

8 Income tax 160

9 Capital gains tax and inheritance tax 181

10 Corporation tax 206

Index 222

Contributors

THE AUTHOR

Benjamin Jones is a senior lecturer in law at the University of South Wales. He has taught and led on a range of undergraduate, postgraduate and professional law courses for over 12 years and is a fellow of Advance HE. He was winner of the LawCareers.Net 'Law Lecturer of the Year Award' in 2016, and he has taught business law and practice and taxation throughout his teaching career.

SERIES EDITORS

Dr Amy Sixsmith is associate professor in law at the University of Sunderland and a senior fellow of Advance HE.

Dr David Sixsmith is assistant professor in law at Northumbria Law School and a senior fellow of Advance HE.

Introduction to Revise SQE

Welcome to *Revise SQE*, a series of revision guides designed to help you in your preparation for, and achievement in, the Solicitors Qualifying Examination 1 (SQE1) assessment. SQE1 is designed to assess what the Solicitors Regulation Authority (SRA) refer to as 'functioning legal knowledge' (FLK); this is the legal knowledge and competencies required of a newly qualified solicitor in England and Wales. The SRA has chosen single best answer multiple-choice questions (MCQs) to test this knowledge, and *Revise SQE* is here to help.

PREPARING YOURSELF FOR SQE

The SQE is the relatively new route to qualification for aspiring solicitors introduced in September 2021 as one of the final stages towards qualification as a solicitor. The SQE consists of two parts:

SQE1
- **Functioning legal knowledge (FLK)**
  - two x 180 MCQs
  - closed book; assessed by two sittings, over 10 hours in total.

SQE2
- **Practical legal skills**
  - 16 written and oral assessments
  - assesses six practical legal skills, over 14 hours in total.

In addition to the above, any candidate will have to undertake two years' qualifying work experience. More information on the SQE assessments can be found on the SRA's dedicated SQE website; this revision guide series will focus on FLK and preparation for SQE1.

It is important to note that the SQE can be perceived to be a 'harder' set of assessments than the Legal Practice Course (LPC). The reason for this, explained by the SRA, is that the LPC is designed to prepare candidates for 'day one' of their training contract; the SQE, on the other hand, is designed to prepare candidates for 'day one' of being a newly qualified solicitor. Indeed, the SRA has chosen the SQE1 assessment to be 'closed book' (ie without permitting use of any materials) on the basis that a newly qualified solicitor would know all of the information tested, without having to refer to books or other sources.

With that in mind, and a different style of assessments in place, it is understandable that many readers may feel nervous or wary of the SQE. This is especially so given that this style of assessment is likely to be different from what readers will have experienced before. In this *Introduction* and revision guide series, we hope to alleviate some of those concerns with guidance on preparing for the SQE assessment, tips on how to approach single best answer MCQs and expertly written guides to aid in your revision.

What does SQE1 entail?

SQE1 consists of two assessments, containing 180 single best answer MCQs each (360 MCQs in total). The table below breaks down what is featured in each of these assessments.

Assessment	Contents of assessment ('functioning legal knowledge')
FLK assessment 1	• Business law and practice • Dispute resolution • Contract • Tort • The legal system (the legal system of England and Wales and sources of law, constitutional and administrative law and European Union law and legal services)
FLK assessment 2	• Property practice • Wills and the administration of estates • Solicitors' accounts • Land law • Trusts • Criminal law and practice

Please be aware that in addition to the above, ethics and professional conduct will be examined pervasively across the two assessments (ie it could crop up anywhere).

Each substantive topic is allocated a percentage of the assessment paper (eg 'legal services' will form 12–16% of the FLK1 assessment) and is broken down further into 'core principles'. Candidates are advised to read the SQE1 Assessment Specification in full (available on the SQE website). We have also provided a *Revise SQE checklist* to help you in your preparation and revision for SQE1 (see below).

HOW DO I PREPARE FOR SQE1?

Given the vastly different nature of SQE1 compared to anything you may have done previously, it can be quite daunting to consider how you could possibly prepare for 360 single best answer MCQs, spanning 11 different substantive topics (especially given that it is 'closed book'). The *Revise SQE FAQ* below, however, will set you off on the right path to success.

Revise SQE FAQ

Question	Answer
1. Where do I start?	We would advise that you begin by reviewing the assessment specification for SQE1. You need to identify what subject matter can be assessed under each substantive topic. For each topic, you should honestly ask yourself whether you would be prepared to answer an MCQ on that topic in SQE1. We have helped you in this process by providing a *Revise SQE checklist* on our website (revise4law.co.uk) that allows you to read the subject matter of each topic and identify where you consider your knowledge to be at any given time. We have also helpfully cross-referenced each topic to a chapter and page of our *Revise SQE* revision guides.
2. Do I need to know legal authorities, such as case law?	In the majority of circumstances, candidates are not required to know or use legal authorities. This includes statutory provisions, case law or procedural rules. Of course, candidates will need to be aware of legal principles deriving from common law and statute. There may be occasions, however, where the assessment specification does identify a legal authority (such as *Rylands v Fletcher* in tort law). In this case, candidates will be required to know the name of that case, the principles of that case and how to apply that case to the facts of an MCQ. These circumstances are clearly highlighted in the assessment specification and candidates are advised to ensure they engage with those legal authorities in full. In each of our texts in the *Revise SQE* series, we detail clearly which authorities are required for that subject. Any authorities provided in addition are designed to assist in your revision by acting as an aide-mémoire.
3. Do I need to know the history behind a certain area of law?	While understanding the history and development of a certain area of law is beneficial, there is no requirement for you to know or prepare for any questions relating to the development of the law

Revise SQE FAQ (continued)

Question	Answer
	(eg in criminal law, candidates will not need to be aware of the development from objective to subjective recklessness). SQE1 will be testing a candidate's knowledge of the law as it stands four calendar months prior to the date of the first assessment in an assessment window. The SRA on the SQE website has helpfully provided the exact cut off date for each assessment in the cycle; it is worth checking this when you are preparing for your assessment.
4. Do I need to be aware of academic opinion or proposed reforms to the law?	Candidates preparing for SQE1 do not need to focus on critical evaluation of the law, or proposed reforms to the law either.
5. How do I prepare for single best answer MCQs?	See our separate *Revise SQE* guide on preparing for single best answer MCQs below.

Where does *Revise SQE* come into it?

The *Revise SQE* series of revision guides is designed to aid your revision and consolidate your understanding; the series is not designed to replace your substantive learning of the SQE1 topics. We hope that this series will provide clarity as to assessment focus, useful tips for sitting SQE1 and act as a general revision aid.

There are also materials on our website to help you prepare and revise for the SQE1, such as a *Revise SQE checklist*. This *checklist* is designed to help you identify which substantive topics you feel confident about heading into the exam - see below for an example.

Revise SQE checklist

Business Law and Practice

SQE content	Corresponding chapter	*Revise SQE checklist*		
Business organisations and their characteristics	Chapter 1, Pages 2–13	I do not know this subject and I am not ready for SQE1 ☐	I partially know this subject, but I am not ready for SQE1 ☐	I know this subject and I am ready for SQE1 ☐

Business Law and Practice (continued)

SQE content	Corresponding chapter	*Revise SQE checklist*		
Legal personality and limited liability	Chapter 1, Pages 7–10	I do not know this subject and I am not ready for SQE1 ☐	I partially know this subject, but I am not ready for SQE1 ☐	I know this subject and I am ready for SQE1 ☐
Procedures and documentation required to incorporate/form a business	Chapter 3, Pages 39–47	I do not know this subject and I am not ready for SQE1 ☐	I partially know this subject, but I am not ready for SQE1 ☐	I know this subject and I am ready for SQE1 ☐

PREPARING FOR SINGLE BEST ANSWER MCQS

As discussed above, SQE1 will be a challenging assessment for all candidates. This is partly due to the quantity of information a candidate must be aware of in two separate sittings. In addition, however, an extra complexity is added due to the nature of the assessment itself: MCQs.

The SRA has identified that MCQs are the most appropriate way to test a candidate's knowledge and understanding of fundamental legal principles. While this may be the case, it is likely that many candidates have little, if any, experience of MCQs as part of their previous study. Even if a candidate does have experience of MCQs, SQE1 will feature a special form of MCQs known as 'single best answer' questions.

What are single best answer MCQs and what do they look like?

Single best answer MCQs are a specialised form of question, used extensively in other fields such as in training medical professionals. The idea behind single best answer MCQs is that the multitude of options available to a candidate may each bear merit, sharing commonalities and correct statements of law or principle, but only one option is absolutely correct (in the sense that it is the 'best' answer). In this regard, single best answer MCQs are different from traditional MCQs.

A traditional MCQ will feature answers that are implausible in the sense that the distractors are 'obviously wrong'. Indeed, distractors in a traditional MCQ are often very dissimilar, resulting in a candidate being able to spot answers that are clearly wrong with greater ease.

In a well-constructed single best answer MCQ, on the other hand, each option should look equally attractive given their similarities and subtle differences. The skill of the candidate will be identifying which, out of the options provided, is the single best answer. This requires a much greater level of engagement with the question than a traditional MCQ would require; candidates must take the time to read the questions carefully in the exam.

How are single best answer MCQs structured?

For SQE1, single best answer MCQs will be structured as follows:

A woman is charged with battery, having thrown a rock towards another person intending to scare them. The rock hits the person in the head, causing no injury. The woman claims that she never intended that the rock hit the person, but the prosecution allege that the woman was reckless as to whether the rock would hit the other person.

The factual scenario. First, the candidate will be provided with a factual scenario that sets the scene for the question to be asked (known as the 'stem').

Which of the following is the most accurate statement regarding the test for recklessness in relation to a battery?

The lead in. Next, the candidate will be provided with the question that they must find the single best answer to.

A. There must have been a risk that force would be applied by the rock, and that the reasonable person would have foreseen that risk and unjustifiably taken it.
B. There must have been a risk that force would be applied by the rock, and that the woman should have foreseen that risk and unjustifiably taken it.
C. There must have been a risk that force would be applied by the rock, and that the woman must have foreseen that risk and unjustifiably taken it.
D. There must have been a risk that force would be applied by the rock, and that both the woman and the reasonable person should have foreseen that risk and unjustifiably taken it.
E. There must have been a risk that force would be applied by the rock, but there is no requirement that the risk be foreseen.

The possible answers. Finally, the candidate will be provided with **five** possible answers. There is only one single best answer that must be chosen. The other answers, known as 'distractors', are not the 'best' answer available.

It will be beneficial to guide you through each aspect of the MCQ to further your understanding of the writing process.

The stem

The stem (ie scenario) will differ according to each MCQ and what it is seeking to test. If the MCQ is seeking simply to test a candidate's basic knowledge of the law, without application, then the stem is likely to be short. Where, however, the MCQ is seeking to have a candidate analyse a factual pattern, and apply it to the options available, the stem will be significantly longer.

In general, however, a stem should be a concise and clear introduction to the issue at hand. A well written stem should contain all material facts relevant to answering the question about to be asked (new facts should not be introduced in the lead in or the distractors). The stem should not be ambiguous or open to interpretation.

The lead in

The lead in will be a short question and can be phrased in a variety of ways. The lead in should provide the candidate with everything they need to answer the question. There should be no ambiguity or double meanings.

The length and nature of the lead in will vary dependent on the type of question being asked. These categories of MCQ are detailed in the table below.

Categories of MCQs	Explanation and example
'Knows' MCQs	To *recall* a specific answer (eg the author of X is Y)
'Shows How' MCQs	To *analyse* a fact pattern and *apply* (eg the application of X in this case is Y)
'Knows How' MCQs	To *know* the answer, and *show* the reason *why* (eg the purpose of X is Y because ...)

Most commonly, a lead in may be phrased as:
- Which of the following statements best describes ...?
- Which of the following statements best summarises ...?
- Which of the following best explains ...?

A lead in will not, however, be phrased as:
- Which of the following is true?
- What is the rule for X?
- Which one of the following is not correct?

The options

You will be provided with five possible answers and only one is correct (whether that be outright correct, or the single best).

The options will not ask a candidate to identify multiple options as being correct (eg 'A, C and D are correct; B and E are wrong'). Nor will the options feature an 'all of the above' option.

A well written MCQ will avoid vague language in the options. Words such as 'rarely', 'usually' etc should be avoided as they present too much ambiguity. On the other hand, absolute words such as 'only', 'always' and 'never' should equally be avoided because they are often obvious distractors (there rarely being a circumstance in English and Welsh law where the legal position is absolute without exception).

If written well, each option should be plausible (meaning that some candidates would choose it). Plausibility can come from drawing on faulty reasoning and common misconceptions. It may be the case that some options share identical wording save for one word (eg a change from 'may' to 'must'). You therefore need to pay close attention to the wording of the options.

To achieve that, all options will be of a fairly equal length to ensure that they are consistent with one another. It is often said that the correct answer is likely to be the longest; so the writers of the MCQs will have that in mind.

In addition, to ensure plausibility, each option is either likely to be a variation of the other, or each option will be entirely different to the others. MCQ drafters will often rely on the rule of 'Three and Two'. The idea behind this rule is that three options will be fairly similar to each other (eg starting with 'Yes'), whilst the remaining two answers will be equally similar to each other (eg starting with 'No'). If you know the answer is definitely 'Yes', that therefore removes the 'No' options immediately. If the MCQ has not adopted the rule of Three and Two, it is likely that you will be able to pick out the 'obvious' distractor.

Now that you know what the MCQs will look like on SQE1, let us talk about how you may go about tackling an MCQ.

How do I tackle single best answer MCQs?

No exact art exists in terms of answering single best answer MCQs; your success depends on your subject knowledge and understanding of how that subject knowledge can be applied. Despite this, there are tips and tricks that may be helpful for you to consider when confronted with a single best answer MCQ.

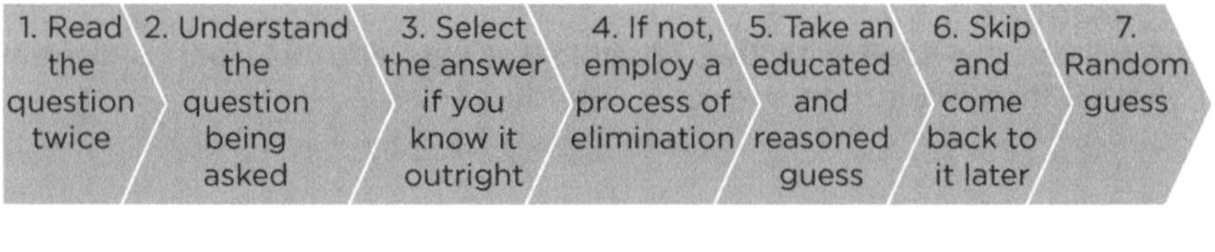

These tips and tricks are essential for preparing you to sit the SQE1 assessment. Each session will involve 90 MCQs, to be answered over 2 hours, 33 minutes. Answering 90 MCQs in that timescale allows *1 minute, 42 seconds per question*, under exam conditions. Of course, some questions will take more or less time to answer than others.

Please take a moment to think about that: on average, within 1 minute and 42 seconds you will have to:

- read the MCQ, including the various answers
- distil from that MCQ what the question is assessing
- work out which of the five possible answers is the correct (or 'single best') answer.

This will be an intensive assessment. You must ensure that you are properly prepared for it, in terms of your subject knowledge and also your mental resilience and time management. Your ability to navigate MCQs will also assist greatly.

1. Read the entire question at least twice

This sounds obvious but is so often overlooked. You are advised to read the entire question once, taking in all relevant pieces of information, understanding what the question is asking you and being aware of the options available. Once you have done that, read the entire question again and this time pay careful attention to the wording that is used.

- **In the factual scenario:** Does it use any words that stand out? Do any words used have legal bearing? What are you told and what are you not told?
- **In the lead in:** What are you being asked? Are there certain words to look out for (eg 'should', 'must', 'will', 'shall')?
- **In the answers:** What are the differences between each option? Are they substantial differences or subtle differences? Do any differences turn on a word or a phrase?

You should be prepared to give each question at least two viewings to mitigate any misunderstandings or oversights.

2. Understand the question being asked

It is important first that you understand what the question is asking of you. The SRA has identified that the FLK assessments may consist of single best answer MCQs that, for example:

- require the candidate to simply identify a correct legal principle or rule
- require the candidate to not only identify the correct legal principle or rule, but also apply that principle or rule to the factual scenario
- provide the candidate with the correct legal principle or rule, but require the candidate to identify how it should be properly applied and/or the outcome of that proper application.

By first identifying what the question is asking you to do, you can then understand what the creators of that question are seeking to test and how to approach the answers available. Many candidates actually find it beneficial to start with the lead in, before reading the scenario. This gives them the opportunity to understand what the scenario will likely entail. You need to decide what works best for you, so take the opportunity to try both ways.

3. Select the answer if you know it outright

You may feel as though a particular answer 'jumps out' at you, and that you are certain it is correct. It is very likely that the answer is correct. While you should be confident in your answers, do not allow your confidence (and perhaps overconfidence) to rush you into making a decision. Review all of your options one final time before you move on to the next question.

4. If you do not know the answer outright, employ a process of elimination

There may be situations in which the answer is not obvious from the outset. This may be due to the close similarities between different answers. Remember, it is the 'single best answer' that you are looking for. If you keep this in your mind, it will thereafter be easier to employ a process of elimination. Identify which answers you are sure are not correct (or not the 'best') and whittle down your options. Get rid of the distractors. Once you have only two options remaining, carefully scrutinise the wording used in both answers and look back to the question being asked. Identify what you consider to be the best answer, in light of that question. Review your answer and move on to the next question.

5. Take an educated and reasoned guess

There may be circumstances, quite commonly, in which you do not know the answer to the question. In this circumstance, you should try as hard as possible to eliminate any distractors that you are positive are incorrect and then take an educated and reasoned guess based on the options available. 'Always select C' will not work in this assessment; the correct answers will be randomly distributed amongst the MCQs as options A–E.

6. Skip and come back to it later

If time permits, you may think it appropriate to skip a question that you are unsure of and return to it before the end of the assessment. The assessment portal will highlight any questions that have not been answered, and you are also able to 'flag' questions for your review later on in the assessment (time permitting). If you do so, we would advise that you:

- make a note of what question you have skipped or click 'Flag for Review' on your screen, and

- ensure you leave sufficient time for you to go back to that question before the end of the assessment.

The same advice is applicable to any question that you have answered but for which you remain unsure.

7. Random guess

As a matter of absolute last resort, being unable even to take an educated and reasoned guess, you should simply choose an answer. There is no negative marking in the SQE1 assessments, so it is better for you to select an answer with the possibility, by sheer luck, of answering it correctly than it is to leave the answer blank and have no chance of scoring a point. The advice is simple: answer all of the questions, even if you have to guess at the end.

We hope that this brief guide will assist you in your preparation towards, and engagement with, single best answer MCQs.

GUIDED TOUR

Each chapter contains a number of features to help you revise, apply and test your knowledge.

Make sure you know Each chapter begins with an overview of the main topics covered and why you need to understand them for the purpose of the SQE1 assessments.

SQE assessment advice This identifies what you need to pay particular attention to in your revision as you work through the chapter.

What do you know already? These questions help you to assess which topics you feel confident with and which topics you may need to spend more time on (and where to find them in the chapter).

Key term Key terms are highlighted in bold where they first appear and defined in a separate box.

Exam warning This feature offers advice on where it is possible to go wrong in the assessments.

Revision tip Throughout the chapters are ideas to help you revise effectively and be best prepared for the assessment.

Summary This handy box brings together key information in an easy to revise and remember form.

Practice example These examples take a similar format to SQE-type questions and provide an opportunity to see how content might be applied to a scenario.

Procedural link Where relevant, this element shows how a concept might apply to another procedural topic in the series.

Key point checklist At the end of each chapter, there is a bullet-point summary of its most important content.

Key terms and concepts These are listed at the end of each chapter to help ensure you know, or can revise, terms and concepts you will need to be familiar with for the assessments.

SQE-style questions Five SQE-style questions on the chapter topic give you an opportunity to test your knowledge.

Answers to questions Check how you did with answers to both the quick knowledge test from the start of the chapter and the SQE-style questions at the end of the chapter.

Key cases, rules, statutes and instruments These list the key sources candidates need to be familiar with for the SQE assessment.

SQE1 TABLE OF LEGAL AUTHORITIES

The SQE1 Assessment Specification states the following in respect of legal authorities and their relevance to SQE1:

> On occasion in legal practice a case name or statutory provision, for example, is the term normally used to describe a legal principle or an area of law, or a rule or procedural step (eg *Rylands v Fletcher*, CPR Part 36, Section 25 notice). In such circumstances, candidates are required to know and be able to use such case names, statutory provisions etc. In all other circumstances candidates are not required to recall specific case names, or cite statutory or regulatory authorities.

This *SQE1 table of legal authorities* identifies the legal authorities you are required to know for the purpose of the SQE1 Functioning Legal Knowledge assessments for *Business Law and Practice*.

Legal authority	Corresponding *Revise SQE* chapter/pages
Salomon v A Salomon and Co Ltd [1897] AC 22 - principle of separate legal personality	**Chapter 1: Types of business medium, page 8**
Partnership Act 1890	**Chapter 2: Partnerships, page 18**
Bushell v Faith [1970] AC 1099 - '*Bushell v Faith clauses*'	**Chapter 4: Limited companies: part 2, page 76**

TABLE OF CASES

Bushell v Faith [1970] AC 1099... xvi, 76, 82, 84

Prest v Petrodel Resources Limited and others [2013] UKSC 34... 8

Salomon v A Salomon and Co Ltd [1897] AC 22... xvi, 8–9, 16, 17

TABLE OF STATUTES AND STATUTORY INSTRUMENTS

Bribery Act 2010... 69

Companies Act 1985 (CA 1985) 43, 46
Companies Act 2006 (CA 2006) 10–11, 20, 38, 41–62, 63–88, 89, 91–103, 106–7, 143
Companies (Model Articles) Regulations 2008... 43
Companies (Registration) Regulations 2008... 46
Company Directors Disqualification Act 1986 (CDDA) 65, 76–7, 83, 130
Company, Limited Liability Partnership and Business Names (Sensitive Words and Expressions) Regulations 2014... 20–1, 40
Company, Limited Liability Partnership and Business (Names and Trading Disclosures) Regulations 2015... 72
Corporate Insolvency and Governance Act 2020 (CIGA 2020) 138
Corporation Tax Act 2009 (CTA 2009) 207
Corporation Tax Act 2010 (CTA 2010) 207, 214

Economic Crime and Corporate Transparency Act 2023 (ECCTA) 38, 41, 42–6, 57, 63, 66, 71, 76–8, 89, 95

Finance Act 2013, s 207... 175

Higher Education Act 2004, s 42... 130

Income Tax Act 2007 (ITA) 150–1, 162
Income Tax (Earnings and Pensions) Act 2003 (ITEPA) 162, 165–6
Income Tax (Trading and Other Income) Act 2005 (ITTOIA) 162, 165
Insolvency Act 1986 (IA) 65, 70–1, 81, 122, 125–9, 132–9, 143

Law of Property Act 1925 (LPA) 136, 138–40
Limited Liability Partnerships Act 2000 (LLPA) 11
Limited Liability Partnerships Regulations 2001... 11

Partnership Act 1890 (PA) xvi, 6–7, 18–37, 130, 186

Small Business, Enterprise and Employment Act 2015... 45

Taxation of Chargeable Gains Act 1992 (TOCGA) 183, 185

Value Added Tax Act 1994 (VATA) 153

1

Starting a new business: types of business medium

MAKE SURE YOU KNOW

This chapter provides an overview of the main types of business medium that are available for an individual or individuals who wish to set up a new business. It also outlines the concept of limited liability. For the SQE1 assessments, you will need to understand the main organisational characteristics of sole traders, partnerships, limited liability partnerships, private companies and unlisted public companies. You will also need to understand the concepts of unlimited liability and limited liability. Your understanding of these subjects will enable you to identify and apply the relevant legal rules and principles to SQE1-style single best answer MCQs.

Types of business medium

- Unincorporated businesses
  - Sole traders
  - Partnerships
- Incorporated businesses
  - Limited companies (private & public)
  - Limited liability partnerships

SQE ASSESSMENT ADVICE

For SQE1, you are required to understand the types of business medium from a practical perspective. It is likely that you will be required to determine the most appropriate business medium in particular circumstances and/or identify the practical implications of the organisational characteristics.

An appreciation of the legal status and organisational characteristics of different types of business medium is important in most areas of legal practice.

As you work through this chapter, remember to pay particular attention in your revision to:

- the key different types of business organisation in England and Wales (ie sole traders, partnerships, limited liability partnerships, private companies and unlisted public companies)

- comparing and contrasting the key organisational characteristics and practical implications of the various types of business organisation
- how you would advise on which type of business medium would be most suitable in particular circumstances.

■ WHAT DO YOU KNOW ALREADY?

Attempt these questions before reading this chapter. If you find some difficult or cannot remember the answers, remember to look more closely at that area during your revision.

1) Which of the following need to be registered at Companies House?
   a) partnership
   b) sole trader
   c) limited liability partnership
   d) private limited company.

   [Introduction to incorporated and unincorporated businesses, page 2]
2) Which of the following statements are true?
   a) If a sole trader's business fails, the sole trader is personally liable and their personal assets are at risk.
   b) If a partnership business fails, the partners are personally liable for the firm's debts and their personal assets are at risk.
   c) If a company limited by shares is wound up (ie shut down), the liability of the shareholders will be limited to any amount unpaid on their shares.

   [Sole traders, partnerships and companies, pages 3–10]
3) Name the infamous case in which the principle of separate legal personality was enshrined.

   [Companies, pages 7–10]
4) True or false? In a private company limited by shares, the directors own the shares and the members/shareholders are responsible for managing the company on a day-to-day basis.

   [Companies, pages 7–10]
5) True or false? In a private company limited by shares, it is not possible for the directors and the members/shareholders to be the same people.

   [Companies, pages 7–10]

INTRODUCTION TO INCORPORATED AND UNINCORPORATED BUSINESSES

When a client wishes to set up a business, they have a number of options from which to choose. For SQE1, you will need to demonstrate that you understand the characteristics of the different options, and advise on which may be most suitable in particular circumstances.

It is necessary to distinguish between **unincorporated businesses** (sole traders and partnerships) and **incorporated businesses** (companies and limited liability partnerships). The fundamental distinction between the two is that an incorporated business has its own legal identity or separate personality (this concept is explored below) and needs to be registered with Companies House. It is an artificial 'person' created by law and is legally distinct from those who own and run the business.

Key term: unincorporated business

An unincorporated business does not have its own legal identity (or separate personality). There is no legal distinction between the business and its owner(s) and manager(s).

Key term: incorporated business

An incorporated business has its own legal identity (or separate personality). There is a legal distinction between the business and its owner(s) and manager(s) (see **Practice example 1.1**).

Practice example 1.1

Niamh is the only director and shareholder of a private limited company. The company has entered into a contract with your client, Linda, and failed to perform its obligations. Should Linda consider legal action against Niamh, the limited company or both?

Linda should consider legal action against the limited company only. As a separate (artificial) legal person, it owes the contractual obligations to her.

Procedural link: civil litigation

Knowing the proper status of the parties to legal proceedings is very important in the context of civil litigation (see ***Revise SQE: Dispute Resolution***).

UNINCORPORATED BUSINESSES

This section will explore unincorporated businesses - sole traders and partnerships. For SQE1, it is crucial that you understand their main characteristics and their advantages/disadvantages.

Sole traders

A **sole trader** or sole proprietor is someone who is self-employed and owns and runs their own unincorporated business. Although they may have employees, they are the sole owner of the business.

Key term: sole trader

A self-employed person who is the sole owner of their unincorporated business.

Sole traders may be involved in any trade, business or profession and can be anything from window cleaners and hairdressers to accountants and solicitors. The term 'sole practitioner' is sometimes used for sole traders/proprietors who have a profession (eg a dentist) rather than a trade (eg a shopkeeper).

As an unincorporated business, there is no legal separation between the business and the sole trader's personal affairs/assets. This has the advantage of keeping ownership and management simple. However, the disadvantage to this is that sole traders have **unlimited liability**.

Key term: unlimited liability

Unlimited liability means that a business owner is personally and directly responsible for all debts and liabilities incurred. Therefore, their personal assets (eg any property they own or money held in bank accounts, even if unrelated to the business) will be at risk, and they can be made bankrupt if the business is unsuccessful (see **Chapter 6**).

For SQE1, it is important to recognise the concept of unlimited liability in the context of sole traders. It is a key disadvantage of carrying on business as a sole trader and its implications can have serious consequences (see **Practice example 1.2**).

Practice example 1.2

Katrina set up business as a hairdresser several years ago, but the liabilities of the business now exceed its assets by over £100,000. Katrina has savings of £50,000 and a house worth £200,000. The realisable assets of the business amount to £20,000. How would you advise Katrina?

As a sole trader, Katrina will be personally liable for the debts of the business. The business is unincorporated, so does not have its own legal identity (or separate personality). There is no legal distinction between the business and its owner and manager. Therefore Katrina's personal assets will be at risk (including her home) if she is unable to satisfy the debts of the business.

Procedural link: insolvency

When considering liability for the debts of an insolvent business (see key term box in **Chapter 6**), it is important to know the legal status of the business concerned. There are different rules for individuals/unincorporated businesses and incorporated businesses, and these are considered in **Chapter 6**.

Although unlimited liability can be a significant disadvantage of being a sole trader, a key advantage is that there are no specific formalities or legal processes required to set up the business. Self-employed people do need to register with HMRC and some sole traders may be required to register for VAT (see **Chapter 7**). However, the additional costs of forming a company are avoided. In addition to this, unlike companies, there are no onerous ongoing formality, decision-making, filing and disclosure requirements (see **Companies** below and **Chapter 3**). This can make being a sole trader more attractive, private and less expensive.

Sole traders pay income tax on their trading profits and capital gains tax on their capital gains (see **Chapters 8 and 9**). They will usually obtain tax advice when deciding on the type of business medium.

Exam warning

For the purposes of SQE1, it is important to consider the particular circumstances of the client when advising on which type of business medium would be most suitable for their particular needs. You should be able to balance competing factors (eg the importance of limited liability, versus onerous disclosure requirements) in order to advise. Make sure that you read the question carefully (see **Practice example 1.3**).

Practice example 1.3

Rylan wants to set up his own business as a window cleaner. His funds are modest and his liabilities (see **Chapter 5**) and financial investment will be low. He is keen to keep things simple and not to incur substantial expense. How would you advise Rylan with regard to the most suitable business medium for him?

Although the benefits of limited liability may be significant for those investing large sums and taking significant risk, it would appear that the costs and administrative burden of setting up a limited company would not be appropriate here. Therefore, in this situation, it would be advisable for Rylan to operate his business as a sole trader.

Partnerships

A **partnership** is an unincorporated business with at least two owners.

Key term: partnership

An unincorporated business that exists when two or more people 'carry on' a business in common with a view of profit (as defined in s 1 Partnership Act 1890 (PA)).

Partnerships under the PA must be distinguished from limited liability partnerships (see **Limited liability partnerships**, below), which are incorporated businesses.

As with sole traders, although the partners may have employees, they are the owners of the business. They may also be involved in any trade, business or profession.

Revision tip

For the purposes of SQE1, it is important to be able to recognise the existence of a partnership. This is very much a question of fact. It arises when two or more people actually carry on a business in common with a view of profit (see **Practice example 1.4**).

Practice example 1.4

Netta and Duncan are friends. They make and sell cakes in the town where they live and split the money they receive 50–50. They think that, as the arrangements are purely informal and there is nothing in writing, this is not a partnership. Is this correct?

They are mistaken. As Netta and Duncan are 'carrying on a business in common with a view of profit', this is a partnership as defined by s 1 PA. There is clearly agreement between the parties (whether oral or implied by conduct) as to how the business is run.

Therefore, as with sole traders, no specific formalities are required to set up the business. A partnership can arise through oral agreement or through conduct. If the parties are actually carrying on business together with a view of profit, a partnership exists.

Although no specific formalities or legal processes are *required* to set up a partnership, it is often *desirable* to have a formal partnership agreement, setting out the terms of the partnership (see **Chapter 2**). This is because many of the provisions of the PA will apply, in the absence of an express or implied agreement to the contrary (the so-called 'default provisions').

Many of the default provisions can have undesirable consequences (see **Chapter 2**).

As an unincorporated business, there is no legal separation between the business and the partners' personal affairs/assets. They are therefore personally and directly responsible for all debts and liabilities incurred whilst they are partners (s 9 PA). Their personal assets are at risk, and they may be made bankrupt if the business is unsuccessful (see **Chapter 6**).

Under the PA, there is no separation of ownership and control (s 5 PA). Every partner may act for the purposes of the partnership business and the acts of any one partner may bind the partnership (see **Chapter 2**). This can make management more straightforward than with companies.

As with sole traders, partners do need to register with HMRC and partnerships may be required to register for VAT (see **Chapter 7**). However, the additional costs of forming a company are avoided (see **Companies**, below). In addition to this, unlike companies, there are no onerous ongoing formality, decision-making, filing and disclosure requirements. This can make being in partnership more attractive, private and less expensive.

Individual partners pay income tax on their share of the trading profits and capital gains tax on their share of the capital gains for the partnership (see **Chapters 8 and 9**, respectively). They will usually obtain tax advice when deciding on the type of business medium.

Revision tip

When advising on which type of business medium would be most suitable to a client's particular needs, you should be able to balance competing factors. Two or more people going into business may be more concerned about ongoing costs and formalities than with the implications of unlimited liability. A professional services firm's main concern may be professional negligence claims, for which insurance may be available, making limited liability less important.

INCORPORATED BUSINESSES

This section will explore incorporated businesses - companies and limited liability partnerships. For SQE1, it is crucial that you understand their main characteristics and their advantages/disadvantages.

Companies

A **company** is an incorporated business with separate legal personality and where the owners (members) usually have limited liability. The company may be limited by shares or by guarantee and can be public or private. These concepts are explored below.

Key term: company

An incorporated business with separate legal personality, where its members can have limited liability.

Unlike sole traders and partnerships, a company is the creation of a legal process and documents must be filed at Companies House in order for a company to be 'born' (see **Chapter 3**). It is not possible for a company to exist without the involvement of Companies House.

Companies may be involved in any trade, business or profession. They range from very small private companies, with just one director and one member/shareholder, to very large, listed public companies (whose shares are traded on a stock exchange).

Exam warning

For the purposes of SQE1, you need to focus on private companies limited by shares and only those public companies whose shares are not traded on a stock exchange (ie unlisted public companies).

The two key hallmarks of a company are separate legal personality and limited liability. We will look at each in turn.

Separate legal personality

The principle of **separate legal personality** was enshrined in the infamous case of *Salomon v A Salomon and Co Ltd* [1897] AC 22, which held that it was not fraud to set up a limited company in order to create a separate legal person, to avoid personal responsibility for debts. Cases where the court will disregard this fundamental principle and impose personal liability are very rare (*Prest v Petrodel Resources Limited and others* [2013] UKSC 34) and are outside the scope of this book.

Key term: separate legal personality

The company is a person separate from its members/shareholders and directors. As a separate legal person, it can own property, enter into contracts and be a party to legal proceedings (by suing or being sued). It is a key advantage of incorporation and, as an artificial person, it can have perpetual succession (ie it can continue indefinitely).

Unlike sole traders and partnerships, a company is not the agent of its shareholders (not even a one-person company with one director and one member/shareholder). In other words, it acts in its own right and not simply on behalf of its owner(s). The basic company model distinguishes between the **shareholders**/members and the **directors**.

Key term: shareholders

The shareholders own the shares in the company (see **Chapter 3**). Sometimes shareholders are referred to as 'members'.

Key term: directors

The directors have general management powers to control what the company does on a day-to-day basis. They run the company.

Directors and shareholders may be the same people, and this can often be the case with smaller companies.

The separation of membership (ownership) and management is a key advantage of incorporation, but it can also be unnecessarily cumbersome for smaller businesses (eg a one member, one director company).

The sale/transfer of a company or any interest in it is also made more straightforward as this can be done through the transfer of shares as an alternative to the transfer of the assets themselves.

Limited liability

The second major hallmark of a company is the potential for **limited liability**. Liability may be limited by shares (more commonly) or by guarantee (usually for non-profit-making entities).

Key term: limited liability

Limited liability means that members have a limit on their liability to contribute towards the company's debts.

Limited by shares - the liability of members (shareholders) is limited to any amount unpaid on their shares (see **Practice example 1.5**).

Limited by guarantee - the liability of members is limited to any amount they promise to pay in the event that the company is wound up (ie when it is brought to an end and ceases to exist - see **Chapter 6**).

Limited liability is a significant advantage of incorporation.

Practice example 1.5

Kobi subscribes and pays for 100 £1 shares in a private limited company. The company is subsequently wound up. What is Kobi's liability?

Kobi will have no further liability as he held fully paid shares. Had payment not been made, or only partially made, he would be liable for the balance.

Advantages and disadvantages of incorporation

Separate personality and limited liability are the most significant advantages of incorporation, but there are also a number of other advantages and disadvantages.

Having a company can be perceived as being more prestigious to both owners and clients/customers. It is the main format for most big businesses and they are recognised internationally.

Companies can grant floating charges, as well as fixed charges. Floating charges are explored further in **Chapter 5**. The key point to make now is that the floating charge is a more flexible form of security, which can improve the banking facilities available to companies.

Although some expense can be taken up in forming a company, this need not be substantial (see **Chapter 2**). However, there are onerous ongoing formality, decision-making, filing and disclosure requirements, which can add to administrative burden and legal expense over time (see **Chapter 3**). The fact that most information kept at Companies House becomes public may not be attractive to those who value commercial secrecy.

Companies pay corporation tax on both their income profits and their capital gains (see **Chapter 10**). Those setting up a company will usually obtain tax advice when deciding on the type of business medium.

Public and private companies

Finally, it is important to know the key distinctions between private companies and public companies (see **Table 1.1**). Remember that for the purposes of SQE1, you need to focus on private companies limited by shares and unlisted public companies.

Table 1.1: Private and public companies compared

Private limited company	**Public limited company**
A company that is not a public company (s 4(1) Companies Act 2006 (CA))	Certificate of Incorporation states that it is a public limited company (see **Chapter 3**)
May be limited by shares or by guarantee	May be limited by shares
Shares cannot be offered to the general public (s 755 CA)	General public can be invited to subscribe for shares

Table 1.1: (continued)

Private limited company	Public limited company
No minimum capital requirements	Minimum capital requirements - £50,000 (ss 761 and 763 CA) Shares must be at least one-quarter paid up (s 586 CA)
	Subject to more stringent/onerous rules (particularly on disclosure), as public money is involved
	Company may apply for shares to be officially listed for trading on a recognised investment exchange (eg London Stock Exchange or alternative investment market)
	Officially listed companies are subject to additional disclosure rules

Limited liability partnerships (LLPs)

A **limited liability partnership** is formed under the Limited Liability Partnerships Act 2000 (LLPA). It is a type of incorporated business and is formed by sending form LLIN01 to Companies House.

Key term: limited liability partnership

A cross between a company and a partnership, formed under the LLPA.

An LLP has a combination of the features of both partnerships and limited companies. For example, they are available for persons 'carrying on a lawful business with a view to profit' (s 2(1)(a) LLPA) and every member is deemed to be an agent of the LLP (s 6 LLPA).

However, when registered at Companies House, an LLP has separate personality (s 1(2) LLPA) and members have limited liability/are not directly responsible for its debts (s 1(4) and (5) LLPA).

Like the PA, the Limited Liability Partnerships Regulations 2001 provide provisions that apply between the partners in default of express or implied agreement to the contrary (see **Chapter 2**). There is therefore more flexibility with regard to management than companies, which have a stricter separation of powers.

Like companies, LLPs may grant fixed and floating charges over their assets. Also like companies, LLPs are subject to ongoing administrative and reporting requirements. However, a key disadvantage of LLPs is that they are not as well recognised internationally as limited companies.

LLP members pay income tax on their share of the trading profits and capital gains tax on their share of the capital gains for the partnership (see **Chapters 8 and 9**, respectively). Those setting up an LLP will usually obtain tax advice when deciding on the type of business medium.

SUMMARY

Table 1.2 provides a summary of key information, which should assist in answering SQE1-style questions (remember to always read the question carefully and provide a tailored response).

Table 1.2: Summary: unincorporated and incorporated businesses

	Sole trader	Partnership	Limited company	LLP
Formalities required for creation	No	No - although partnership agreement recommended	Yes	Yes
Incorporated - separate personality	No	No	Yes	Yes
Limited liability	No	No	Yes	Yes
Personal liability for debts	Yes	Yes	No	No
Finance	Can grant fixed charges only	Can grant fixed charges only	Can grant fixed and floating charges	Can grant fixed and floating charges
Management - board structure (separation of powers)	No	No	Yes	No
Stricter formalities/ more onerous administration/ greater expense/ publicity	No	No	Yes	Yes

Table 1.2: (continued)

	Sole trader	Partnership	Limited company	LLP
Status	Less prestigious	Less prestigious	More prestigious	More prestigious – although less recognised internationally
Transferrable shares	No	No	Yes	No

■ KEY POINT CHECKLIST

This chapter has covered the following key knowledge points. You can use these to structure your revision, ensuring you recall the key details from each point.

- The key different types of business organisation in England and Wales are sole traders, partnerships, companies and LLPs.
- The key types of business organisation can be separated into unincorporated businesses (sole traders and partnerships) and incorporated businesses (companies and LLPs).
- You need to focus on private and unlisted public companies for the purposes of SQE1 and do not need to have detailed knowledge of listed public companies.
- Each type of business organisation has different organisational characteristics and practical implications.
- You need to have good working knowledge of the organisational characteristics and practical implications in order to provide tailored advice to a client on the most appropriate medium for them and the consequences of such a decision. Remember to consider a client's individual circumstances.

■ KEY TERMS AND CONCEPTS

- unincorporated business (**page 3**)
- incorporated business (**page 3**)
- sole trader (**page 4**)
- unlimited liability (**page 4**)
- partnership (**page 6**)
- company (**page 8**)
- separate legal personality (**page 8**)
- shareholders (**page 9**)
- directors (**page 9**)

- limited liability (**page 9**)
- limited liability partnership (**page 11**)

SQE1-STYLE QUESTIONS

QUESTION 1

A client wishes to set up business on their own, providing light gardening services. The client is keen to keep things as straightforward as possible and to minimise costs. They do not foresee a substantial capital outlay and they have no plans to take on employees or to borrow money.

Which of the following best describes the type of business medium the client should choose for their business and why?

A. A private limited company. This is because there is little administrative burden in setting up and running a private limited company.

B. A sole trader. Although limited liability would be of benefit to the client, their needs are straightforward and their investment and overheads would not be substantial. The additional burdens of starting and running a limited company would not be justified.

C. A limited company in any event. The benefits of separate personality and limited liability are so great that they outweigh all other considerations.

D. A private limited company. The client will be able to separate ownership and control and grant floating charges over the company's assets when they wish to expand the business.

E. A public limited company. It will give the client better flexibility to expand and will enable shares to be offered to the public.

QUESTION 2

A client wishes to start up a manufacturing business with a long-standing friend and business associate. The pair plan to buy premises, employ several staff, expand very quickly and trade internationally. In the medium term, the pair will need to borrow considerable funds.

Which of the following best describes the type of business medium the client and their friend should choose?

A. A private limited company.

B. A partnership.

C. A public limited company.

D. A limited liability partnership.

E. A private company, limited by guarantee.

QUESTION 3

A client holds 10,000 £1 ordinary shares in a private limited company, representing a 5% shareholding. The shares are fully paid and the company is being wound up, with substantial debts.

How much will the client be required to contribute on winding-up?

A. The client will not be required to contribute on winding-up.
B. The client will be required to contribute 5% of the company's outstanding debt.
C. The client will be required to contribute £10,000.
D. The client's liability will be unlimited.
E. The client will be required to contribute towards the costs of winding-up.

QUESTION 4

A client is a sole trader whose business is in financial difficulty. However, they have substantial personal assets and are keen to ascertain their liability for the debts of the business.

Which of the following best describes the client's liability?

A. The business is a separate legal person, and the client will be able to keep their personal assets separate.
B. The client will be personally liable for the debts of the business.
C. The client's liability will be limited to the amount they contributed to the business.
D. The client will be jointly and severally liable for the debts of the business.
E. The client will not be liable as the business has not been registered at Companies House.

QUESTION 5

A client is looking to set up a manufacturing business with two friends who are both experienced executives. They plan to expand quickly, have substantial borrowings and appoint over 50 employees. The client is happy not to be involved in the day-to-day management of the business, but he wants to make sure that his liability is limited to his investment. The client may also wish to sell his share in the business on his retirement in a few years' time.

Which of the following best describes the type of business medium the client and his two friends should choose?

A. A private company, limited by shares.

B. A partnership.

C. A public limited company.

D. A limited liability partnership.

E. A private company, limited by guarantee.

■ ANSWERS TO QUESTIONS

Answers to 'What do you know already?' questions at the start of the chapter

1) The correct answer was (c) and (d) as these are incorporated businesses, so need to be registered at Companies House. The other two are unincorporated businesses, so do not need to be registered at Companies House.
2) The correct answer was (a), (b) and (c). Sole traders and partners have unlimited liability and are personally liable for the debts of the business. Their personal assets are at risk if their business fails. Where a company is limited by shares, shareholders have limited liability and are not personally liable.
3) *Salomon v A Salomon and Co Ltd* [1897] AC 22. Although SQE1 does not require you to recall specific case names, this is a seminal case and you need to be aware of its fundamental implications.
4) False. In a private company limited by shares, the members/shareholders own the shares and the directors are generally responsible for managing the company on a day-to-day basis.
5) False. In a private company limited by shares, it is possible for the directors and the members/shareholders to be the same people. This is often the case with smaller 'owner managed' companies.

Answers to end-of-chapter SQE1-style questions

Question 1

The correct answer was B. Although separate personality and limited liability have clear benefits, they are not the client's main concern, particularly in view of the low capital outlay/risk. Therefore, option C is incorrect. The additional costs of forming and managing a company would be unjustified, making option A incorrect. Option D is incorrect as separation of ownership and control would be unnecessarily complicated, and they have no plans to borrow money, so the ability to grant floating charges is not a concern. Option E is incorrect as a public limited company (plc) would be even less appropriate than a private company; they have no desire to offer shares to the public and would be unlikely to meet the minimum capital requirements.

Question 2

The correct answer was A. The ambitious plans, nature of the business and need to borrow make a private limited company the obvious choice.

There are likely to be significant liabilities and the ability to grant floating charges will be a clear advantage. Option B would be inappropriate as partners have unlimited liability and partnerships cannot grant floating charges. Limited companies are more recognised across the world than LLPs, which makes option D incorrect. A plc would be inappropriate in the short term as there are no plans to offer shares to the public (which makes option C incorrect). Option E is incorrect as a private company limited by guarantee would be more appropriate for a non-profit-making entity.

Question 3

The correct answer was A. The client's liability will be limited to any amount unpaid on their shares, which in this case is nothing. Therefore, options B, C, D and E are incorrect. The client would only be required to contribute on winding-up if the shares were not fully paid. In these circumstances, liability would be limited to the unpaid amount.

Question 4

The correct answer was B. The client's liability will be personal, without limit, as the business is unincorporated and does not have separate legal personality. Therefore, options A and C are incorrect. There is no requirement to register the business at Companies House, so option E is incorrect. Joint and several liability is inappropriate for a sole trader but would be relevant if the client were a partner. Therefore, option D is incorrect.

Question 5

The correct answer was A. The client's key concerns are having limited liability, not being involved in the day-to-day management of the business and having transferrable shares. Therefore, option B is incorrect. The board structure (separation of ownership and control) and ambitious plans make this the obvious choice. There will be significant benefit to limited liability and the ability to grant floating charges. A public company would be less appropriate, although it would be possible to re-register as a public company later. Therefore, option C is incorrect. Companies limited by guarantee are usually non-profit-making entities, so option E is incorrect. Option D is incorrect as limited companies are more widely recognised than LLPs for trading purposes.

■ KEY CASES, RULES, STATUTES AND INSTRUMENTS

The SQE1 Assessment Specification does not require you to know any statutory authorities or specific case names for this topic. However, you should be aware of the implications of the case of *Salomon v A Salomon and Co Ltd* [1897] AC 22. Specific sections of statutes are set out for ease of reference.

2

Partnerships

MAKE SURE YOU KNOW

This chapter provides an overview of partnerships under the Partnership Act 1890 (PA). For the SQE1 assessments, you will need to understand how and when partnerships are formed, the key 'default provisions' of the PA and the desirability of having a formal partnership agreement. You will also need to understand how partners can bind the partnership in their relationships with third parties and advise on liability for debts. Your understanding of these subjects will enable you to identify and apply the relevant legal rules and principles to SQE1-style single best answer MCQs.

SQE ASSESSMENT ADVICE

For SQE1, you are required to understand partnerships from a practical perspective. It is likely that you will be required to identify whether a partnership is in existence and apply the key 'default provisions' under the PA to problem-based, single best answer MCQs. You may also be required to advise on the necessity of a formal written partnership agreement in order to contract out of some of the more undesirable default provisions, based on particular client circumstances. It is also likely that you will be required to advise on liability for debts and how partners should protect themselves from future liability when leaving a partnership.

As you work through this chapter, remember to pay particular attention in your revision to:

- the requirements for forming a partnership
- the key 'default provisions' under the PA
- the desirability of having a formal written partnership agreement in light of the 'default provisions' and particular client circumstances
- the liability of partners for debts to third parties and ways of limiting liability when leaving a partnership.

WHAT DO YOU KNOW ALREADY?

Attempt these questions before reading this chapter. If you find some difficult or cannot remember the answers, remember to look more closely at that area during your revision.

1) True or false? Formalities are a strict requirement in order to form a partnership.

   [Formation of partnerships and the PA, page 19]

2) Where there is a partnership at will, without a formal written partnership agreement, and no other express or implied agreement to the contrary, how much notice must a partner give in order to leave the partnership?

   a) None.

   b) The partner may leave immediately, provided that they give notice to the other partners.

   c) The partner must give reasonable notice.

   d) The partner must give at least one month's notice.

   [Partnership agreements and the PA, page 21]

3) Jesper and Laurits are in partnership. Jesper invests 60% of the capital of the business and Laurits invests 40%. Jesper works full-time for the business and Laurits works part-time. In the absence of a formal partnership agreement or informal agreement, how will income profits be shared?

   a) Equally.

   b) Split 60/40 in accordance with the capital contributions.

   c) Split in accordance with how many hours each partner works in the business.

   [Partnership agreements and the PA, page 21]

4) In a partnership at will, without a formal written partnership agreement, what is the impact of death or insolvency of a partner on the partnership?

   [Partnership agreements and the PA, page 21]

5) Fill in the blank in the following statement: 'Where a partner acts beyond the scope of his actual authority in making a deal with a third party, that deal may still be binding on the partnership if the partner had ________ authority to make it.'

   [Liability to third parties, page 27]

FORMATION OF PARTNERSHIPS AND THE PA

For the purposes of SQE1, it is important to understand the definition of a partnership and how one is formed.

What is a partnership and how is one formed?

A partnership is one medium through which a business may be run. A partnership is an unincorporated business (see **Chapter 1**) and is not a separate legal entity from its partners. As outlined in **Chapter 1**, a partnership exists where two or more persons agree that they will run a business together, and actually do so. The existence of a partnership is very much a question of fact. The agreement to operate in partnership can be oral or in writing, or may even be implied by conduct. There is therefore no legal requirement for, although there are several advantages in, drawing up a **partnership agreement**.

Key term: partnership agreement

A formal document setting out the terms of a partnership. It usually deals with the relationship between the partners and their relationships with third parties. It will often vary or amend key default provisions under the Partnership Act 1890 (PA).

Exam warning

As outlined in **Chapter 1**, it is important that you are able to identify when a partnership exists. Remember, no specific formalities are required, and simply carrying on business with another or others will usually mean that the criteria under s 1 of the PA are met.

Who can be a partner?

Generally, any legally capable person may enter into a partnership. Companies, as well as individuals, may be partners with other companies/individuals.

The maximum number of persons who may be members of a partnership used to be 20. However, certain professions (including solicitors and accountants) were exempt from this limit. Since 2002, no limits apply in any circumstances.

The partnership name

The law relating to business names is contained in Part 41 of the Companies Act 2006 (CA).

No restrictions will apply if the partnership name consists only of the surnames of all partners, with or without forenames or initials. In any other case, the CA will apply and certain words or expressions forming part of the business name will require prior approval. These include words and expressions contained in the Company, Limited Liability Partnership and Business Names (Sensitive Words and Expressions) Regulations 2014.

Any partnership that uses a business name must also comply with the prescribed disclosure requirements under the CA (ss 1200–1206). Generally, details about the partners must appear at the main place of business and on partnership stationery.

Exam warning

Although it is not a requirement to know statutory authorities and the sensitive words and expressions in the 2014 regulations, you should be aware of the requirement to seek approval for some names and the general requirement to disclose business names.

PARTNERSHIP AGREEMENTS AND THE PA

For the purposes of SQE1, it is important to understand the desirability of having a formal partnership agreement and what a typical partnership agreement should include.

Purpose of a written partnership agreement

A formal partnership agreement is not a strict requirement, but it does have clear benefits, such as:

- It provides evidence of the partners' relations and of the partnership's terms.
- It overrides some of the provisions of the PA, which will automatically apply, except to the extent that there is contrary agreement. Many of these 'default provisions' may have undesirable consequences for modern partnerships.

Usual clauses in a partnership agreement

For the purposes of SQE1, it is important to appreciate the 'default provisions' within the PA that apply in the absence of express or implied agreement to the contrary. These may be unsuitable for specific client circumstances and so it is helpful to look at them in the context of what a typical partnership agreement would include.

The parties

The parties to the agreement will be the partners. No new partner may be admitted without the consent of all of the partners (s 24(7) PA). Although sensible for smaller partnerships, this may be unworkable for larger ones.

Commencement date

Remember that the existence of a partnership is a question of fact; the partnership will exist from the date the s 1 PA criteria are satisfied. Therefore, an agreement subsequent to that date will only govern rights and responsibilities from that date.

Nature and place of business

The nature of the business is important to the question of a partner's authority and the extent to which a partner may bind the partnership (see **Liability to third parties**, below).

Unanimity is required by the partners in order to change the nature of the business (s 24(8) PA).

It is usual to specify the place(s) at which the business will be carried on.

Partnership name

See above.

Duration

A partnership may run for a specific venture or a fixed term. A fixed-term partnership that continues after expiry will be presumed to continue on terms that are consistent with a **partnership at will** (s 27(1) PA), otherwise it will be dissolved (s 32 PA).

Key term: partnership at will

A partnership where no specific duration or fixed term is set. It is the most common type of partnership.

With a partnership at will, the following will apply:

- Any partner may determine the partnership (ie bring it to an end) at any time on giving notice to the other partners. There is no requirement for written notice, unless the partnership agreement was made by deed (s 26(1) PA).
- The partnership shall be dissolved from the date specified in the notice, or if none is specified, the date of communication of the notice (s 32 PA).

Therefore, there is potential for the dissolution to be immediate and this can have serious consequences for the business. This would be a technical dissolution and the remaining partners may seek to continue in what would be a 'new' business (see **Practice example 2.1**).

Accordingly, it is usual to provide in the agreement that the partnership will continue despite the retirement, death, expulsion or bankruptcy of a partner.

Practice example 2.1

Kikki and Carola are in partnership together. There is no formal partnership agreement in place and Kikki decides one day to leave the business to travel the world. How much notice does Kikki need to give Carola and what will the impact be on the partnership?

Kikki needs to give notice to Carola. It does not need to be in writing and it may take effect immediately. The partnership will be dissolved.

Capital

It is important to specify what each partner is contributing to the business and how capital profits/losses will be shared between the partners. In the absence of express or implied agreement to the contrary, the PA provides that capital profits and losses will be shared equally (s 24(1)). Although it may be implied that unequal contributions of capital result in the right to make unequal withdrawals of capital, a formal written partnership agreement should make this clear.

The agreement may also provide for interest to be paid on partners' capital contributions. There is no right to interest on capital under the PA (s 24(4)), but this may be important, particularly where large capital contributions have been made. Provision should also be made for how future capital contributions will be made.

Income

The agreement should specify how the income profits/losses of the business will be shared between the partners. In the absence of express or implied agreement to the contrary, income profits and losses will be shared equally (s 24(1) PA) and this may not be suitable to clients' specific circumstances.

The agreement should also deal with the payment of salaries from profits before the final profit shares are divided. The PA does not provide for salaries to be paid to partners (s 24(6)) and this could be particularly important where, for example, not all partners work full-time for the business.

The final key point here is drawings (the amounts that partners withdraw on account of profits). A well-drafted agreement should deal with how and when drawings are made and provide for repayment (with interest) if too much is taken.

Practice example 2.2 provides an example of how capital and income profits are dealt with under the PA.

Practice example 2.2

James and Surie are in partnership together. There is no formal partnership agreement in place or any express or implied agreement as to how they will share income and capital profits. Both of them contributed the same amount of capital, but Surie only works part-time for the business. How are their income and capital profits shared?

In the absence of an express or implied agreement to the contrary, income and capital profits will be shared equally.

Partnership property

The assets belonging to the firm should be specified, so that they are clearly distinguishable from those assets that belong to the individual partners. For example, a freehold or leasehold property may remain owned by one individual partner but be used for the purposes of the business. A failure to deal with this properly can lead to disputes on dissolution and problems with taxation.

Management

All partners are entitled to take part in the management of the business (s 24(5) PA). This may not be what is desired between the partners. For example, one partner may wish to take the role of a 'sleeping partner' and simply invest in the business.

All matters connected with the partnership business may be decided by a majority of the partners (s 24(8) PA). This is except for changing the nature of the business, where unanimity is required.

Thought should be given to whether unanimity should be required for other decisions and whether a majority decision should always be applicable. For example, the partners may wish for certain issues to be decided upon by the senior partners only.

Authority of the partners to bind the partners is also significant (see **Liability to third parties**, below).

Absences should also be catered for (eg leave and illness).

Retirement

Retirement, in this context, simply means leaving the partnership. The PA does not provide for the possibility of a partner leaving a partnership without the partnership being dissolved. This is a significant shortcoming of the PA and can have serious consequences for the continuing partners.

The agreement should include a mechanism for a partner to leave, following appropriate notice, and get what is owing to them, without dissolving the firm (see **Payment for outgoing partner's share** below).

Death and bankruptcy

Unless otherwise agreed by the partners, a partnership will be dissolved by the death or bankruptcy (see **Chapter 6**) of any partner (s 33(1) PA). Again, this can have serious consequences for the continuing partners.

Provision should be made in the agreement for the continuation of the firm by the surviving/solvent partners and for payment of the deceased/ bankrupt partner's share (see **Payment for outgoing partner's share** below).

Expulsion

Under the PA, no majority may expel any partner (s 25 PA - see **Practice example 2.3**). Therefore, an express power to expel a 'problem' partner should be included in the agreement, specifying the grounds for expulsion and providing for payment of the expelled partner's share in the partnership (see **Payment for outgoing partner's share** below). There should also be provision that the partnership should continue as regards the remaining partners.

Practice example 2.3

Tom, Alexandra and Fred are in partnership together. There is no formal partnership agreement in place. Tom and Alexandra become disappointed with Fred's performance and want to remove him from the partnership. Are they able to do this?

Tom and Alexandra cannot force Fred to leave without his consent. If he does not agree to do so, they must carry on in business with him or dissolve the partnership.

Payment for outgoing partner's share

Specific provision should be made for the following:

- the remaining partners to have the option to purchase the outgoing partner's share
- valuation of the outgoing partner's share (eg preparation of partnership accounts, agreement on value, or independent determination, if agreement cannot be reached)
- payment of the outgoing partner's share (eg payment by instalments or in a lump sum)
- dissolution, if the option to purchase is not exercised.

On a full dissolution, the winding-up (see **Chapter 6**) will take place in accordance with the provisions of the partnership agreement, or s 44 of the PA.

Under s 44, the proceeds of sale are used to:

- repay third party creditors
- repay partner creditors
- repay partners' capital entitlements.

Any balance is then divided between the partners in accordance with their profit-sharing ratios.

Partnership losses are met from:

- income profits
- capital
- contributions made by the partners in the same proportion as their profit-sharing ratio.

See **Chapter 5**, **Business accounts**, for more information on income, capital and profit-sharing ratios.

There may be a financial advantage in selling the business as a going concern (ie a business that is still running), rather than dissolving the business. This is because there may be value in the goodwill of the business (ie the fact the business is already established, with a sound reputation and with a pre-existing client/customer base and business connections).

Restrictive covenants

Consideration should be given as to whether there should be a restriction on ex-partners competing with the partnership business, approaching employees or former clients or dealing with former clients. No such covenants will be implied by the general law or through the PA, so specific provision will need to be made.

Careful drafting of any covenant is required if it is to be enforceable. The goodwill of the business is a valuable and legitimate interest to protect and the clause must be reasonable in scope (eg in terms of duration and area). The more limited/reasonable the clause, the more likely it will be upheld.

Revision tip

When revising for SQE1, you need to be able to advise on whether a restraint of trade clause/restrictive covenant is likely to be reasonable. For example, a clause restricting involvement with the same type of business as the partnership in the same geographical area for a year is more likely to be successful than one restricting involvement in the same type of business, across a much wider area and/or for a longer period.

Administrative provisions

The partnership agreement will also need to contain sufficient administrative provisions to make it workable. For example, definitions and interpretation, service of notices, costs and arbitration in the event of disputes.

PARTNERS' DUTIES TO EACH OTHER

Partners owe each other a duty of good faith and the PA provides for three fiduciary duties (ie duties of trust and confidence: see ***Revise SQE: Trusts Law***):

- duty to provide true accounts and full information on partnership matters (s 28 PA)
- duty to account for profits derived from the position as partner (s 29 PA)
- duty to account for profits from a competing business (s 30 PA).

Many partnership agreements will contain further provisions, for example that the partners are to devote their whole time and attention to the partnership and are not to start or join any other business whilst they are a partner.

Further provisions of the PA relate to the relationship between partners. In the usual way, these can be varied by contrary agreement. These include the right to inspect partnership books (s 24(9)) and the payment of 5% interest on loans made by the partners (s 24(3)).

Practice example 2.4 provides an illustration of s 30 PA in practice.

Practice example 2.4

Dana and Conchita are in partnership together as performers. They always perform together, but it transpires that Dana has been performing as a solo artist. What is Dana's duty to Conchita?

Dana must account to Conchita for her 'secret profit' (ie reimburse her for her proper share).

LIABILITY TO THIRD PARTIES

It is a requirement of SQE1 that you are able to identify liability for the firm's debts to third parties who deal with the partnership business.

Is the partnership liable?

The starting point for determining whether a partnership is liable is s 5 of the PA, which is based on the law of agency. Section 5 provides that each partner is an agent of their fellow partners and, as such, a partner acting within the scope of their **actual authority** or **apparent/ostensible authority** will bind the partnership as a whole.

Key term: actual authority

The partner is actually authorised to bind the partnership in the circumstances, whether under any partnership agreement or through authority given outside of one (specifically, generally or through a course of conduct).

Key term: apparent/ostensible authority

It would appear to the third party that the transaction is authorised by the partnership in the circumstances.

Apparent authority asks four questions:

- Is the transaction related to the partnership business?
- Would a partner usually be expected to have authority to enter into the transaction?
- Does the third party know that the partner has no actual authority?
- Does the third party know that the 'partner' concerned is not, in fact, a partner of the firm or do they have suspicions that this is the case?

If a partner has entered into a transaction with *either* actual or apparent authority, then the partnership *will* be bound by that act.

If a partner has entered into a transaction with *neither* actual nor apparent authority, then the partnership will *not* be bound by that act and only the partner concerned will be fully liable.

If a partner has entered into a transaction with *only* apparent authority, he will be liable to his fellow partners for breach of warranty of authority. In other words, the partnership will still be bound and the third party contract will not be affected. However, the individual partner will be liable personally, to account to his fellow partners for any loss to the partnership as a result of acting outside of the scope of what he was actually authorised to do.

Revision tip

It is important to distinguish between the relationship between the partners *themselves* and their relationship with *third parties*. A partnership agreement will often include provisions limiting any given partner's activities (for example, purchases of over £5,000 require the consent of all of the partners). However, the partner(s) will not be able to rely on these limitations as against a third party, unless that third party knew of them.

Practice example 2.5 illustrates how partnership authority may work in practice.

Practice example 2.5

Michael and Linda are partners in a restaurant business. There is no formal written partnership agreement, but the two partners each make regular orders for supplies. Michael enters into a contract to buy a new oven for the business. Who will be liable?

Michael and Linda clearly have actual authority (implied through a course of dealings) to purchase supplies for the business. However,

the scope of this transaction is wider. The transaction relates to the partnership business and it is arguable that a partner would usually be expected to have authority to enter into the transaction. Unless the third party knew that Michael had no authority, or knew or suspected Michael was not a partner in the business, the firm will be liable. Michael will be liable by virtue of privity of contract (see *Revise SQE: Contract Law*), in any event.

Which partners are liable?

Once it has been established whether the partnership as a whole is bound by a transaction with a third party, it must then be established precisely which partners are liable.

Partners are jointly liable for the debts and obligations of the partnership without limit (s 9 PA). Where a partnership is unable to pay its debts out of partnership assets, a creditor is entitled to obtain payment from the private assets of the partners (see **Chapter 1** for more information on unlimited liability).

Practice example 2.6 provides an example of how joint liability works in practice.

Practice example 2.6

Terry and Ulrika run a record shop in partnership. Terry orders food worth £500 from a caterer for an event at the shop. There is a formal partnership agreement in place, which provides that any partner has authority to purchase items up to the value of £1,000. Who is liable to pay the caterer?

Terry is liable on the basis that he made the contract and is therefore personally liable under it. The partnership as a whole is also liable as Terry had actual authority to enter into the transaction. Furthermore, Ulrika is liable on the basis that as the partnership itself is liable for the debt, she (as a partner at the time the deal was done) is jointly liable for the firm's debts. After judgment has been obtained in the county court, the partners become severally liable and the caterer could proceed against one or all of the partners. If Ulrika were sued for the full amount, she would be entitled to an indemnity from Terry for his proper share of the debt.

Change of partners

For the purpose of SQE1, it is important that you are able to advise on liability following a change in composition of a partnership. When doing so, it is crucial to distinguish between *existing debts* (those incurred prior to the change) and *future debts* (those incurred after the change).

- A partner is liable for the debts incurred whilst they are a partner (s 9 PA).
- A new partner is not liable for debts incurred by the partnership before they became a partner (s 17(1) PA).
- A retiring partner is not released from debts incurred by the partnership whilst they were a partner (s 17(2) PA).

A retiring partner may seek to protect themselves from liability for *existing debts* through a deed of release, a novation agreement, or an indemnity (see **Table 2.1**).

Table 2.1: Protection from liability for existing debts

Type of document	Description	Effect
Deed of release from willing creditors	A release of the outgoing partner from any outstanding debt/liability	Release of outgoing partner
Novation agreement from willing creditors	A *tripartite* arrangement between (1) the creditor (2) the partnership as constituted before the retirement (3) the partnership as constituted following the retirement Consideration or a deed will be required in order for it to be valid/binding	The newly constituted partnership stands in the shoes of the old one as regards the debt/liability
Indemnity from the continuing partners	A *bipartite* arrangement between (1) the outgoing partner and (2) the continuing partners	Not binding on third parties. The outgoing partner will still be liable but will be able to seek indemnity from the continuing partners

A retired partner may be liable for debts incurred after their retirement (ie *future debts*) if they fail to comply with ss 36 and 14 of the PA.

Section 36 of the PA says that a retiring partner must give notice to third parties of their leaving the partnership. This is because people who deal or who have dealt with the firm are entitled to assume there has been no change in composition of the partnership unless they have notice of it.

There are two types of notice under s 36 - actual and constructive (see **Table 2.2**).

Table 2.2: Protection from liability for future debts – s 36 PA

Type of notice	Section of PA	Who to?	How?
Actual	36(1)	Existing/ former clients/ customers	Inform them directly (eg send out standard letters)
Constructive	36(2)	Potential/ future clients/ customers	Place advertisement in the *London Gazette* (for partnerships in England and Wales)

A retiring partner must also avoid being **held out** as a partner under s 14 of the PA.

Key term: holding out

Holding out involves:

- doing something or allowing something to be done or represented that suggests one is a partner
- which is relied upon by someone
- who gives credit to the firm as a result.

Holding out is explained in **Practice example 2.7**.

Practice example 2.7

Toto was a partner in a brewery business and retired a year ago. The partnership has continued to supply beer to a number of local pubs. Toto, who is embarrassed not to have been in business or gainful employment since his departure, is a regular in one of the pubs and tells the landlord that he is still a partner in the business. The partnership also continues to use old stationery for orders, which states that Toto is one of the partners in the business. Will Toto be liable under future contracts of the partnership?

By telling the landlord that he is still a partner, Toto is clearly *doing something* that suggests that he is still a partner. By failing to destroy the old stationery, Toto is also *allowing something to be done* that suggests he is still a partner. He should have insisted that the old business stationery was destroyed on his departure. Toto may still be liable under future contracts as these representations are likely to have been relied upon in the course of business.

Exam warning

Make sure you read any question on liability for debts carefully. As well as any authority issues, ascertain who the partners were at the relevant time and consider whether the case involves existing or future liability.

Figure 2.1 summarises the approach for ascertaining partnership liability for debts.

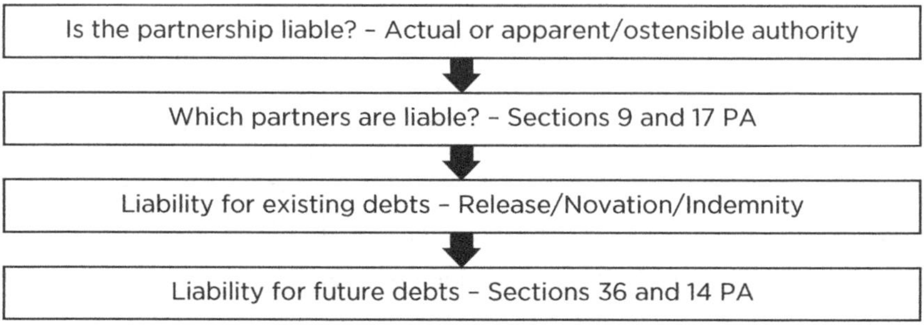

Figure 2.1: Ascertaining liability for debts

Practice example 2.8 shows how liability for future debts works in practice.

Practice example 2.8

The facts remain as in **Practice example 2.6**. Terry and Ulrika run a record shop in partnership. Terry orders food worth £500 from a caterer for an event at the shop. There is a formal partnership agreement in place, which provides that any partner has authority to purchase items up to the value of £1,000. However, the caterer brings an action against Terry, Ulrika and Katie. Katie was a former partner of the firm, who left one year before the contract was made. The caterer has contracted with the partnership for many years. Will Katie be liable under the contract?

As this is a future debt of the partnership (ie it was incurred after Katie left, rather than when she was still a partner), she will be liable unless she served actual notice on the caterer under s 36(1) of the PA. She may also be liable if she has done anything or allowed anything to be done which holds herself out as still being a partner (eg by not destroying old business stationery).

■ KEY POINT CHECKLIST

This chapter has covered the following key knowledge points. You can use these to structure your revision, ensuring you recall the key details for each point, as covered in this chapter.

- The formation of a partnership is a question of fact. It depends on whether the s 1 PA criteria are met and no specific formalities are required.
- There are real advantages to having a formal written partnership agreement. Most importantly, it can vary some of the key default

provisions under the PA. The most significant ones to be aware of are entitlement to capital and income profits, duration (retirement, death and bankruptcy), management and expulsion.
- Liability of the firm for debts to third parties depends on whether a partner had actual or apparent authority to contract on behalf of the partnership.
- Liability of the individual partners for debts depends on whether they were a partner at the time. Former partners do not automatically cease to be liable for debts incurred when they were a partner and new partners do not automatically become liable for debts incurred before they were a partner.
- Limiting an outgoing partner's liability for existing debts (ie those incurred before the change in composition - when they were still a partner) can be achieved through a deed of release, novation agreement or an indemnity.
- Limiting an outgoing partner's liability for future debts (ie those incurred after the change in composition - when they were no longer a partner) can be achieved through serving notice under s 36 PA and avoiding being held out as a partner under s 14 PA.

■ KEY TERMS AND CONCEPTS

- partnership agreement (**page 20**)
- partnership at will (**page 22**)
- actual authority (**page 27**)
- apparent/ostensible authority (**page 27**)
- holding out (**page 31**)

■ SQE1-STYLE QUESTIONS

QUESTION 1

Two clients start a business together. They each invest 50% of the capital and share profits equally. After a number of years, the business makes a loss.

Have the two clients been in partnership together?

A. Yes, because they are in business together with a view to making a profit.

B. Yes, but only because they agreed to invest equal amounts of capital.

C. No, because they have not entered into a formal written partnership agreement.

D. No, because the partnership has not been registered at Companies House.

E. No, because they did not agree on how losses should be shared between them.

QUESTION 2

A client seeks advice from a solicitor in setting up a partnership business.

Which of the following most accurately describes the position under the Partnership Act 1890, in the absence of an express or implied agreement to the contrary?

A. Partners will have an equal share of income profits, retirement of a partner will not dissolve the partnership, all partners are entitled to take part in the management of the business and a rogue partner may not be expelled by majority vote.

B. Partners will have an equal share of income profits, retirement of a partner will dissolve the partnership and a rogue partner may be expelled by majority vote.

C. Partners will have an equal share of income profits, retirement of a partner will dissolve the partnership, all partners are entitled to take part in the management of the business and a rogue partner may not be expelled by majority vote.

D. Partners will receive income profits proportionate to their capital share, retirement of a partner will not dissolve the partnership and all partners are entitled to take part in the management of the business.

E. Partners will receive income profits proportionate to their capital share, retirement of a partner will not dissolve the partnership and a rogue partner may not be expelled by majority vote.

QUESTION 3

A client starts a partnership business with a friend, and they make unequal capital contributions. One of the partners works full-time for the business and the other works part-time. There is no formal written partnership agreement or any agreement as to how income and capital profits will be shared.

Which of the following best describes the position on the share of income and capital profits?

A. Income and capital profits will be shared in accordance with the partners' respective capital contributions.

B. Income and capital profits will be shared in accordance with the hours worked by each partner in the business.

C. Income profits will be shared according to the hours worked by each partner and capital profits will be shared equally.

D. The partners must enter into a formal written partnership agreement as the Partnership Act 1890 does not make any provision for this type of situation.

E. Income profits will be shared equally, although it will most probably be implied that capital will be shared in proportion to the contributions made.

QUESTION 4

A client is a partner in a bakery business and enters into a transaction to buy a conservatory for his home, with partnership money.

Which of the following best describes the liability of the firm for this transaction?

A. The partnership as a whole will be liable. Individual partners, as joint owners of the business, always have authority to bind the firm, as agents of it. They do not need to act jointly.

B. Only the contracting partner will be liable. Individual partners, despite being joint owners of the business, do not have authority to bind the firm, as agents of it. They must make decisions jointly.

C. If the transaction was entered into with actual or apparent authority on the part of the contracting partner, the firm will be liable. It is unlikely that there will be apparent authority as the deal did not relate to the type of business in which the partnership normally deals.

D. If the transaction was entered into with actual or apparent authority on the part of the contracting partner, the firm will be liable. It is unlikely that there will be apparent authority unless the third party actually knew that the person they were dealing with was a partner.

E. If the transaction was entered into with actual or apparent authority on the part of the contracting partner, the firm will be liable. It is likely that there will be apparent authority on the facts.

QUESTION 5

A client leaving a partnership has sought advice as to whether she will have any ongoing liability for the partnership's existing and future debts. The client has already written to the firm's existing and previous clients informing them of her departure.

Which of the following most accurately describes the position of the client?

A. Upon leaving the partnership, the client will automatically cease to be liable for existing and future debts.

B. The client can avoid liability for existing debts through deeds of release or novation. She can avoid liability for future debts by giving constructive notice to potential clients and avoiding being held out as a partner.

C. The client will be liable for existing and future debts unless she enters into deeds of release or novation with the continuing partners and willing creditors.

D. Provided that the client gives constructive notice to potential clients and does everything possible to avoid being held out as a partner, she will have no liability for existing and future debts.

E. Upon leaving the partnership, the client will automatically cease to be liable for future debts.

■ ANSWERS TO QUESTIONS

Answers to 'What do you know already?' questions at the start of the chapter

1) False. Formalities are not a strict requirement in order to form a partnership. The agreement to operate a partnership can be oral or in writing, or may even be implied by conduct.
2) The correct answer was (b). In the absence of any written (or oral) agreement as to how long the partnership should last, or how it should be ended, it is a 'partnership at will' under s 26 of the PA and can be dissolved immediately by any party giving notice to the other(s) at any time.
3) The correct answer was (a). In the absence of an express or implied agreement to the contrary, the income and capital profits will be shared equally. It would most probably be implied that they would be able to withdraw capital unequally. In these circumstances, the parties would be best advised to enter into a formal written partnership agreement.
4) The partnership will be dissolved (s 33(1) PA).
5) Apparent/ostensible: under the principle of ostensible (or apparent) authority, the firm may be liable for actions which were not actually authorised, but which may have appeared to an outsider to be authorised.

Answers to end-of-chapter SQE1-style questions

Question 1

The correct answer was A, as the s 1 PA criteria are met. Equal investment in capital, agreement as to how profits and losses are to be shared, and registration at Companies House are not requirements. Therefore, options B, E and D are incorrect. A formal partnership agreement is not required, but one is usually recommended. Therefore, option C is also incorrect.

Question 2

The correct answer was C. Partners will have an equal share of income profits regardless of capital input. Therefore, options D and

E are incorrect on this point. Retirement of a partner will dissolve the partnership, therefore, options A, D and E are incorrect here. All partners are entitled to take part in the management of the business and a rogue partner may not be expelled by majority vote. Therefore, option B is also incorrect in this final respect.

Question 3

The correct answer was E. Income profits will be shared equally, irrespective of partners' capital contributions and their hours worked. Therefore, options A, B and C are incorrect. It will most probably be implied that capital is shared in proportion to the contributions made, also making options A, B and C incorrect. Although a partnership agreement would be advisable in these circumstances, it is not a requirement, so option D is incorrect.

Question 4

The correct answer was C. Although partners are agents of the business and may bind the partnership as individuals, actual and apparent authority need to be considered. Therefore, options A and B are incorrect. Option D is also incorrect - watch out for the exact wording in the question. The third party does not have to show that they *actually knew* that the person with whom they were dealing was a partner in the firm. They merely need to show that they *believed* that person to be a partner *or* had *no reason to suspect* that they were not. Option E is incorrect as apparent authority is unlikely on the facts.

Question 5

The correct answer was B. The client will need to take action to avoid liability for existing and future debts, so options A and E are incorrect. In respect of future debts, the client has already given actual notice to existing and former clients, so needs to give constructive notice and avoid being held out as a partner. As for existing debts, she will need deeds of release or novation. Note that an indemnity will not stop her being liable to the creditors but will entitle the outgoing partner to be indemnified by the continuing partners. Watch out for the fundamental distinction between existing and future debts. Options C and D are incorrect, as they do not make this distinction.

■ KEY CASES, RULES, STATUTES AND INSTRUMENTS

The SQE1 Assessment Specification does not generally require you to know statutory authorities or specific case names for this topic, but it does make specific reference to the PA 1890. Therefore, it may be referred to in questions and you should be aware of the principles behind the key provisions from a practical point of view. Sections of the PA are set out for ease of reference, but ss 36 and 14 are particularly important.

3

Limited companies: part 1

The Economic Crime and Corporate Transparency Act 2023 (ECCTA) received Royal Assent on 26 October 2023 and has made some changes to the Companies Act 2006. Not all of its provisions are in force and further changes are likely to be implemented in the course of 2026/27. Useful updates on implementation can be found on the 'Changes to UK company law' pages of the gov.uk website.

MAKE SURE YOU KNOW

This chapter provides an overview of company formation and constitution, as well as company management and decision-making. It will also outline some of the key documentary, record-keeping, statutory filing and disclosure requirements relevant to private limited companies. For SQE1, you will need to understand how limited companies are formed, the nature of the main constitutional document (the articles of association) and who is responsible for making key decisions in the life of a company. You will also need to understand the rules dealing with how those decisions are made, recorded and reported. Your understanding of these subjects will enable you to identify and apply the relevant legal rules and principles to SQE1-style single best answer MCQs.

SQE ASSESSMENT ADVICE

For SQE1, you are required to understand company formation and management from a practical perspective. It is likely that you will be required to identify the requirements and formalities of forming a private limited company. You may also be required to advise on the key requirements of corporate decision-making (ie who is responsible for key decisions and how those decisions are made, recorded and reported). At the heart of this is the separation between ownership (the shareholders/members) and management (the directors). In all aspects of this topic, you will be required to apply law and practice to problem-based, single best answer MCQs.

As you work through this chapter, remember to pay particular attention in your revision to the following:

- the key requirements for forming a company and the information/documentation required
- the importance of the articles of association as a company's key constitutional document
- the separation between shareholders/members and directors, as well as the key requirements of board meetings and general meetings

- the formality and reporting requirements relevant to company decision-making (including internal administration and Companies House filing requirements).

■ WHAT DO YOU KNOW ALREADY?

Attempt these questions before reading this chapter. If you find some difficult or cannot remember the answers, remember to look more closely at that area during your revision.

1) True or false? When setting up a private limited company, it is necessary to adopt the model articles of association.

   [Company formation and constitution, page 39]

2) True or false? The first directors of a company are automatically appointed on incorporation.

   [Company formation and constitution, page 39]

3) True or false? The directors are responsible for day-to-day decision-making in a company by passing board resolutions in general meetings.

   [Company meetings and resolutions, page 48]

4) What majority is required to pass an ordinary resolution and is it necessary to file one at Companies House?

   [Company meetings and resolutions, page 48]

5) What notice is required to hold a board meeting?

   [Company meetings and resolutions, page 48]

COMPANY FORMATION AND CONSTITUTION

For SQE1, it is necessary to know:

- the mechanics of company formation - procedure, documentation and relevant considerations
- post-incorporation steps and considerations.

Remember that a company is one medium through which a business may be run. In law, a company is an artificial legal 'person' (ie a separate legal entity with rights and obligations distinct from those of its shareholders/ members and directors - see **Chapter 1**). The creation of a company involves a legal process of producing documentation and filing it with the Registrar of Companies at Companies House.

Incorporating a company

There are two ways to provide a business client with a company:

- incorporating a new company (a 'tailor-made' company)
- acquiring a company that has already been incorporated, but which has not traded (an 'off the peg' or **shelf company**).

Key term: shelf company

A company that has already been set up, often by solicitors or a company formation agent. It is already live and has directors and shareholders (usually employees of the solicitors/agent) that will need to be changed. It can be an efficient way of providing a company to a client where time is of the essence.

Incorporation procedure, forms and documents

For a new company to be registered, the following must be sent to Companies House:

- application to register a company (form IN01)
- memorandum of association
- articles of association (in some circumstances) - see **Articles of association**, below
- the requisite fee.

The application may be made by post or online and a same day incorporation service (with an increased fee) is available. Company formation agents may also incorporate companies using specialist software.

Form IN01

Form IN01 requires the following information:

Form IN01 Part 1: company details

Company name

Subject to very limited exceptions, the name of a company must end with:

- limited or Ltd (or the Welsh language equivalents) - for private limited companies
- public limited company or plc (or the Welsh language equivalents) - for public limited companies.

In addition, a company name cannot be chosen which:

- is the same as that of an existing registered company
- in the opinion of the Secretary of State is offensive or constitutes a criminal offence (eg it contains swear words or refers to an activity prohibited by law)
- (unless previously approved) includes words suggesting a connection with the Government or a local authority or particular 'sensitive' words specified in the Company, Limited Liability Partnerships and Business Names (Sensitive Words and Expressions) Regulations 2014
- exceeds 160 characters, including spaces
- is intended to facilitate dishonesty or deception, contains computer code, or which could give a false impression of an association with a foreign government or international organisation.

Revision tip

For the purposes of SQE1, you do not need to know the 2014 regulations in detail; however, you should look over Schedule 1 of them to get a general appreciation of sensitive words and expressions.

Before the incorporation documents are sent to Companies House, it is therefore important to check the online index of company names kept there and whether any words in the proposed company name require approval. The trademarks register should also be checked to avoid possible trademark infringement.

If a name is chosen which is the same as, or similar to, that of an existing business and the business is likely to be affected by the similarity, the company may be subject to a passing off action in tort (see ***Revise SQE: Tort Law***). This is an action against someone who is misrepresenting themselves as being the same as/connected to another business. Following ECCTA, Companies House now has wider powers to reject company names and order a change of name (eg where it contains computer code). The detail of these provisions is beyond the scope of this book.

A company may change its name by special resolution (see **Company meetings and resolutions** below and s 77 Companies Act 2006 (CA)). Form NM01 must be filed at Companies House, together with a copy of the special resolution and the required fee.

Exam warning

It is important to appreciate that companies may also adopt a separate *trading/business* name. This does not have to be disclosed to Companies House and can be decided upon by the directors. Whilst a company's name requires a *special resolution* to be changed, a *trading/business* name may be changed by *board resolution* (see **Company meetings and resolutions**, and **Practice example 3.1** below).

Practice example 3.1

Your client, Sweet Dreams Desserts and Catering Limited, decides to trade under the name 'Sweet Dreams'. What is the required procedure?

A board resolution will be required to authorise the use of this trading name.

Company type

Public or private, limited by shares or guarantee (see **Chapter 1**).

Principal business activity

Companies House provides a list of code numbers to select from to define the principal business activity/activities.

Situation of registered office and registered office address (ss 86–88 CA)

The registered office is the official correspondence address for a company and where key documents must usually be kept (eg minutes and (where required) statutory books – see **Post-incorporation steps**, below).

Form IN01 will state whether the company's registered office is situated in:

- England and Wales
- Wales
- Scotland
- Northern Ireland.

The registered office must be consistent with where the company is registered. Following ECCTA, the company's registered office must be at an 'appropriate' address. This means an address where documents sent there would be expected to come to the attention of a person acting on behalf of the company and where delivery of documents can be acknowledged as delivered (s 86 CA).

Once incorporated, a company's registered office may be changed by board resolution (s 87 CA) and form AD01 must be filed at Companies House.

Under ECCTA, from 18 November 2025, it is no longer a requirement for companies to keep their own **statutory books**, save for the register of members. However, some companies may continue to choose to hold them. From 26 January 2026, companies can no longer elect to hold membership information solely on the central register.

Key term: statutory books

The statutory books traditionally include the following registers:

- register of secretaries
- register of directors
- register of directors' residential addresses
- register of members
- PSC register.

Email address

Following ECCTA, the company must also give and maintain an 'appropriate' registered email address. This must be an address, where in the ordinary course of events, emails sent to it by the registrar would be expected to come to the attention of a person acting on behalf of the company (s 88A CA).

Articles of association

The **articles of association** form a particularly important constitutional document for a company. They are a contract between (1) a shareholder and the company and (2) a shareholder and other shareholders (s 33(1) CA).

Key term: articles of association (articles)

The company's internal rulebook dealing with directors, shareholders, meetings and key administrative requirements.

The CA provides for standard sets of articles, known as **model articles**.

Key term: model articles

There are standard sets of articles for different types of company, set out in the Companies (Model Articles) Regulations 2008, which were introduced on 1 October 2009. The model articles for private companies limited by shares (the MAs) are set out in Schedule 1 of the regulations.

It is not compulsory to use the MAs and companies have the option of adopting:

- the MAs in their entirety
- the MAs with specific amendments
- a specifically drafted (bespoke) set of articles.

The important point here is that a copy of the company's articles must accompany the application *unless* the company intends to adopt the MAs in their entirety.

The MAs will automatically apply by default unless they are excluded or modified in the company's articles. Even if a company registers articles on incorporation, the MAs will still form part of the company's articles insofar as they are not specifically excluded or amended by the registered articles (s 20 CA).

It is very common to adopt the MAs with amendments. Popular amendments include deleting MA14 and MA13 (see **Company meetings and resolutions**, below) and supplementing the standard provisions on transfer and issue of shares (see **Chapter 5**).

For companies incorporated prior to 1 October 2009, it is usual to find 'Table A' as the basis for articles. Table A is the equivalent of the MAs for companies registered under the Companies Act 1985.

A special resolution is required to change the articles (s 21(1) CA). A copy of the special resolution and the amended articles must be filed at Companies House within 15 days (ss 26(1), 29 and 30 CA).

Practice example 3.2 deals with the selection of articles in practice.

Practice example 3.2

Agnetha approaches you for advice on setting up a private limited company with her friend Benny and wants to know their options with regard to the articles. How would you advise Agnetha?

On incorporation, the company may adopt all or some of the provisions of the MAs (with or without additional special articles) or have entirely bespoke articles. There is no obligation to adopt the MAs in whole or in part, although the MAs will apply in default.

Form IN01 Part 2: proposed officers

Verification of identity

Under ECCTA, identity verification requirements (IDV) are being gradually introduced for directors, people with significant control (PSCs) (see below) and those delivering documents to Companies House (s 1110A and s 1110B CA). A 12-month transition phase began on 18 November 2025, although voluntary IDV became possible from 8 April 2025. The procedure is now compulsory on incorporation and for both new and existing individual directors and PSCs and members of LLPs. IDV requirements for others (including those who file documents at Companies House) is expected to follow in November 2026. Existing directors must confirm their identity as part of the company's next Confirmation Statement, and PSCs are given a 14-day period for compliance. Under the procedure, relevant individuals must have their identity verified at Companies House online, at a post office, or by an 'Authorised Corporate Services Provider' (ACSP), registered with Companies House. There are criminal penalties for non-compliance.

Company secretary

The company secretary is the person responsible for keeping records and filing documents at Companies House. It is not a requirement of the CA for a private limited company to have a company secretary, but if there is one, their name and address for service must be given. No particular qualifications are required to act as a company secretary of a private limited company.

Directors

The name, month and year of birth, and nationality of all directors must be set out (see **Chapter 4** for more on directors).

An address for service and usual residential address must be given, although directors may apply for an exemption if they would be at risk of violence or intimidation if their residential address were to be made publicly available (eg they are a celebrity or are involved in a controversial business).

A private company must have at least one director (public companies require a minimum of two). Human directors must be at least 16 years of age and although corporate directors are permitted, at least one director must be a natural person. In other words, a company may be a director of another company (usually acting through its own directors), but it is not possible for a company to be the sole director of another company. There always needs to be at least one human being taking the role. There is no limit on the number of directors unless the articles provide for this, and it is possible for a director to hold the position of company secretary. No particular qualifications are required to act as a director of a private limited company.

Exam warning

The law on corporate directors could change in the future. The Small Business, Enterprise and Employment Act 2015 inserted a new s 156A into the CA, but the provision is not yet in force. If put into force, it will only be possible to have human directors, although exceptions may be provided for in regulations.

Form IN01 Part 3: statement of capital and initial shareholdings

The statement of capital and initial shareholdings show the following:

- initial share capital - the number of shares of each type and their nominal value
- rights attaching to the different types/classes of share (eg voting and dividends - see **Exercise of shareholders' powers - GMs** below, and **Chapters 4 and 5**)
- initial shareholdings - names and addresses of shareholders, details of their individual shareholdings and any amount unpaid on their shares.

A minimum of one shareholder is required. ECCTA will introduce a required statement in form IN01 that none of the proposed officers, subscribers to the memorandum or people with significant control (see below) have been disqualified as directors or are otherwise ineligible to hold that office.

Form IN01 Part 4: statement of guarantee

This is only applicable for companies limited by guarantee (see **Chapter 1**).

Form IN01 Part 5: people with significant control

Details of **people with significant control** (PSC) must be set out.

Key term: people with significant control

Generally, these people meet one or more of the following conditions:

- they hold more than 25% of the shares
- they have more than 25% of the voting rights
- they have the right to appoint or remove the majority of the board.

See **Practice example 3.3**.

Practice example 3.3

Songs for Europe Limited has 1,000 £1 shares with voting rights that are issued as follows:
Mike - 150 shares
Bobby - 250 shares
Cheryl - 550 shares
Jay - 50 shares

Who needs to be entered onto the PSC register?

Only Cheryl needs to be entered onto the PSC register for the company. She is the only one with more than 25% of the shares.

The relevant Companies House PSC forms (PSC01-09) must be filed whenever changes are made (eg PSC01 to appoint a new individual PSC).

Form IN01 Part 6: consent to act

In all cases, the subscriber(s) must make a statement that the proposed officers (director(s) and the company secretary, if applicable) have consented to act in the relevant role(s).

Form IN01 Part 7: statement about individual PSC particulars

The subscribers must make a statement that the PSCs know their details have been provided as part of the application.

Form IN01 Part 8: lawful purpose statement

This confirms that the subscribers wish to form the company for lawful purposes.

Form IN01 Part 9: statement of compliance

This confirms that the requirements of the CA as to registration have been complied with.

Memorandum of association

The memorandum of association is a statement of intention of the subscriber(s) to form a company and become shareholders, taking at least one share each. The prescribed form of memorandum is set out in the Companies (Registration) Regulations 2008 and can be accessed online at Companies House. Under the CA 1985, the memorandum of association was an important ongoing constitutional document, setting out the objects of the company. Following the CA 2006, the objects are moved to the articles and may be changed by special resolution.

Certificate of incorporation

The documents are examined by Companies House and, provided that they are in order, a certificate of incorporation (COI) will be issued which will include the company name, the company number and the date of incorporation (s 15 CA). It is essentially the company's 'birth certificate' and although the company may change its name, its number remains consistent throughout its life.

The company cannot enter into contracts until the COI has been issued (s 51 CA).

Post-incorporation steps

Once the COI has been issued, a number of practical steps should be taken and statutory provisions complied with, namely:

- *ordering the company seal (optional)*: this is an optional alternative way of executing documents and can make them look more official (MA49)
- *publicising the company's name*: outside the company's office(s) or place(s) of business and in all its correspondence
- *including the correct particulars on business stationery*: the company stationery must include the company's name, registered office and number (s 82 CA 2006)
- *registering for VAT with HMRC* (see **Chapter 7**)
- *dealing with all matters relating to the company's employees*: for example, contracts of employment, setting up PAYE (see **Chapter 8**) and National Insurance for employees
- *arranging insurances* (eg buildings insurance, public liability, employers' liability and professional indemnity policies)
- *opening a company bank account*
- *obtaining all requisite licences/consents to operate the business*
- *maintaining the statutory books (where kept – see above)*
- *keeping other documents at the registered office*: these include copies of charges (see **Chapter 5**), directors' service (employment) contracts and minute books (see **Company meetings and resolutions**, below).

First board meeting

Once incorporated, the company should call its first board meeting to make decisions on a variety of matters. These include:

- appointing a chairperson of the board (MA12)
- adopting the company seal
- appointing bankers/formalising bank mandates

- appointing auditors (if the company needs to file audited accounts – see **Accounts**, below)
- fixing an accounting reference date (ie the date up to which it must prepare its annual accounts), otherwise it will be the last day of the month of incorporation. Following a change, form AA01 must be filed at Companies House (see **Practice example 3.4**)
- awarding directors' service contracts (see **Chapter 4**)
- authorising use of a business/trading name
- allotting shares and issuing share certificates (see **Chapter 5**)
- approving the cost of formation
- registering with HMRC for corporation tax, PAYE, National Insurance and VAT
- taking out insurances
- calling a general meeting (see **Company meetings and resolutions**, below), if required (eg to give the directors authority to issue shares etc).

Practice example 3.4

Esther sets up One Night Limited to carry on a hotel business. The company is incorporated on 16 March. What will be the accounting reference date for the company?

Unless the company nominates an alternative accounting reference date by filing form AA01 at Companies House following its incorporation, an accounting reference date will be allocated which corresponds to the last day of the month in which the company was incorporated (ie 31 March).

COMPANY MEETINGS AND RESOLUTIONS

For SQE1, you need to have good working knowledge of the ways in which companies make and implement decisions in the forum of both **board meetings** and **general meetings**.

Key term: board meetings (BMs)

Meetings of the directors, who pass board resolutions (BRs) to make decisions (see **Exercise of directors' powers: BMs**, below).

Key term: general meetings (GMs)

Meetings of the members/shareholders, who pass ordinary resolutions (ORs) and special resolutions (SRs) to make decisions (see **Exercise of shareholders' powers: GMs**, below).

The division of decision-making between the directors and the members of a company is a fundamental aspect of company law. There are two key questions here:

- Can the board, without reference to the members, make the decision?
- Must the members first sanction the decision of the board?

The directors can make most day-to-day decisions, but some key decisions must be approved/authorised by the members first. This can be because of the provisions of the CA or the articles. If this is the case, the directors usually call a BM in order to pass a BR to call a GM. The original BM will then be closed or adjourned, pending the decision of the members in a GM. A second or reconvened BM is then called in order for the directors to implement the decision and deal with the necessary administrative formalities (see **Figure 3.1**).

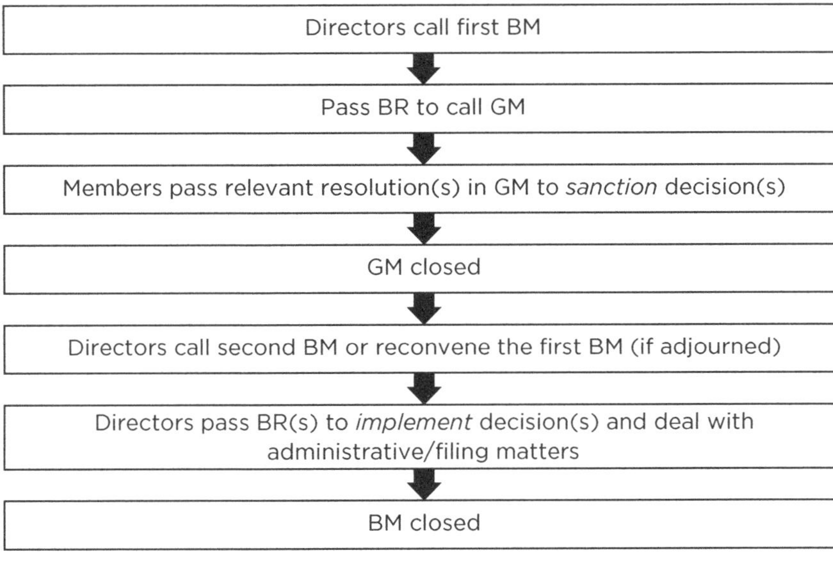

Figure 3.1: Sanction of shareholders required

Exercise of directors' powers: BMs

The directors are the people who manage the company.

The powers of the directors are laid down in the company's articles and MA3, by far one of the most important provisions of the MAs, gives the directors wide powers to manage the business of the company.

Generally, directors make decisions at BMs by majority vote (MA7) or otherwise by unanimous decision of the directors (MA8).

It is common to give the directors the right to delegate any of their powers (MA5).

The key provisions of BMs are set out in **Table 3.1**.

Table 3.1: Key provisions of BMs

Calling and notice	Any director may call a BM at any time or require the company secretary to do so (MA9) Reasonable notice must be given (not necessarily in writing unless the articles provide) (MA9(1)) All directors must be given notice, wherever they are (MA9(3)) Notice contents - date, time, place and means of communication (MA9(2)) Permitted forms of communication include telephone calls, video calls, text message, instant messaging (MA10(1)) Director(s) can waive the right to notice (MA9(4)) An agenda is not a legal requirement Implications of failure to give notice - a new meeting can be demanded
Quorum	Two is the **quorum** (MA11(2))
Voting	Show of hands or oral assent (MA7(1)) Chairperson's casting vote in the event of deadlock (MA13) MA14 and ss 177 and 182 - See **Conflicts of interest**
Resolutions and majority	BRs - simple majority required (deadlock if equality of votes and MA13 does not apply)

NB: Statutory references are to the CA.

Key term: quorum

The minimum number of people required to be present in order for valid decisions to be made. If the minimum number is not present, then the meeting is not 'quorate' and decisions cannot be made.

Conflicts of interest

MA14 prevents a director from voting and counting towards the quorum on any decision in which they have a personal interest. A classic example of a conflict would be a director agreeing to buy property from, or sell property to, the company. In such circumstances, the director will want the best possible deal for himself, but this will conflict with the fiduciary duties he owes to the company (see **Chapter 4**). MA14 is subject to limited exceptions in MA14(3) and (4), the most important of which is where a director subscribes for shares in the company.

MA14(3)(a) allows a company to suspend or relax the general application of MA14 by OR.

Sections 177 and 182 CA require a director to declare a personal interest in a proposed (s 177) or existing (s 182) transaction or arrangement. This is subject to limited exceptions in sections 177(6) and 182(6) of the CA respectively, the most important of which is where a director's service (employment) contract is being considered (see **Chapter 4**). Breach of s 182 is a criminal offence (s 183 CA).

Revision tip

It is crucially important to appreciate that the *declaration* of a conflict of interest under ss 177 and 182 is a separate and distinct requirement from the ability to *vote and count towards the quorum* under MA14. Candidates often misunderstand and conflate the two requirements, but both should be considered separately. It is also worth remembering the two key exceptions set out above.

Practice example 3.5 provides an example of conflicts of interest in practice.

Practice example 3.5

Hanne is a director and shareholder of Swing Entertainments Limited, a company with unamended MAs. She agrees to subscribe for some additional shares in the company and has been offered a new service contract, subject to board approval. The company has also agreed, subject to contract, to buy a commercial property from Elisabeth, an existing shareholder. What is the position with regard to potential conflicts of interest?

As an existing director, Hanne must declare her interest in the proposed share acquisition but will be able to vote and count towards the quorum in relation to their issue at BM, due to the exception in MA14(4). She does not need to declare her interest in the proposed service contract, due to the exception in s 177(6)(c), but she will be prevented from voting and counting towards the quorum in relation to it, under MA14. Although Elisabeth clearly has a personal interest in the property transaction, ss 177 and 182 and MA14 will only apply if she is also a director, as the provisions relate to BMs. If so, she would need to declare her interest at the BM and would be unable to vote and count towards the quorum on the decision.

Minutes of BMs

Minutes must be kept of all BMs for at least 10 years (s 248 CA and MA15) and will usually be signed by the chair of the BM.

Unanimous decisions

MA8 provides that a procedure for unanimous decision-making may be used instead of holding a BM. This enables the directors to make decisions in writing or more informally, provided that they all agree.

Exercise of shareholders' powers: GMs

The powers of the members are laid down in the CA and the company's articles and they generally exercise their powers by passing resolutions in GMs. There are two types of GM - an **AGM** and an **(E)GM**.

Key term: AGM

An annual general meeting. A private company formed on or after 1 October 2006 does not need to have an AGM, unless a special article provides so. A company formed before that date is required to hold an AGM, unless its articles have been amended. AGMs can be useful if there are a number of shareholders who are not directors.

Key term: (E)GM

Any meeting of the members other than an AGM. GMs used to be referred to as 'extraordinary general meetings' (EGMs), but under the CA, they are now simply GMs.

There are two types of resolution - an **ordinary resolution** (OR) and a **special resolution** (SR).

Key term: ordinary resolution

An OR requires a simple majority (*more than* 50%) of shareholders attending and voting at a GM.

Key term: special resolution

An SR requires a 75% majority (ie 75% *or more*) of shareholders attending and voting at a GM.

Exam warning

It is important to appreciate the difference between an OR and an SR and not to confuse them with BRs. The majority required for an OR is *more than* 50%, so if exactly 50% are in favour of passing it, it will not be passed and will result in deadlock. However, the majority required for an SR is 75% *or more*, so if exactly 75% are in favour of passing an SR, it will be passed.

The key provisions of GMs are set out in **Table 3.2**.

Table 3.2: Key provisions of GMs

Calling and notice	Usually the directors call a GM (s 302) Written or electronic notice may be given (ss 308 and 1168 and MA48) Shareholders' power to requisition a GM (see main text) (ss 303–305) 14 *clear* days' notice required (s 307(1)) (in effect 16 days as you do not include date of service and date of meeting (s 360)) to (inter alia) all members and directors (s 310) Add an extra two days' notice if serving by email or post (in effect 14 *clear* days = 18 days) (s 1147) Short notice may be agreed by (1) a majority in number of members (2) holding at least 90% of the company's voting shares (s 307(4)–(6)) (both conditions have to be satisfied – see **Practice example 3.7**) Contents of notice: Date, time, place and nature of business (s 311) Full text of any SR proposed and sufficient detail re ORs (s 283) Reasonably prominent proxy notice (s 325) – a notice informing the shareholder of their right to send someone to attend and vote in their stead (s 324 and MA45)
Quorum	Two (unless a one-member company) (s 318(2)) Meeting must remain quorate throughout (MA40(1))
Voting	Show of hands (one vote per member) (ss 282–283 and MA42) unless poll vote demanded Poll may be demanded by – (1) the chairperson, (2) at least two voting members, (3) any member(s) holding at least 10% of the voting shares (MA 44) One vote per share on a poll vote (s 284(3))
Resolutions and majorities	OR – >50% – simple majority of those voting SR – 75% majority of those voting

NB: Statutory references are to the CA.

Shareholders' power to requisition a GM (ss 303–305 CA)

Although it is usually the directors who call GMs, the members of a company may also indirectly call them (ss 303–305 CA). These sections provide that the directors must call a GM when members holding at least 5% of the company's paid-up share capital with voting rights requisition them to do so. The directors then have 21 days from the date of the requisition to call a GM, which must be held within 28 days from the date the GM is called. If the meeting is not called, the shareholders may call the meeting themselves and recover the costs from the company.

Written resolutions

As an alternative to holding a GM, a private company may pass resolutions in writing (ss 288–300 CA), with shareholders having one vote per share.

Formalities

Minutes must be kept of all GMs for at least 10 years (s 355 CA).

A signed copy of every SR and some ORs must be filed at Companies House within 15 days of being passed. The most important example of an OR that needs to be filed is one which authorises the issue of shares (see **Chapter 5**).

Where the resolution alters the company's articles, a copy of the amended document must be filed.

Any appropriate form must also be filed at Companies House.

Where appropriate and required (see above), the company's statutory books must be updated.

Practice examples 3.6–3.8 put some of the key principles relating to GMs into practice.

Practice example 3.6

Your firm acts for Wurst Transformations Limited, a company that has adopted MAs, unamended. The directors wish to change the company's name to Phoenix Properties Limited and propose to call a GM to sanction this. They will personally hand over the notices of the GM. How much notice will be required?

At least 14 clear days' notice is required. Short notice may be agreed, but a majority in number of the members must sanction this and those members must hold at least 90% of the company's voting shares. If the

notices were not physically being handed over, an extra two days' notice would need to be added to allow for the service rules.

Practice example 3.7

Napoleon (Waterloo) Properties Limited has an issued share capital of 100,000 £1 ordinary shares held as follows:

- Sonia - 80,000 shares
- Björn - 5,000 shares
- Anni-Frid - 5,000 shares
- Gina - 4,000 shares
- Loreen - 4,000 shares
- Engelbert - 2,000 shares.

The company has adopted the MAs, unamended, and wishes to authorise short notice of a GM. What combination of shareholders will be required to do this?

The required percentage shareholding (90%) is met with the support of Sonia, Björn and Anni-Frid, but this combination (three shareholders) does not represent a majority in number of the shareholders (ie the support of at least four of the six shareholders is required, who hold the requisite 90% shareholding).

Practice example 3.8

Your client, Diva Developments Limited, has queried whether a company resolution needs to be filed at Companies House. How would you advise them?

BRs never need to be filed, but SRs must always be filed at Companies House. The general rule is that ORs are not required to be filed, but an OR under s 551 CA 2006 (authority to issue shares) is an exception to that general rule (see Chapter 5).

Summary of key decisions

Company decision-making involves a number of formality and reporting requirements (including internal administration and Companies House filing requirements). It is important to know these in the context of particular transactions. The transactions dealt with in this chapter are summarised in **Table 3.3**.

Table 3.3: Summary of key decisions

Change of company name		
Substantive legal requirements	**Procedural requirements (PR) and Directors' declaration of personal interests (DOI)**	**Filing/Administration requirements**
Check whether company name requires approval SR (s 77)	PR: BM > GM > BM DOI: Usually not applicable	Filing: Copy SR Form NM01 Change of name fee Admin: Update company stationery BM and GM minutes
Change of trading name		
MA3 (BR)	PR: BM DOI: Usually not applicable	Admin: Update company stationery BM minutes
Change registered office		
MA3 (BR) (s 87)	PR: BM DOI: Usually not applicable	Filing: Form AD01 Admin: Update company stationery BM minutes
Change articles		
SR (s 21(1))	PR: BM > GM > BM DOI: Usually not applicable	Filing: SR Amended articles Admin: BM and GM minutes
Appointment of chairperson		
MA3 (BR) MA12	PR: BM DOI: s 177 and MA14	Admin: Update company stationery BM minutes
Change of accounting reference date		
MA3 (BR)	PR: BM DOI: Usually not applicable	Filing: AA01 Admin: BM minutes

NB: Statutory references are to the CA.

ACCOUNTS

Directors must file accounts each financial year with Companies House (s 394 CA). It is a criminal offence not to do so (s 387 CA).

Small companies are exempt from the requirement for accounts to be audited (s 477 CA).

Key term: small companies

Small companies are those that satisfy two or more of the following:

- turnover of not more than £15m
- balance sheet of no more than £7.5m
- not more than 50 employees.

The directors must also prepare a financial report for each financial year (s 415 CA). Small companies and 'micro entities' (s 384A CA) are exempt.

Accounts for private companies must usually be filed with Companies House within nine months from the end of the accounting reference period (s 442 CA).

Note that ECCTA will bring into effect changes to requirements on accounts filing, although Companies House has confirmed that companies will receive at least 21 months to prepare for the changes. Changes will include requirements to file accounts by software only, changes to filing options for small companies, further requirements when claiming an audit exemption, and limitations on changing accounting reference periods on multiple occasions.

CONFIRMATION STATEMENT

A confirmation statement (form CS01) must be filed each year within 14 days of the anniversary of the company's incorporation (s 853A CA). The form confirms that all information required to be delivered to Companies House has been duly filed and provides details of any changes (eg to shareholdings). This ensures that Companies House has the most up-to-date information about the company and its composition. Failure to do so is a criminal offence. The confirmation statement was formerly known as an 'annual return'. ECCTA has introduced a statement in the confirmation statement that the intended future activities of the company are lawful.

■ KEY POINT CHECKLIST

This chapter has covered the following key knowledge points. You can use these to structure your revision, ensuring you recall the key details for each point, as covered in this chapter.

- In order to create a company, form IN01 must be filed at Companies House, together with a memorandum of association, the requisite fee and, in some cases, the articles.

- The articles form the company's internal rulebook.
- MAs are available, which provide a standard set of rules. If the company wishes to adopt the MAs in their entirety, the articles do not need to be submitted with form IN01.
- Once incorporated, the company is 'born' as an artificial 'person' and a COI will be issued. There are a number of post-incorporation matters to attend to and the company will hold its first BM.
- The separation between shareholders/members and directors is fundamental to company law.
- Directors decide matters in BMs and pass BRs by simple majority. They have general management powers (MA3), but the CA or articles may specify that the approval of the shareholders/members is required for some matters/transactions.
- The shareholders/members have GMs and pass ORs (simple majority) and SRs (majority of 75%) to make decisions. The CA, or the articles, will specify the type of resolution required.
- The key requirements of BMs and GMs are very important, and you need to have a good working knowledge of them. It is also important to know these in the context of particular transactions.

■ KEY TERMS AND CONCEPTS

- shelf company (**page 39**)
- statutory books (**page 42**)
- articles of association (**page 43**)
- model articles (**page 43**)
- people with significant control (**page 45**)
- board meetings (**page 48**)
- general meetings (**page 48**)
- quorum (**page 50**)
- AGM (**page 52**)
- (E)GM (**page 52**)
- ordinary resolution (**page 52**)
- special resolution (**page 52**)
- small companies (**page 57**)

■ SQE1-STYLE QUESTIONS

QUESTION 1

Two new clients wish to set up a private company limited by shares.

Which of the following best describes the information required in order to complete form IN01?

A. Full details of the shareholders, directors and company secretary (if any), the registered office, the name of the company, how many shares the company will have, their type and nominal value, and instructions on the articles.

B. Full details of the shareholders, directors and company secretary (if any), the registered office, the name of the company, its trading name, how many shares the company will have, their type and nominal value and instructions on the articles.

C. Full details of the shareholders, directors and company secretary (if any), the registered office, the name of the company, how many shares the company will have, their type and nominal value, instructions on the articles and details of any service contracts to be issued to the directors.

D. Full details of the shareholders, directors and company secretary (if any), the registered office, the name of the company, how many shares the company will have, their type and nominal value, instructions on the articles and confirmation of registration with HMRC.

E. Full details of the shareholders, directors and company secretary (if any), the registered office, the name of the company, how many shares the company will have, their type and nominal value, instructions on the articles, confirmation of the auditor and instructions on whether to adopt a company seal.

QUESTION 2

A client was a sole trader who recently incorporated their hairdressing business into a private limited company. They are the sole director and joint and equal shareholder with their spouse. Prior to receiving the certificate of incorporation, the client entered into a contract with a shampoo supplier. The contract was signed by the sole trader on behalf of the company.

With whom, if anyone, does the benefit of the contract reside?

A. The company.

B. The shareholders.

C. The sole trader.

D. The sole trader and the company jointly.

E. The contract is void.

QUESTION 3

A private limited company was incorporated with unamended model articles of association but has since adopted amended articles.

What must be filed with Companies House following the adoption of the amended articles of association?

A. The board minutes relating to the change and the shareholders' resolution sanctioning the adoption.

B. The shareholders' resolution to adopt the amended articles of association only.

C. The amended articles of association only.
D. The shareholders' resolution to adopt the amended articles of association and the amended articles of association.
E. The board resolution relating to the change and the new articles of association.

QUESTION 4

A company wishes to call a general meeting to amend the articles of association. There are seven shareholders, all with ordinary voting shares. The client has 52,000 shares, a man has 20,000 shares and a woman has 20,000 shares. The remaining four shareholders have 2,000 shares each.

Which of the following best describes who would be required to agree to hold the meeting on short notice?

A. The client, the man and the woman.
B. Any four - a simple majority in number is required.
C. The client, the man, the woman and any other shareholder.
D. The client, as majority shareholder.
E. The client, the man, the woman and any other two shareholders.

QUESTION 5

A client private limited company with unamended model articles of association has six directors and needs to approve the purchase of property worth £3,000 that is jointly owned by two of the directors (the 'selling directors'). Two directors do not support the transaction, but the remaining four (including the two selling directors and one of the other directors, who is also the chairperson) wish to vote in favour of it.

Which of the following best describes the situation should all directors attend and vote at the board meeting?

A. The four directors in favour will be able to pass a board resolution (BR) as they represent the majority.
B. The four directors in favour will be able to pass a BR as they represent the majority. However, the two selling directors will need to declare their personal interests in the transaction.
C. The four directors in favour will be unable to pass the BR. The two selling directors will need to declare their personal interests in the transaction and will be unable to vote and count towards the quorum.
D. The four directors in favour will be able to pass the BR. The two selling directors will need to declare their personal interests in the transaction

and will be unable to vote and count towards the quorum. In the event of deadlock (which is anticipated on the facts), the chairperson will be able to exercise her casting vote.

E. The decision must be authorised by an ordinary resolution of the shareholders.

■ ANSWERS TO QUESTIONS

Answers to 'What do you know already?' questions at the start of the chapter

1) False. When setting up a private limited company, it is not necessary to adopt the model articles in their entirety, but it is possible to do so. The model articles may also be adopted with amendments, or completely bespoke articles may be chosen.
2) True. The first directors of a company are automatically appointed on incorporation (s 16 CA). They cannot take office until the company is incorporated and there is no requirement for them to be formally appointed in meetings after incorporation.
3) False. The directors are responsible for day-to-day decision-making in a company and they do pass board resolutions; however, they are passed in board meetings. The shareholders pass ordinary resolutions and special resolutions in general meetings.
4) A simple majority (*more than* 50%) of shareholders attending and voting at a general meeting is required to pass an ordinary resolution. Special resolutions require a 75% majority (ie 75% *or more*). Special resolutions need to be filed at Companies House, but ordinary resolutions usually do not.
5) Reasonable notice is required to call a board meeting. Fourteen clear days' notice is required to call a general meeting (although short notice may be possible).

Answers to end-of-chapter SQE1-style questions

Question 1

The correct answer was A. The trading name (option B), directors' service contracts (option C), registration with HMRC (option D) and whether to have a company seal (option E) can all be decided after incorporation. Depending on the size and value of the company, an auditor may not be required (option E) and their appointment may be decided after incorporation.

Question 2

The correct answer was C. The company is not able to enter into contracts until the certificate of incorporation has been issued. Until then, the company can have no liability, so options A and D are incorrect. If made after incorporation, the company would have the benefit of the contract as a separate legal person. The shareholders' liability would be limited thereafter, but they can have no liability until the company is incorporated, so option B is incorrect. The contract is not void as the sole trader will still be liable by virtue of privity of contract, so option E is incorrect.

Question 3

The correct answer was D. It is the shareholders who need to pass a special resolution (SR) in general meeting (GM) in order to approve the amendment. Although the directors will usually pass a board resolution (BR) to call the GM, the amendment of the articles is not their decision to make. The company is under a duty to keep minutes of both meetings, but these do not need to be filed at Companies House, so option A is incorrect. BRs and most ordinary resolutions do not need to be filed, but SRs do, so option E is incorrect. Both the SR and the amended articles need to be filed, so options B and C are incorrect.

Question 4

The correct answer was C. In order to satisfy the conditions, there has to be a majority in number of shareholders, who together hold at least 90% of the company's voting shares. Both pre-conditions have to be satisfied. Option A is incorrect as it does not satisfy the 'majority in number' point. Option B is incorrect as it may not satisfy the shareholding threshold. Option D is incorrect as it satisfies neither. Option E exceeds the minimum requirements but could also authorise the decision.

Question 5

The correct answer was D. The two selling directors will need to declare their personal interests in the transaction and will be unable to vote and count towards the quorum when the decision is made, so options A, B and C are incorrect. That leaves four directors who are eligible to vote, two in favour and two against. The chairperson will have a casting vote to break the deadlock. An ordinary resolution will not be required as the transaction falls within the directors' general management powers and is not a substantial property transaction (see **Chapter 4**). Therefore, option E is incorrect.

■ KEY CASES, RULES, STATUTES AND INSTRUMENTS

The SQE1 Assessment Specification does not require you to know any statutory authorities or specific case names for this topic, so references to the CA and the MAs are for information purposes only. However, MA3, MA14 and s 177 CA are particularly important, so you should be aware of the principles behind these key provisions from a practical point of view.

4

Limited companies: part 2

The Economic Crime and Corporate Transparency Act 2023 (ECCTA) received Royal Assent on 26 October 2023 and has made some changes to the Companies Act 2006. Not all of its provisions are in force and further changes are likely to be implemented in the course of 2026/27. Useful updates on implementation can be found on the 'Changes to UK company law' pages of the gov.uk website.

■ MAKE SURE YOU KNOW

This chapter provides an overview of the appointment and removal of directors and the company secretary and the rights, duties, obligations, liabilities, restrictions and powers of the key stakeholders in a company (the directors and shareholders). It sets out important documentary, record-keeping, and statutory filing and disclosure requirements relevant to directors, the company secretary and shareholders. It also outlines minority shareholder protection. Your understanding of these subjects will enable you to identify and apply the relevant legal rules and principles to SQE1-style single best answer MCQs.

■ SQE ASSESSMENT ADVICE

For SQE1, you are required to understand the law relating to directors and shareholders from a practical perspective. It is likely that you will be required to understand the requirement for a company to have directors (and in some cases a company secretary), and how they are appointed and removed. You will also need to understand their duties, obligations and powers, recognise where breaches may have occurred and appreciate where shareholder approval is necessary. It is likely that you will be required to identify the rights, duties and powers of shareholders, their ability to be involved in key decisions and what they can do when issues occur. At the heart of this chapter is the separation between ownership (the shareholders) and management/control (the directors) and there is a clear link with the procedural aspects of company decision-making referred to in **Chapter 3**.

As you work through this chapter, remember to pay particular attention in your revision to the following:

- the need for directors (and in some cases a company secretary) and how they are appointed and removed
- the rights, duties, obligations, liabilities and powers of directors and restrictions they are under
- the need for shareholders and their rights, duties and powers

- minority shareholder protection
- the formality and reporting requirements relevant to directors, company secretaries and shareholders (including internal administration and Companies House filing requirements).

WHAT DO YOU KNOW ALREADY?

Attempt these questions before reading this chapter. If you find some difficult or cannot remember the answers, remember to look more closely at that area during your revision.

1) True or false? The shareholders always appoint new directors.
   [Appointment of directors, page 65]
2) When do directors' service contracts require shareholder approval?
   [Restrictions on directors: directors' service contracts (s 188 CA), page 72]
3) True or false? The shareholders must always approve a property transaction which exceeds £100,000 in value.
   [Restrictions on directors: substantial property transactions, page 73]
4) What type of resolution is required to remove a director from office?
   [Removal of directors, page 75]
5) Explain what is meant by the term 'minority shareholder'.
   [Members' powers, page 79]

DIRECTORS

For SQE1, it is important to understand the law relating to the appointment and removal of **directors** and directors' duties, liabilities, restrictions and powers.

Key term: director

A director is *'any person occupying the position of director, by whatever name called'* (s 250(1) Companies Act 2006 (CA)).

Accordingly, the definition of director is very wide and includes **shadow directors** and **de facto directors**.

Key term: shadow director

A person who, although not properly appointed as a director, exercises a major influence on the directors; the directors are accustomed to act in accordance with their instructions (s 251 CA).

Key term: de facto director

Either a director who has not been properly appointed under the CA, but performs the role of director, or a person who continues in the role of director after their term of office has expired.

Many of the provisions of the CA and the Insolvency Act 1986 (IA) apply to shadow and de facto directors. This is to prevent people escaping liability where it would be unjust for them to do so.

APPOINTMENT OF DIRECTORS

This section deals with the need for, and appointment of, directors.

Requirement for directors

A private company must have at least one director (s 154(1) CA) and a public company must have at least two directors (s 154(2) CA).

It is possible for a company to be a director, although there must be at least one director who is a 'natural person' (s 155 CA) (ie one company cannot be the sole director of another company - see **Chapter 3**). As indicated in **Chapter 3**, the law on corporate directors could change in the future.

Human directors must be at least 16 years of age (s 157 CA), not disqualified from being a director (Company Directors Disqualification Act 1986 (CDDA)), physically and mentally capable and not bankrupt (Model Article 18 (MA18)).

First directors

The first director(s) named in Part 2 of form IN01 are automatically appointed on incorporation (see **Chapter 3**).

Subsequent directors

The company's articles may specify the permitted minimum and any maximum number of directors. The model articles (MAs, see **Chapter 3**) assume a minimum of two directors because of the quorum requirement (MA11, see **Chapter 3**), although sole directors may act alone (MA7(2)).

The company's articles will provide for the appointment of subsequent directors.

It is important to understand that directorship is an office (a **non-executive** position) but it can also be an **executive** position, in addition to an office.

Key term: non-executive director

A person who holds the office of director. They have rights, duties, restrictions and obligations under the CA, but they do not work for the company in a paid position. They do not have an employment/service contract but will be entitled to fees for their duties.

Key term: executive director

A person who, as well as holding the office of director, also works for the company in a paid position. They will usually have an employment/service contract (see **Restrictions on directors: directors' service contracts**, below), and will be entitled to a salary. They will often have a particular role and job title linked to their duties or specialism, such as managing director, finance director, sales director or marketing director.

Revision tip

When considering the appointment of directors, it is important to distinguish between appointment to the office (MA17) and the *separate* requirement to appoint in an executive capacity (MA19).

Appointment of non-executive director

Appointment as a non-executive director is dealt with under MA17 and may be done by either an ordinary resolution (OR) of the shareholders or a board resolution (BR) of the directors (see **Chapter 3** for ORs and BRs).

A BR is more straightforward, but if a general meeting (GM, see **Chapter 3**) is required to approve other business, or if not all directors are shareholders, it may be preferable to obtain an OR in order to gain the sanction of the shareholders.

Appointment of executive director

Appointment as an executive director is dealt with under MA19 and may be done by BR. **Practice example 4.1** sets out how this would work in practice.

Practice example 4.1

Provence Beauty Limited, a company that has adopted unamended MAs, wishes to appoint Nicki as a sales and marketing director, with a salary of £50,000 per annum. What resolutions will be required?

Under MA17, appointment to the office of director may be made by way of BR or OR. Appointment to the paid position will be by way of BR (MA19).

Following appointment, the company must:

- update the register of directors and the register of directors' residential addresses (if held - see **Chapter 3**, particularly on the impact of ECCTA in this respect)
- file form AP01 (individual directors) or AP02 (corporate directors), as appropriate, with Companies House within 14 days.

DIRECTORS' DUTIES

Directors owe fiduciary duties to their company (ie a duty not to make a secret profit out of their position and to act in the best interests of the company). In comparison, shareholders may act in their own interests.

Under ss 170–180 of the CA, directors have statutory general duties. For SQE1, it is important to have a good general appreciation of the nature and extent of these duties so you can recognise breaches.

To act within the company's constitution and to exercise their powers for proper purposes (s 171)

Directors must adhere to the provisions of the company's articles and exercise their powers in the best interests of the company. Their own personal interests, for example when issuing shares (see **Chapter 5**) or entering into contracts, should not sway them (see **Practice example 4.2**).

Practice example 4.2

Olivia is a director of a private limited company with unamended MAs. She enters into a transaction worth £5,000 on behalf of the company, when the articles state that the shareholders must approve transactions over £2,000. She also authorises the purchase of materials from her family trading company, at an inflated price. Is there a potential breach of s 171 here?

In breaching the articles and failing to exercise her powers for proper purposes, Olivia has potentially breached s 171 CA.

To promote the success of the company (s 172)

Directors must act in a way *they consider*, in good faith, would be most likely to promote the success of the company, for the benefit of the members as a whole. The test is subjective, and in acting, directors must have regard to six (non-exhaustive) factors:

- the likely long-term consequences
- employees' interests
- the need to foster good business relationships
- impact on the community and the environment
- the desirability of maintaining a reputation for high standards of business conduct
- the need to act fairly between members.

The subjective nature of the test and the lack of weight given to the respective factors is a key criticism of this provision, as it can make it very difficult to establish a breach. Directors only need to 'have regard' to the factors and the need to promote the success of the company will usually take precedence (see **Practice example 4.3**).

Practice example 4.3

The directors of a private limited company authorise the purchase of new machinery. Although it is expensive, it is anticipated that it will help improve productivity and profits. It is likely to lead to redundancies, will use more energy and will create more noise than the old machinery. Is there a potential breach of s 172 here?

If the directors have at least had regard to the relevant factors here, it is unlikely that there will be a breach of s 172. The directors will have made the decision in good faith, to promote the success of the company.

To exercise independent judgement (s 173)

A director must not do anything to fetter (ie compromise or undermine) their right to exercise independent judgement (eg agree to vote in a particular way, unless it is done in good faith and in the best interests of the company). They may take legal or financial advice without being in breach of this section.

To exercise reasonable care, skill and diligence (s 174)

The standard of care here is of a reasonably diligent person. There is a minimum objective standard (the standard knowledge, skill and experience that may reasonably be expected of a director) which may be raised, based on the actual knowledge, skill and experience that the director has (a subjective standard). See **Practice example 4.4** for how this may apply in practice.

Practice example 4.4

Eva is a director of a private limited company and an experienced commercial solicitor. She authorises the company to enter into a contract without reading the terms and it transpires that the terms are unusually onerous. Is there a potential breach of s 174 here?

It is likely that there will be a breach of s 174. A director would usually be expected to consider commercial terms carefully or seek professional advice. One would expect an experienced solicitor to be even more careful in the circumstances.

To avoid conflicts of interest (s 175)

This usually involves taking advantage of property, information or opportunities that belong to the company (whether or not the company was in a position to exploit these) (see **Practice example 4.5**). The directors of a private company may authorise a breach of this duty by BR (although the interested director's vote will not count).

Practice example 4.5

Blas is a director of a private limited company. The company is busy, so will be unable to carry out some work when required by a regular customer. He agrees to undertake it in his personal capacity. Is there a potential breach of s 175 here?

It is likely that there will be a breach of s 175, although the other directors may authorise the breach of duty.

Not to accept benefits from third parties (s 176)

There will be no breach of this duty if the acceptance of the benefit cannot reasonably be regarded as likely to give rise to a conflict (eg it is minimal or relates to normal corporate hospitality). However, receipt of a benefit may constitute bribery under the Bribery Act 2010, which is a criminal offence (see **Practice example 4.6**).

Practice example 4.6

Kate is a director of a private limited company. A regular customer invites her to rugby matches and also offers to give her a new car if the company enters into a significant contract. Is there a potential breach of s 176 here?

It is likely that there will be a breach of s 176, as well as potential liability under the Bribery Act 2010. The corporate entertainment alone, in normal circumstances, would not usually constitute a breach.

To declare interest in a proposed transaction with the company (s 177)

See **Chapter 3, Conflicts of interest**.

Remedies and ratification

As directors' duties are owed to the company, the company is the proper claimant in any action for their breach. Shareholders may consider taking 'derivative action' (see **Minority shareholder protection**, below) if the directors fail to act. Remedies can include an account for profits (payment to the company), damages or an injunction.

Shareholders may ratify (authorise) a breach of duty by OR (s 239 CA). The vote(s) of any interested director who is also a shareholder, and those persons they are connected with (see **Substantial property transactions**, below), will not count.

PERSONAL LIABILITY OF DIRECTORS

A director will be personally liable to third parties dealing with the company where the director has given a personal guarantee or is guilty of **wrongful trading**, **fraudulent trading** or **misfeasance**. For SQE1, you need to have an understanding of these concepts.

Personal guarantee

Lenders often insist upon personal guarantees from director-shareholders, particularly when a company is newly formed. It makes them personally liable for the liabilities of the company and takes away the real benefit of limited liability (see **Chapter 1**).

Wrongful trading (s 214 Insolvency Act 1986 (IA))

Key term: wrongful trading

A director of an insolvent company (see **Chapter 6**) may be liable to contribute to the assets of a company (see **Chapter 5**) where the company continued to trade, and they knew, or ought to have concluded, that there was no reasonable prospect of the company avoiding insolvency proceedings.

Like under s 174 CA, the test is a combined objective/subjective test. However, there will be a defence if the director took every step to minimise potential loss to creditors as ought to have been taken (see **Practice example 4.7**).

Practice example 4.7

Lena is a director of a private limited company and an experienced, professionally qualified accountant. She is aware that the company is in financial difficulty but is confident that things will improve. She takes professional advice from other experts, cuts outgoings, personally authorises all expenses to make sure they are strictly necessary, makes some redundancies and checks the accounts daily. Will she be liable for wrongful trading?

It is likely that she will have a defence to wrongful trading. She will be subject to a higher standard of care, based on her professional qualification and experience, but her actions seem genuine and to a high standard.

Fraudulent trading (s 213 IA)

Key term: fraudulent trading

A director of an insolvent company (see **Chapter 6**) may be liable to contribute to the assets of a company (see **Chapter 5**) where the company carried on business with intent to defraud creditors or for any fraudulent purposes.

Fraudulent trading is harder to prove than wrongful trading, due to the need to show 'intention to defraud'. It is a criminal offence (s 993 CA).

Misfeasance (s 212 IA)

Key term: misfeasance

Misfeasance is essentially a breach of directors' duties discovered on winding-up (see **Chapter 6**). Personal liability may be imposed in these circumstances.

POWERS OF DIRECTORS

The powers of the directors are set out in the company's articles. The directors' wide powers of management (MA3) are subject to any instruction given to the board by special resolution (see **Chapter 3**) of the members (MA4).

Directors' powers are exercised either by making decisions at board meetings or by unanimous agreement (MA8, see **Chapter 3**). MA5 also contains wide powers of delegation (eg to a managing director).

The company's articles may make provision for the appointment of an alternate director (ie a substitute director, for example, to cover absence), but the MAs do not make such provision.

A number of provisions under the CA require the sanction of the members (see **Chapter 3**).

DISCLOSURE OF INFORMATION UNDER CA 2006

Companies were previously required to maintain a register of directors (s 162) and a register of directors' residential addresses (s 165), unless they applied for exemption (s 167A). However, under ECCTA, the requirement to keep and maintain both of these registers has been removed (see **Chapter 3**).

If a director's particulars change, they must be reported to Companies House using form CH01 (individual directors) or CH02 (corporate directors).

The company registered name must be displayed at its registered office and appear in certain communications, sometimes with further particulars (eg registered number and registered office in business letters). Directors do not need to be named in business letters etc, but if they are, all of them must be included (s 82 CA and the Company, Limited Liability Partnership and Business (Names and Trading Disclosures) Regulations 2015).

Copies of directors' service contracts or a memorandum of their terms must be kept by the company for up to one year after expiry/determination (s 228 CA). Members have a right to inspect directors' service contracts (s 229 CA).

RESTRICTIONS ON DIRECTORS

The CA contains a number of restrictions on directors. For SQE1, you need to have a good working knowledge of these (particularly substantial property transactions).

Restrictions on directors: directors' service contracts (s 188 CA)

Service (employment) contracts for executive directors are usually granted by the directors under their general management powers (MA3) and specifically MA19 (power to make executive appointments).

Shareholders' approval by ordinary resolution (OR, see **Chapter 3**) is required for directors' service contracts of a guaranteed fixed term of *more than* two years' duration (see **Practice example 4.8**). This is because such contracts could lead to significant liability for the company if wrongfully terminated (the starting point for damages would be the remuneration for the entire remaining term). Only the 'guaranteed term' element requires shareholders' approval.

If the guaranteed term is not duly approved by OR, the service contract will be terminable on reasonable notice.

Although the director will not need to declare their interest in the proposed service contract (due to the exception in s 177(6)(c) CA), they will be unable to vote and count towards the quorum in the board meeting where it is approved (unless MA14 is temporarily disapplied by OR (MA14(3)) or has been removed) (see **Chapter 3, Conflicts of interest**).

A memorandum of the proposed terms must be made available for inspection for at least 15 days prior to the meeting and at the meeting itself (s 188(5) CA).

Practice example 4.8

Mikolas is a director of a private limited company and has negotiated a guaranteed fixed-term service contract for 10 years. Will shareholder approval be required?

The shareholders must approve the guaranteed term element by OR. The directors may decide the other terms, under MA3.

Restrictions on directors: substantial property transactions (ss 190–196 CA)

The directors under their general management powers (MA3) may approve most property transactions involving the company. However, **substantial property transactions (SPTs)** require shareholders' approval by OR.

Key term: substantial property transaction (SPT)

An SPT involves the *acquisition/disposal* of a *non-cash asset* where:

- The *parties* involved are the company and a director or a **person connected to a director** (as defined); AND
- The asset is *substantial*, ie its value is not £5,000 or less and is either more than £100,000 or more than 10% of the company's net asset value.

Therefore:

- If the value of the transaction is £5,000 or less, it will *never* be substantial.
- If the value of the transaction is over £100,000, it will *always* be substantial.
- If the value of the transaction is more than £5,000, but equal to or less than £100,000, it will only be substantial *if the value exceeds 10% of the company's net asset value.*

Key term: person connected to a director (ss 252–257 CA)

- *Family:* includes spouse, civil partner, romantic partner in an enduring relationship, children, stepchildren, parents and children of romantic partners (but not brothers, sisters, grandparents, grandchildren, uncles, aunts, nephews and nieces) (s 253 CA).
- *Body corporate:* director and persons connected with the director who own at least 20% of the company's voting shares (s 254 CA).

Exam warning

For the purposes of SQE1, you should have a good working knowledge of the provisions relating to SPTs (including the definition of connected persons). Remember that in order to be an SPT, the transaction must be between the company and a director (not someone who is just a shareholder) or connected person. Candidates often focus on the value alone, rather than the need for a connection. The fact that siblings are omitted from the definition may be of surprise to you.

If there is a breach of s 190 CA, the transaction is voidable (s 195 CA).

Figure 4.1 sets out how to approach SPT issues and **Practice example 4.9** provides an example of an SPT in practice.

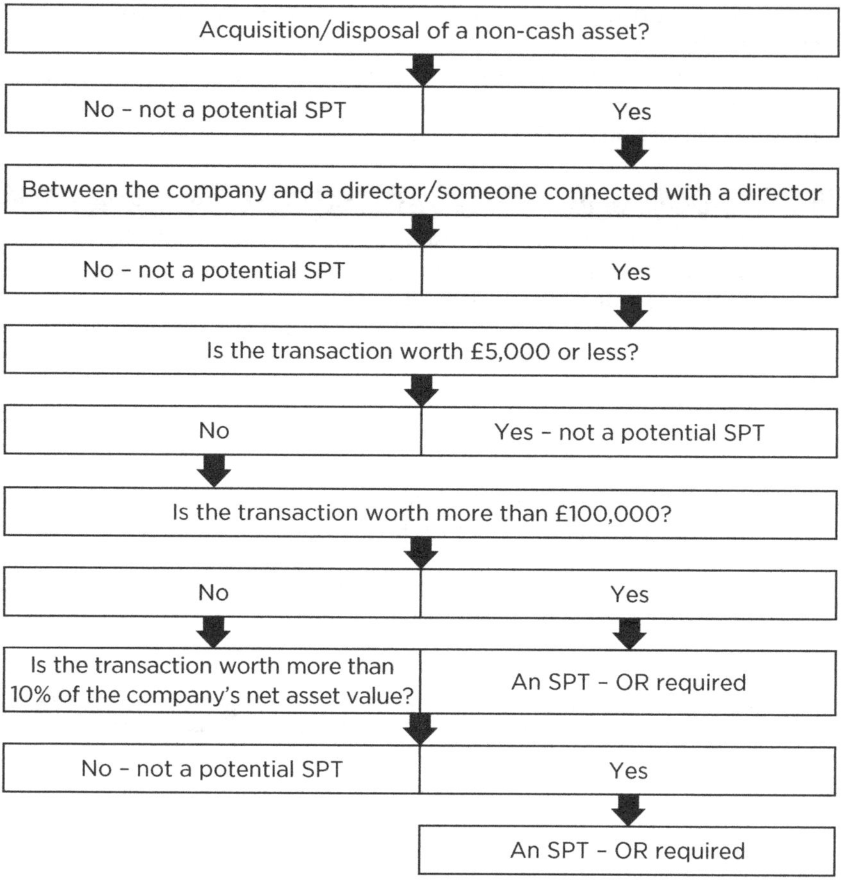

Figure 4.1: Substantial property transactions

Practice example 4.9

Birthe is a director of a private limited company, with a net asset value of £950,000. She has agreed to buy an investment property from the company worth £80,000. Will shareholder approval be required?

Shareholder approval will not be required as this is not an SPT. Although it is a transaction between the company and a director, it is not substantial, as it does not exceed 10% of the company's net assets.

Restrictions on directors: loans to directors (s 197 CA)

Subject to limited exceptions, loans made to a director of more than £10,000 in total require the approval of the members by OR.

The transaction will be voidable if not approved, unless ratified by OR of the shareholders within a reasonable time.

A memorandum of the proposed terms must be available for inspection for 15 days prior to the meeting and at the meeting itself (s 197(3)).

Restrictions on directors: payments for loss of office (ss 215–222 CA)

Certain payments to directors for loss of office (ie on termination of their role) require approval of the members by OR if they exceed £200. This does not include payments properly due under existing contracts or pursuant to a legal obligation (eg due as part of an employment law claim).

REMOVAL OF DIRECTORS

Once appointed, a director holds office until death, voluntary retirement, removal or disqualification.

Voluntary retirement/resignation

A director may resign by serving notification of resignation on the company (MA18(f)). An executive director will also have to adhere to the terms of any service contract/general employment law.

Removal: bankruptcy order, entering into a composition with creditors (see Chapter 6), physical or mental incapacity

The director's office ceases in these circumstances (MA18(b), (c) and (d)).

Removal under s 168 CA

The right of the shareholders to remove directors by OR is an important, inherent right and, for SQE1, it is imperative that you understand the procedure.

Special notice of the OR is required to be given to the company of the proposed resolution – ss 168(2) and 312(1) CA.

Key term: special notice
At least 28 days' notice of the proposed resolution must be given to the company, otherwise the resolution will be ineffective.

The director concerned has the right to be informed and to make representations to argue against their removal (both through written representations and at the meeting itself) (s 169 CA). Therefore, the written resolution procedure cannot be used here (see **Chapter 3**).

The company must then serve notice of the GM (s 312(4)).

The members may need to requisition a GM if the board is uncooperative (see **Chapter 3**).

Removal of a director is without prejudice to any right to compensation which the director may have. Therefore, it is important to check the director's service contract to ascertain the potential contractual liability to the director.

It is also important to check the company's articles for any ***Bushell v Faith* clause**.

Key term: *Bushell v Faith* clause

A clause giving shareholder-directors weighted voting rights (eg two votes for every one they would normally have) on a resolution to remove them as a director (and usually on a resolution to amend the relevant provision in the articles).

Any shareholders' agreement (see **Shareholders' agreements**, below) should also be consulted as it may contain an agreement as to how voting powers are to be exercised.

Following resignation/removal, the company must:
- update the register of directors and the register of directors' residential addresses (if held - see **Chapter 3** on the impact of ECCTA in this regard)
- file form TM01 (individual directors) or TM02 (corporate directors) as appropriate with Companies House within 14 days.

Disqualification by the court under the Company Directors Disqualification Act 1986 (CDDA)

Directors may be disqualified by the court from acting as director (without leave of the court) for any period from 2 to 15 years. For SQE1, you need to have a general appreciation of these provisions.

The potential grounds include the following:
- conviction of an indictable offence (see ***Revise SQE: Criminal Law***)
- persistent breaches of companies legislation
- fraud in winding-up (see **Chapter 6**)
- summary conviction (see ***Revise SQE: Criminal Law***) for failure to comply with companies legislation

- wrongful or fraudulent trading
- being an unfit director of an insolvent company (see **Chapter 6**).

The most significant ground is the final one. The court will consider whether the director has breached their duties or the requirements of the CA and has particular personal responsibility for dubious behaviour or transactions. If a company is in financial difficulty, directors should exercise extra diligence to avoid disqualification (in a similar way to avoiding wrongful trading, see **Wrongful trading**, above).

It is a criminal offence to breach a disqualification order and the director will be personally liable.

THE COMPANY SECRETARY

For SQE1, you need to have an appreciation of the role of **company secretary**.

Key term: company secretary

The person who is usually responsible for:

- keeping the various records of the company
- filing documents at Companies House
- the general administration of the company.

A private company is not required to have a company secretary (s 270(1) CA), although a public company is (s 271 CA).

If a company chooses to appoint a secretary, its first secretary, named in Part 2 of form IN01, is automatically appointed on incorporation (see **Chapter 3**). The company must confirm on form IN01 on behalf of the secretary that they consent to act as such.

It is possible for another company to act as company secretary (although it must act through its officers) and no specific qualifications are required for a company secretary in a private company.

The directors have the power to remove an existing company secretary and appoint a replacement by BR, under MA3.

The administrative formalities for a change of company secretary are as follows:

- update register of secretaries (if held - see **Chapter 3** on the impact of ECCTA in this regard); and
- file form AP03 (appointment - individual), AP04 (appointment - corporate) or TM02 (termination), as appropriate, with Companies House within 14 days.

Form CH03 (individual) or CH04 (corporate) are required to change the particulars of a company secretary.

COMPANY MEMBERS

This section deals with:

- the procedure for becoming a company member
- members' powers
- minority shareholder protection.

How to become a company member

Every private company must have at least one member (s 123 CA). There is no legal maximum and it is possible for a company to be a shareholder in another company.

The first members of the company are those subscribers who have signed the company's memorandum prior to incorporation and have agreed to become members of the company (s 112 CA).

Subsequent members of the company are those who acquire shares in the company and who are registered as such in its register of members. They may have new shares issued to them by the company or may have existing shares that are transferred (ie purchased, gifted or transmitted to them - see **Chapter 5**).

Registration of membership

Every company must keep a register of its members (s 113 CA).

Shareholders may inspect the register (s 116 CA) and it is a criminal offence to refuse to allow them to do so (s 118 CA). ECCTA has withdrawn a company's option to elect to keep the records centrally (see **Chapter 3**).

Classes of share

Different classes of share may be issued, with different rights attaching to them (eg relating to voting rights and dividends) (see **Chapter 5**).

Holders of ordinary shares usually have the right to vote and receive dividends, and holders of preference shares usually have preferential rights (eg the right to receive dividends first).

It is for the company to decide the rights that will attach to the different classes of share.

Shareholders' agreements

These may be entered into between shareholders to govern their relationship in a private way (eg agreements as to how voting rights will be exercised, to protect minority shareholders).

Liability of members

A company is a legal person in its own right and, as such, is liable for its own debts.

In the absence of personal guarantees (see **Personal guarantee** above), the liability of a member to contribute to the debts of the company is usually 'limited' to the extent of their investment in that company (see **Chapter 1**).

Members' powers

The powers of the members are laid down by statute and in the company's articles.

The members exercise their powers by passing resolutions in GMs or by written resolutions (see **Chapter 3**).

The powers and rights given to members depend in many cases on the holding of a particular proportion of the company's voting shares, although members have some powers irrespective of their shareholding.

Examples of members' powers

These include the right to:

- receive a share certificate(s)
- receive notice of GMs, vote at GMs (provided shares are voting shares) or appoint a proxy (see **Chapter 3**)
- receive a copy of the company's annual accounts (see **Chapter 5**)
- inspect minutes of the GMs, the company books and directors' service contracts
- receive dividends where payable and declared (see **Chapter 5**)
- request the court hold a GM (s 306 CA)
- bring winding-up proceedings (see **Chapter 6**)
- claim minority shareholder protection (see **Minority shareholder protection**, below).

Minority and majority shareholders

It is important to realise the difference between **majority shareholders** and **minority shareholders**.

Key term: majority shareholder

Majority shareholders are those who individually hold *more than* 50% of the company's voting shares.

Key term: minority shareholder

Minority shareholders are those who individually hold 50% or less of the company's voting shares.

One of the most significant powers majority shareholders have is the right to remove a director under s 168 CA. Directors may be removed from office by OR (see **Chapter 3**) under this section, notwithstanding any provision in the company's articles or the directors' service contracts (see **Removal of directors**, above).

A summary of shareholders' rights, based on their shareholding, is set out in **Table 4.1**.

Table 4.1: Summary of shareholders' rights

Percentage shareholding	Powers
100%	Control of the company
75%	Can pass a special resolution
50%	Can block an ordinary resolution
More than 50%	Can pass an ordinary resolution
More than 25%	Can block a special resolution (negative control)
Majority in number holding at least 90% of the voting shares	Can consent to short notice of a GM
Any two voting members or any member(s) holding at least 10% of the voting shares	Can demand a poll vote (see **Chapter 3**)
More than 10%	May refuse consent to short notice of a GM
5% or more with voting rights	May circulate written resolutions (s 292 CA) May circulate a written statement as to proposed resolution(s) (s 292 CA)
5%	May requisition a GM

Minority shareholder protection

For SQE1, you need to appreciate and understand the following three remedies available to minority shareholders. These are valuable remedies, particularly when they do not have the same control as majority shareholders.

Petition for unfairly prejudicial conduct (s 994 CA)

A member may petition the court for an order that the company's affairs have been, or are proposed to be, conducted in a way that is both prejudicial and unfair to them. In this case, *the shareholder is the proper claimant.* This can cover a whole range of conduct (eg refusing to pay dividends when they are properly payable, exclusion from management, or excessive pay being awarded to directors). The most popular order of the court is usually that the prejudiced shareholder be bought out.

Derivative action (ss 260–264 CA)

A derivative action is a claim brought by a shareholder for an act or omission of a director (usually in breach of directors' duties). It is a claim brought for a wrong done to the company, where *the company is the proper claimant.* It is a complex legal process, designed to enable non-director shareholders to take action.

Winding-up on the just and equitable ground (s 122(1)(g) IA 1986)

This is the most drastic 'remedy' of all and enables a member to apply to wind up the company (see **Chapter 6**) on the basis that it is just and equitable to do so. This could, for example, be on the basis of a total breakdown of communication or a total deadlock/inability to make decisions.

SUMMARY OF KEY TRANSACTIONS

It is important to know company decision-making in the context of specific transactions. The transactions dealt with in this chapter are summarised in **Table 4.2**.

Table 4.2: Summary of key transactions

Appointment of director		
Substantive legal requirements	**Procedural requirements (PR) and Directors' declaration of personal interests (DOI)**	**Filing/Administration requirements**
MA17 - to appoint to office, either BR or OR MA19 - to appoint in executive capacity (BR)	PR: Board meeting (BM) or PR: BM > GM > BM DOI: s 177 and MA14	Filing: Form AP01 or AP02 Admin: Update register of directors and register of directors' residential addresses (if held) BM minutes or BM and GM minutes

Table 4.2: (continued)

Director's service contract - guaranteed fixed term of more than two years		
MA19 - BR s 188 CA - OR s 188(5): Memorandum of proposed terms	PR: BM > GM > BM DOI: s 177(6)(c) and MA14	Admin: Seal/execute service contract ss 228 and 229 CA 2006 - inspection requirements BM and GM minutes
Substantial property transaction		
s 190 - OR	PR: BM > GM > BM DOI: s 177 and MA14	Admin: Seal/execute necessary documents BM and GM minutes (Stamp Duty Land Tax/ Land Transaction Tax and registration if real property purchase)
Loans to directors exceeding £10,000		
s 197 - OR s 197(3): Memorandum of proposed terms	PR: BM > GM > BM DOI: s 177 and MA14	Admin: Seal/execute necessary documents BM and GM minutes
Payment to director for loss of office exceeding £200		
s 215-222 - OR	PR: BM > GM > BM DOI: s 177 and MA14	Admin: Seal/execute necessary documents BM and GM minutes
Removal of director		
s 168 CA 2006 - OR Check service contract Check articles of association - is there an effective *Bushell v Faith* clause? Check shareholders' agreement	PR: BM > GM > BM NB s 303 if uncooperative board DOI: s 177 and MA14	Filing: Form TM01 or TM02 to be filed with Companies House

Table 4.2: (continued)

s 168(2) - special notice must be given to the company (28 days) s 312 - minimum of 14 clear days' notice of meeting required s 169 - rights of directors subject to resolution		Admin: Update register of directors and register of directors' residential addresses (if held) BM and GM minutes
Appointment/Removal of company secretary		
MA3 - BR	BM DOI: s 177 and MA14	Filing: Form AP03 or AP04 (if appointing) Form TM02 (if removing) Admin: Update register of secretaries (if held) BM minutes

NB: Statutory references are to the CA.

KEY POINT CHECKLIST

This chapter has covered the following key knowledge points. You can use these to structure your revision, ensuring you recall the key details for each point, as covered in this chapter.

- The first directors of a company are automatically appointed on incorporation. Subsequent directors may be appointed to office by way of an OR or BR, and may be appointed to an executive position by way of BR.
- Directors owe statutory duties to the company and may be personally liable through personal guarantees or in the event of wrongful trading, fraudulent trading or misfeasance.
- Directors are subject to a number of restrictions under the CA, most importantly in relation to guaranteed term service contracts and SPTs.
- Directors may be removed by OR.
- Directors may be disqualified, under the CDDA for any period from 2 to 15 years.
- A private company does not need to have a company secretary, but they may be appointed and removed by BR, if required.

- Different rights and remedies are available to shareholders, depending on their percentage shareholding, but some powers are common to all shareholders.

KEY TERMS AND CONCEPTS

- director (**page 64**)
- shadow director (**page 64**)
- de facto director (**page 64**)
- non-executive director (**page 65**)
- executive director (**page 66**)
- wrongful trading (**page 70**)
- fraudulent trading (**page 70**)
- misfeasance (**page 71**)
- substantial property transaction (**page 73**)
- person connected to a director (**page 73**)
- special notice (**page 75**)
- *Bushell v Faith* clause (**page 76**)
- company secretary (**page 77**)
- majority shareholder (**page 79**)
- minority shareholder (**page 80**)

SQE1-STYLE QUESTIONS

QUESTION 1

A private limited company with unamended model articles of association wishes to sell some of its land to the father of one of the directors. All of the directors are shareholders. The property has been independently valued at £70,000 and the net asset value of the company is £600,000.

Does the proposed sale of land require shareholder approval?

A. No, because the property has been independently valued.

B. Yes, because the transaction is more than 10% of the company's net asset value.

C. Yes, because the company's directors are also shareholders.

D. No, because the transaction falls within the directors' general management powers.

E. No, because the transaction does not exceed £100,000.

QUESTION 2

A private limited company with unamended model articles of association and a net asset value of £85,000 wishes to enter into some property transactions.

The finance director has agreed to buy a van from the company, for the sum of £3,000. The brother of the marketing director has agreed to sell an investment property to the company for the sum of £150,000. Finally, the company has agreed to purchase freehold premises for £90,000 from another company in which the sales director has a 15% shareholding and his wife has a 10% shareholding.

Which of the following best describes the required resolutions to authorise these transactions?

A. A board resolution for the van and ordinary resolutions for the investment property and freehold premises.
B. Ordinary resolutions for the van, investment property and freehold premises.
C. Board resolutions for the van and investment property and an ordinary resolution for the freehold premises.
D. Board resolutions for the van, investment property and freehold premises.
E. A board resolution for the van and freehold premises and an ordinary resolution for the investment property.

QUESTION 3

A private limited company with unamended model articles of association wishes to grant a two-year guaranteed fixed-term service contract to an existing director.

Which of the following best describes the required formalities?

A. A board resolution will be required. The director will need to declare his interest in the proposed transaction, will be unable to vote, and will not count towards the quorum when the decision is made.
B. An ordinary resolution will be required. In the board meeting that follows, the director will need to declare his interest in the proposed transaction, will be unable to vote and will not count towards the quorum when the decision is made.
C. An ordinary resolution will be required. In the board meeting that follows, the director will not need to declare his interest in the proposed transaction but will be unable to vote and will not count towards the quorum when the decision is made.
D. An ordinary resolution will be required. In the board meeting that follows, the director will not need to declare his interest in the proposed transaction, will be able to vote and will count towards the quorum when the decision is made.
E. A board resolution will be required. The director will not need to declare his interest in the proposed transaction but will be unable to vote, and will not count towards the quorum when the decision is made.

QUESTION 4

A director of a private company, limited by shares, has taken, for their own personal benefit, a contract that was initially being negotiated by the company. The same director has also been awarded an excessive pay rise and the company has persistently failed to pay dividends when profits are available. The client, who has a 25% shareholding in the company, wishes to take action.

Which of the following best describes the legal position?

A. The director has potentially breached the duty to avoid conflicts of interest. The directors may authorise a breach of this duty by board resolution, but the interested director's vote will not count. The client could remove the director from office.

B. The director has potentially breached the duty to avoid conflicts of interest. The directors may authorise a breach of this duty by board resolution, but the interested director's vote will not count. The client may take derivative action or seek relief for unfairly prejudicial conduct.

C. The director has potentially breached the duty to declare an interest in a transaction. The client may take derivative action or seek relief for unfairly prejudicial conduct.

D. The director has potentially breached the duty to avoid conflicts of interest. The directors may authorise a breach of this duty by board resolution, but the interested director's vote will not count. The client may take derivative action or seek to remove the director from office.

E The director has potentially breached the duty to avoid conflicts of interest. The directors may authorise a breach of this duty by board resolution, but the interested director's vote will not count. The client may seek relief for unfairly prejudicial conduct or seek to remove the director from office.

QUESTION 5

A director of a private company limited by shares negotiated a contract that caused the company a significant loss. Since then, the director has cut outgoings, personally authorised all expenses to make sure they are strictly necessary and made some redundancies. The director checks the accounts on a daily basis, but despite the director's best efforts, the company loses a lucrative contract and becomes insolvent.

Which of the following best sets out the position of the director?

A. The director may be liable for wrongful trading but is likely to have a defence on the facts.

B. The director may be liable for wrongful trading and fraudulent trading.

C. The director may be liable for wrongful trading.

D. The director may be liable for fraudulent trading.

E. The director may be liable for misfeasance.

■ ANSWERS TO QUESTIONS

Answers to 'What do you know already?' questions at the start of the chapter

1) False. Directors may be appointed to office by either board resolution (BR) or ordinary resolution (OR).
2) The term of directors' service contracts requires shareholders' approval where they are for a guaranteed term of more than two years.
3) False. The shareholders must approve a property transaction, which exceeds £100,000 in value, only where it is between the company and a director or the company and a person connected with a director.
4) An ordinary resolution is required to remove a director from office.
5) A minority shareholder holds 50% or less of the company's voting shares.

Answers to end-of-chapter SQE1-style questions

Question 1

The correct answer was B. The independent valuation is not a factor in determining whether shareholder approval is required (option A), neither is the fact that all shareholders are directors (option C) (although an SPT must be between the company and a director/someone connected with a director). The transaction would fall within general management powers (option D) if it were not an SPT as defined. Option E is incorrect as if the value of the transaction is more than £5,000, but up to and including £100,000, it may still be an SPT if it is more than 10% of the company's net asset value.

Question 2

The correct answer was C. A board resolution is required for the van as the value is £5,000 or less, even though the transaction involves a director. Therefore, option B is incorrect on this point. An ordinary resolution is required for the freehold premises as the director is connected with the selling company (he and his wife, a connected person, own at least 20% of the shares) and the value exceeds 10% of the purchasing company's net asset value. Options D and E are wrong here. A board resolution is required for the investment property as, despite the value, siblings are not connected persons in the context of SPTs. Therefore, options A, B and E are incorrect in this respect.

Question 3

The correct answer was E. An ordinary resolution will not be required as the service contract is not for a guaranteed term of *more than* two years.

Therefore, options B, C and D are incorrect on this point. The director will not be required to declare his interest as there is an exception to the general rule that applies, where a director's service contract is being considered (s 177(6)(c) CA), therefore options A and B are incorrect here. The director will not be able to vote and count towards the quorum of the board meeting, so option D is also incorrect here.

Question 4

The correct answer was B. The client could not remove the director from office based on their voting power alone, as they are a minority shareholder. Therefore, options A, D and E are incorrect in this respect. On the facts, there has been no breach of the duty to declare an interest in a proposed transaction, so option C is incorrect. Option D also fails to mention the possibility of a petition for unfairly prejudicial conduct, option E does not mention a derivative action, and option A does not mention either of them. Both are relevant on the facts.

Question 5

The correct answer was A. Although there is the potential for wrongful trading here, the director is likely to have a defence, as they could argue that they took every step to minimise potential loss to creditors as ought to have been taken. Therefore, options B and C are incorrect here. The director is unlikely to have had an intention to defraud here, so fraudulent trading is unlikely (as suggested in options B and D). Misfeasance is also unlikely here as there is no clear breach of directors' duties, so option E is incorrect.

■ KEY CASES, RULES, STATUTES AND INSTRUMENTS

The SQE1 Assessment Specification does not require you to know any statutory authorities or specific case names for this topic. References to the CA and the MAs are for information purposes only.

5

Financing a business, financial records and accounting requirements

The Economic Crime and Corporate Transparency Act 2023 (ECCTA) received Royal Assent on 26 October 2023 and has made some changes to the Companies Act 2006. Not all of its provisions are in force and further changes are likely to be implemented in the course of 2026/27. Useful updates on implementation can be found on the 'Changes to UK company law' pages of the gov.uk website.

■ MAKE SURE YOU KNOW

This chapter provides an overview of financing a business, financial records and accounting requirements. For the SQE1 assessments, you will need to understand the two main funding options available to businesses (equity finance and debt finance). For equity finance, you should know the processes and requirements for share issue, share transfer, declaration of dividends (as a distribution of a company's profits), and buyback of shares (within the context of capital maintenance). For debt finance, you will need to appreciate the nature and key types of debt finance, types of security, rights of debenture holders and the order of priority. For business accounts, you should have an appreciation of the nature of business accounts, their preparation (including adjustments), composition, structure and importance (for both unincorporated and incorporated businesses), as well as the relevant legal requirements. Your understanding of these subjects will enable you to identify and apply the relevant legal rules and principles to SQE1-style single best answer MCQs.

■ SQE ASSESSMENT ADVICE

For SQE1, you are required to understand equity finance, debt finance and business accounts from a practical perspective. It is likely that you will be required to know the procedures involved in equity finance, including the requirements for a buyback of shares. You will also need to appreciate the nature of debt finance and the priority of different types of security, as well as how business accounts are constructed. As you work through this chapter, remember to pay particular attention in your revision to:

- the nature and requirements of share issue, the process of share transfer and their respective differences
- when a company may declare dividends
- the principle of capital maintenance and the process by which a company may buy back its own shares
- the nature of debt finance and security and the options available to different types of business
- the rights of secured lenders and their order of priority
- how business accounts are compiled and the differences between sole trader, partnership and company accounts
- the key reporting requirements in relation to accounts.

■ WHAT DO YOU KNOW ALREADY?

Attempt these questions before reading this chapter. If you find some difficult or cannot remember the answers, remember to look more closely at that area during your revision.

1) True or false? The directors of a private company, with unamended model articles of association, will always be able to authorise the issue of shares without recourse to the members.

   [Share issue, page 91]
2) Explain what is meant by 'pre-emption' in the context of share issue.

   [Share issue, page 91]
3) True or false? A fixed charge will usually have priority over a floating charge, and only companies and LLPs may grant floating charges.

   [Types of security, page 103, and Priority of security, page 105]
4) True or false? A charge against a company's assets must always be registered at Companies House.

   [Registration of charges, page 106]
5) Explain the nature of a profit and loss account and a balance sheet.

   [Preparation of accounts, page 108]

EQUITY FINANCE

All businesses need money/assets (see **Business accounts**, below) to operate and it is important to appreciate the difference between **equity finance** (which is discussed in this section) and **debt finance** (which will be discussed later on).

Key term: equity finance

Equity finance (or share finance) is the issue (creation) of new shares in exchange for consideration (ie where something of value is given in exchange for a promise) received by a company. It generates money/ assets for a company.

Key term: debt finance

Debt finance (or loan finance) involves borrowing money in order to finance a business (incorporated or unincorporated - see **Chapter 1**). The debt may be secured or unsecured (see **Types of security**, below).

Share issue

A company must have a minimum of one shareholder on incorporation (see **Chapter 3**).

Following incorporation, the directors of a company are responsible for **share issue**.

Key term: share issue

The process whereby new shares are allotted (created) in exchange for consideration received by the company, and the member is entered onto the register of members in respect of those shares (see **Chapter 3**). It can change the control of a company, as the number of shares increases (see **Pre-emption rights**, below).

For SQE1, it is necessary to have a good working knowledge of the process involved so that you can apply it to a given scenario. There are two key questions:

- Do the *directors* have *authority* to issue the shares?
- Do pre-emption rights apply?

Directors' authority

In *private companies with unamended model articles of association (in this respect)* (MAs, see **Chapter 3**) and only one class of shares (see **Chapter 4**), before and after the issue, the directors are free to issue further shares of the same class by board resolution (BR, see **Chapter 3**), under MA3. This can be done without prior reference to the members (s 550 Companies Act 2006 (CA)).

Otherwise, the proposed issue of shares by the directors will require the advance authority of the members by ordinary resolution (OR, see **Chapter 3**) or by provision in the *company's articles* (s 551 CA):

- *For companies incorporated prior to 1 October 2009*: The memorandum of association (see **Chapter 3**) will set out the authorised

share capital (the maximum number of shares that may be issued). Following the CA, this provision is transferred to the articles (s 28(1) CA) and may be amended by OR. A copy of the OR must be filed at Companies House.
- *For companies incorporated on or after 1 October 2009*: It is necessary to check the articles for restrictions and amend, if necessary, by special resolution (SR, see **Chapter 3** and s 21 CA). There are no such restrictions in the MAs.

Any authority to issue (whether in the articles or by way of OR) must state:
- the maximum number of shares the directors are allowed to issue
- the date when the authority will expire (generally not more than five years from the date the authority is given).

If an OR is passed, this must be filed at Companies House within 15 days (ss 551(8), (9), 29 and 30 CA). It is one of the rare occasions where an OR needs to be filed.

See **Figure 5.1** for a summary of the approach to take for ascertaining authority to issue shares.

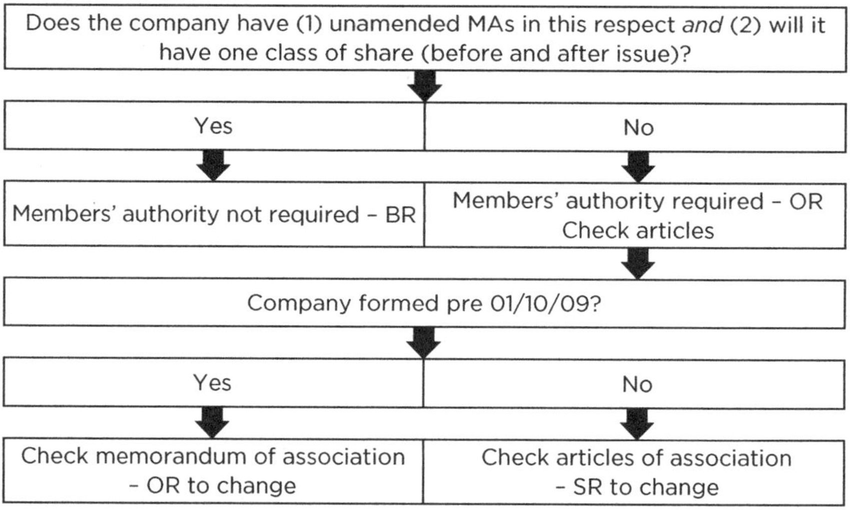

Figure 5.1: Directors' authority

Pre-emption rights

If it is proposed to issue shares *wholly for cash* (s 565 CA), the statutory **pre-emption rights** may apply.

Key term: pre-emption rights

The statutory pre-emption rights dictate that generally, on an issue of new shares, they must first be offered to the existing members, on the same or more favourable terms, in proportion to their existing shareholdings. They have a 'right of first refusal' for a period of at least 14 days (ss 561–562 CA).

The statutory rights may be:
- varied or removed for private companies by contrary provision in the articles (s 567 CA), either on incorporation, or subsequently by SR; *the MAs do not vary the statutory rights*
- disapplied by SR of the members (ss 569, 570 and 571 CA)
- formally waived in relation to a specific issue (if all the members intend to decline the offer).

It is important to understand the rationale behind pre-emption rights. They protect members, where the effect of issuing shares would be to weaken their control of the company (see **Practice example 5.1**). This is because, where new shares are issued, there is potential for an individual's percentage shareholding to decrease.

Practice example 5.1

Clodagh has 55 of the 100 voting shares in a private limited company, which has unamended MAs. What would be the consequences if a further 20 shares were issued to a new shareholder, for cash?

Clodagh's shareholding would be reduced to approximately 46%, so she could no longer pass or block ORs. On the facts, the statutory pre-emption rights would apply to protect her; she would have first refusal on 11 (55%) of the new shares.

Revision tip

When considering share issue, the most important things to ascertain are how many types of shares the company has (authority) and whether the shares are issued *wholly* for cash (pre-emption). If shares are issued *wholly or partly* for non-cash assets, the transaction could also be a substantial property transaction (SPT – see **Chapter 4** and **Practice example 5.2**), and an additional OR would be required. Many candidates do not appreciate this.

Greater protection will be given if the company's articles provide for pre-emption rights on any issue of shares (eg for both cash and non-cash consideration).

See **Figure 5.2** for a summary of the approach to take to ascertain pre-emption rights.

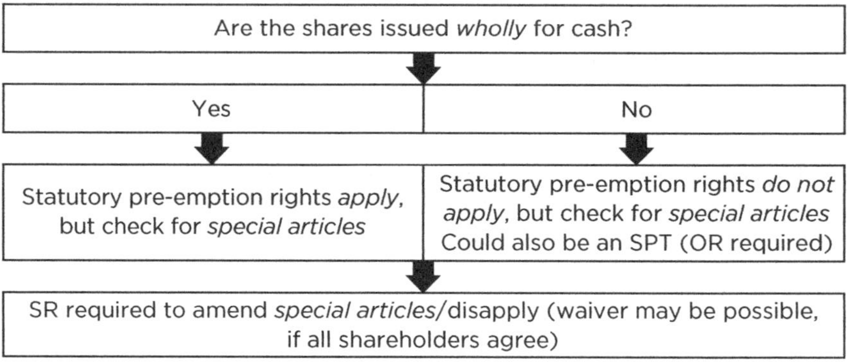

Figure 5.2: Pre-emption rights

Practice example 5.2 sets out how share issue (authority and pre-emption) may work in practice.

Practice example 5.2

Groth and Emanuel Limited is a private limited company, incorporated on 28 December 2015, with unamended MAs. It has 50,000 ordinary shares and 50,000 preference shares, and wishes to issue 20,000 new ordinary shares for cash. Will authority be required, and will the pre-emption rights apply?

Authority will be required as the company has more than one class of shares (before and after issue). The pre-emption rights apply but may be disapplied by SR or waived if all of the shareholders agree. If the shares were issued for non-cash consideration (eg the transfer of property), the pre-emption rights would not apply. However, it would be an SPT if a director or connected person was buying the shares and the value of the asset(s) was substantial (see Chapter 4).

Payment for shares and administration/filing

Shares may be issued fully paid or partly paid, although for private companies with MAs, MA21 states they must be fully paid.

Shares are quite commonly issued at a premium (ie for a price exceeding their base/nominal/par value). Any premium paid must be shown in the share premium account on the balance sheet (s 610 CA) (see **Accounts**, below). Shares may not be issued at a discount - ie below their base/nominal/par value (s 580 CA).

A return of allotments (form SH01) must be sent to Companies House within one month of the share issue (s 555(2) CA).

Copies of any OR or SR must be sent to Companies House within 15 days. Any relevant PSC forms must also be filed (see **Chapter 3**).

The register of members must be updated and share certificate(s) issued within two months. The PSC register should also be updated, if kept (see **Chapter 3**). However, note that under ECCTA a PSC register is no longer required, but companies are required to maintain their own register of members and are no longer allowed to elect to rely on the central records kept at Companies House (see **Chapter 3**).

A summary of the share issue process is set out in **Table 5.1**.

Share transfer

For SQE1, it is important to appreciate that **share transfer** and **share transmission** are fundamentally different to a share issue. You should understand the processes involved and their potential impact.

Key term: share transfer

Share transfer involves dealing with existing shares (eg on sale or gift). No new money or assets are generated for the company, as it is essentially a transaction between the transferor and transferee, whereby ownership changes. The number of shares remains the same, but there is potential for an individual's control of the company to change (see **Practice example 5.3**).

Key term: share transmission

Transmission is the transfer of shares by operation of law (eg to personal representatives (PRs)) on death (see ***Revise SQE: Wills and the Administration of Estates***), or a trustee in bankruptcy (TIB - see **Chapter 6**). When shares are transmitted, the PR/TIB may receive the dividends (see **Dividends**, below), but they do not become shareholders (MA27). They may apply to be registered as a member or sell in their capacity as PR/TIB.

Table 5.1: Summary of the share issue process

Substantive legal requirements	**Procedural requirements (PR) and Directors' declaration of personal interests (DOI)**	**Filing/Administration requirements**
MA3 – General management powers of directors – BR s 550 – *Authority* not required if company has MAs and only one class of shares s 551 – Otherwise need members' authority – OR Company incorporated prior to 01/10/09 – Check articles, OR required to change Company incorporated from 01/10/09 – Check articles, SR required to change s 561 – *Pre-emption rights* apply if shares issued for cash s 569 – SR required for disapplication of statutory pre-emption rights or to change the articles (or specific issue can be waived if all shareholders agree) s 190 – May be an SPT – OR required	PR: BM (Board Meeting) or PR: BM > GM (General Meeting) > BM DOI: s 177 MA14 – N/A due to exception re issue of shares (see **Chapter 3**)	Filing: Copy OR (s 551(9)) Copy SR Form SH01 PSC form(s) Admin: Register of members PSC register (if kept) Seal/execute and issue share certificate BM and GM minutes

NB: Statutory references are to the CA.

Practice example 5.3

Mary has a 26% shareholding in Waterloo and Robinson Limited. The remaining shares are owned by Caroline (30%), Russ (25%), Natalie (15%) and David (4%). All of the shares have voting rights. Caroline transfers her shares to Russ. What will the impact be on Mary?

With 26%, Mary will still be able to block special resolutions, but Russ (55%) will now be able to pass and block ordinary resolutions.

The share transfer process is straightforward and is summarised in **Figure 5.3**.

Transferor completes and signs a *stock transfer form* (STF) and sends it with the *share certificate(s)* to the transferee (ss 770–772 CA)

↓

Transferee pays *stamp duty* on the STF (calculated at 0.5% of the consideration paid, rounded up to the nearest £5)

↓

Transferee sends the *stamped STF* and the *share certificate(s)* to the company

↓

Directors pass BR to approve/reject the transfer
Directors have absolute discretion under MA26 – Check for special articles

↓

Transfer must be *registered* and the *new share certificate* sent to the new member within two months of the application (ss 771(1) and 776 CA) (unless the directors have the right to refuse to register the transfer)

↓

The company will update details of shareholders annually on the *Confirmation Statement* (see **Chapter 3**)

Figure 5.3: Share transfer

Whether or not the directors will have the right to refuse to register the proposed transfer will depend on the terms of the company's articles.

The transfer of shares under the MAs is dealt with in MA26, the effect of which is that directors have an absolute discretion to refuse to register the transfer of shares.

The transferee will become a member when entered onto the register of members (s 113 CA). Until then, the transferor holds the shares on trust for the transferee (see ***Revise SQE: Trusts Law***), so if the directors exercise their discretion not to register, the transferee may never be the legal owner. However, the transferor must vote according to the wishes of the transferee and must hold any dividends on trust for them.

Some companies may decide to adopt other types of restriction on the right to transfer shares in their articles, for example:

- requiring a member who wishes to sell to first offer shares to the existing members pro rata (ie in proportion to their existing shareholding)
- allowing the members freedom only to transfer to family or other company members.

Note that the electronic CREST system may also be used to transfer shares for some companies. The detail of this system is beyond the scope of this book.

Dividends

For SQE1, it is important to appreciate when and how a company may issue a **dividend** to its shareholders.

> **Key term: dividend**
>
> A dividend is a payment the company makes to its members, which provides them with a return on their financial investment in the company.

A dividend may only be made out of 'profits available for the purpose' (s 830 CA). This means that the company must calculate its accumulated realised profits to date (ie its actual net profits to date - see **Accounts**, below) and deduct its accumulated realised losses to date. Accordingly, a dividend may be paid even if a loss has occurred in that year, provided that, over the years, the accumulated profits exceed the accumulated losses.

The company's articles will further regulate when and how a dividend is to be paid. The relevant parts in the MAs are MAs 30–35 and the procedure is summarised in **Figure 5.4**.

Check profits are available (s 830 CA)
↓
MAs 30–35 - Check special articles
↓
Directors decide whether a dividend ought to be declared and make a recommendation to the members in general meeting (GM)
↓
Members vote (by OR) to pay themselves the amount as recommended by the directors or less (note that they cannot vote to pay themselves *more* than the recommended sum)

Figure 5.4: Declaration of dividend

If the company does not declare a dividend when it is properly payable, this may be grounds for unfairly prejudicial conduct (see **Chapter 4**). However, a company will often wish to ensure that it has sufficient reserves available to deal with future liability (see **Company balance sheet**, below).

Buyback of shares

Buyback of shares is permitted in limited circumstances, due to the principle of **capital maintenance**.

Key term: buyback of shares

Where a company buys back its own shares, and the shares are cancelled.

Key term: capital maintenance

A fundamental principle which states that capital provided by shareholders must be maintained and must not be returned to them, as creditors rely on it.

Buyback of shares is heavily regulated as it could leave the company in a financially precarious position (reducing available profits and/or capital). There are different rules for the buyback of shares on the stock market, but for SQE1, you should focus on off-stock market purchases. Shares may be bought back out of profits or, in some circumstances, capital, and you should know the rules and processes involved.

Buyback from profits

The procedure for **buyback from profits** is outlined below in **Figure 5.5**.

Key term: buyback from profits

A buyback of shares that is only permitted where distributable profits (s 830 CA - see **Dividends**, above) are available.

Check *shares are fully paid* (s 691)

↓

Check *articles do not prohibit buyback* (s 690(1))

↓

Directors should consider their *duties* under ss 172 and 174 (see **Chapter 4**)

↓

Check profits are available by producing accounts - *Distributable profits* must be available or payment made from a fresh issue (s 692(2))

↓

OR required to approve contract (s 694(2))
Holders of shares being bought cannot vote and their votes do not count (s 695)

Figure 5.5: Buyback of shares from profits

NB: Statutory references are to the CA.

Copy buyback contract or a summary of it must be sent with written resolution or made available for inspection at least 15 days before the GM and at the GM (s 696(2))
Payment must be made at the time of buyback (s 691(2))

↓

File forms SH03 and SH06 within 28 days (ss 707 and 708)
Cancel shares, update register of members, file relevant PSC forms and update PSC register (if kept)
Make contract/summary available for inspection for 10 years at the registered office once completed (s 702)

Figure 5.5: (continued)

Buyback from capital

The procedure for **buyback from capital** is outlined below in **Figure 5.6**. Only private companies may buyback shares out of capital and the procedure is more tightly regulated.

> **Key term: buyback from capital**
>
> A buyback of shares that is only permitted to the extent that distributable profits are unavailable. *In other words, a company cannot buy back out of capital if profits are available; they must use these first.*

Check *shares are fully paid* (s 691)

↓

Check *articles do not prohibit buyback* (s 709(1))

↓

Directors should consider their *duties* under ss 172 and 174 (see **Chapter 4**)

↓

Check whether profits are available by producing accounts (prepared *no more than three months* before the statement of solvency (SOS)) (s 712)

↓

No earlier than one week before the meeting, directors must make an SOS (with auditors' report annexed) that the company will remain solvent (see **Chapter 6**) for a year after the transaction (ss 714 and 716(2))
They may face personal liability and criminal sanctions if they do this negligently (s 715)
The auditors' report must confirm that the SOS is not unreasonable (s 714(6))

Figure 5.6: Buyback of shares from capital

NB: Statutory references are to the CA.

OR required to approve contract (s 694(2))
SR required to approve buyback from capital (s 716(1))
Holders of shares being bought cannot vote and their votes do not count (s 717)

↓

Copy buyback contract or a summary of it must be sent with written resolution or made available for inspection at least *15 days before the GM* and at the GM (s 696(2))

↓

Copy SOS and auditors' report must be available for inspection before and at the meeting, otherwise the resolution will be ineffective (s 718(2))

↓

Notice must be published in the *London Gazette* as well as a national newspaper or actual notice to each creditor *within seven days of the SR* (s 719) stating where the SOS and auditors' report will be available and that creditors have *five weeks* to apply for an order preventing the buyback (s 721). Before, or at the same time, the SOS and report must be filed at Companies House (s 719(4))

↓

Copy SOS and auditors' report must be available for inspection until *five weeks* after the SR (s 720)

↓

Payment must be made in the *two weeks* following five weeks of the SR (s 723(1))
File form SH03 and SH06 within 28 days (ss 707 and 708)
File SR at CH within 15 days
Cancel shares, update register of members, file relevant PSC forms and update the PSC register (if kept)
Contract/summary available for inspection for 10 years at the registered office once completed (s 702)

Figure 5.6: (continued)

Table 5.2 sets out a timeline for this process.

Table 5.2: Buyback of shares out of capital – timeline

Prepare accounts	**Contract available for inspection**	**SOS**	**Publish notice to creditors**	**SOS to be made available/filed at Companies House/objection period**	**Make payment**
Within three months before SOS	At least 15 days before GM	Within one week before GM	Within one week of SR	Within five weeks of SR	Within weeks six and seven after SR

Practice example 5.4 provides an example of how buyback of shares could work in practice.

Practice example 5.4

Flying Flags Limited, a private company with unamended MAs, has distributable profits of £500,000 and net assets of £1m. It wishes to buy back 50,000 fully paid £1 ordinary shares at their nominal value. Can this be done?

This could be achieved through a purchase from profits only, not from capital (as distributable profits are available). An OR will be required to approve the contract.

Revision tip

The buyback procedure is complex, particularly for buyback from capital. For SQE1, the most important things to be aware of are when buyback is permitted and what resolutions are required.

DEBT FINANCE

This section deals with the issues involved in debt (loan) finance (a business borrowing money and, sometimes, giving security for that borrowing). For SQE1, you need to have a good working knowledge of the law and procedures involved.

The power to borrow/give security

The first issue with borrowing is to ascertain whether the business has power to borrow and give security (see **Types of security**, below).

For a *partnership* (see **Chapter 2**), this will involve checking any partnership agreement.

A *company* (see **Chapter 3**) will have the power to borrow and grant security, unless its articles say otherwise (s 31(1) CA). The process is summarised in **Figure 5.7**.

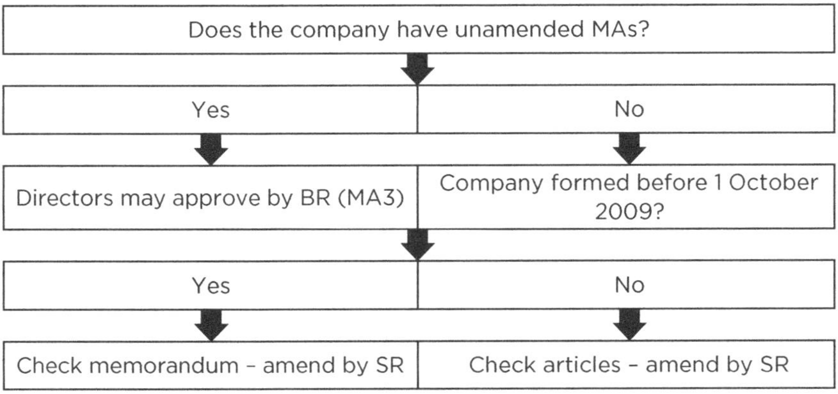

Figure 5.7: Authority to borrow/give security

The usual rules apply on declaration of interests and voting/counting towards the quorum when a director votes (see **Chapter 3**).

Borrowing options available to a business include loans (secured and unsecured), overdrafts and **revolving credit facilities**.

> **Key term: revolving credit facility**
>
> A hybrid between a loan and an overdraft. The business can borrow up to a certain amount and may repay and re-borrow, when needed.

Types of security

A lender will usually require **security** for a loan - a **mortgage** or **charge** (**fixed** and/or **floating**). They will normally carry out **due diligence** in any secured lending.

> **Key term: security**
>
> A charge document (eg a **debenture** - see below) will usually provide a lender with security for a loan. This means that in the event of default (eg failure to repay), the charge holder will have priority over unsecured creditors (see **Chapter 6**) and may sell the charged assets (see **Business accounts**, below) to settle sums owed.

> **Key term: due diligence**
>
> A process of investigation by the lender to ensure its interests are protected, the security will be validly granted and enforceable, and that title to the assets over which the charge will be made will be sound. This may involve company, Land Registry, bankruptcy and winding-up searches, as well as investigation of title. The detail of these processes is beyond the scope of this book, but see ***Revise SQE: Property Practice*** for investigation of title to land.

Key term: mortgage

A mortgage is the highest form of security. It involves the transfer of legal title to the mortgagee (lender) with re-conveyance/transfer back to the mortgagor (borrower) when the debt is satisfied (ie paid off in full). As such, it gives the lender an immediate right to possession. In the case of land, a mortgage is usually created by a fixed charge (see below) by deed.

Key term: charge

A charge provides the lender with an interest in the property, but unlike a mortgage in the traditional sense, it does not transfer legal title.

Key term: fixed charge

A fixed charge is a charge taken over a particular asset or assets. The consent of the lender is required in order to deal with the asset(s).

Key term: floating charge

A floating charge is a charge taken over a particular *class of asset(s)* owned from time to time (tangible, eg stock and/or intangible, eg intellectual property) and can only be granted by a company or LLP. The company/LLP can deal with the asset(s) without the consent of the lender until **crystallisation**, as until then, it 'floats over' rather than 'fixes on' the assets.

Key term: crystallisation

On crystallisation, a floating charge 'fixes' on the assets in the particular class at that time (it becomes a fixed charge). Crystallisation usually occurs when a company becomes insolvent (see **Chapter 6**) or any other event occurs which the charge specifies will cause crystallisation (eg non-payment, ceasing to trade or other default).

A key advantage of a floating charge for the borrower is that it gives them flexibility to deal with assets that are constantly changing (eg stock). It is common for such a charge to be over the whole 'undertaking' or business. The borrower can therefore charge more assets and will be able to give more security for borrowing, which may give them better terms. The key advantage for the lender is that they have security when it matters (on crystallisation - see **Practice example 5.5**). On the negative side, the lender takes the risk that assets may not be replaced, and the security will usually be postponed to fixed charge holders and preferential creditors, or may even be set aside (see **Chapter 6**).

Practice example 5.5

Clark-Neal Stores Limited carries on business as a convenience store. There is a floating charge in favour of a bank over all of its assets, including the stock. Can the company sell a can of baked beans to a customer, Scott, without the permission of the bank?

Yes, this is possible before crystallisation, after which, the consent of the bank would be required. The consequences of having a fixed charge prior to crystallisation here would be ludicrous, as there needs to be a constant turnover of stock to make a profit.

Companies frequently give security in the form of a debenture.

Key term: debenture

A debenture is a document which includes security in the form of a floating charge or sometimes both fixed and floating charges. Because they contain a floating charge, they can only be granted by a company or LLP.

Although not a form of security as such, director-shareholders may also give personal guarantees (see **Chapter 4**).

Priority of security

For SQE1, it is important to know, and be able to apply, the general rules as to priority of security, which are as follows (subject to *registration* - see below and **Practice example 5.6**):

- As between validly created charges of the same type, the first in time (date of creation) will have priority.
- As between a validly created fixed charge or mortgage and a floating charge, the fixed charge or mortgage will take priority (even if granted later) unless:
  - the document creating the floating charge contains a **negative pledge clause**; and
  - the later fixed chargee has notice of this prohibition at the time when it takes its charge (see **Practice example 5.6**).

Key term: negative pledge clause

A clause in a debenture which prohibits the creation of later fixed charges without permission.

Practice example 5.6

Miller-Heidke Associates Limited granted a fixed charge over its London premises in 2010, a floating charge over its whole undertaking in 2015, and a fixed charge over its Birmingham office in 2020. The first charge was not correctly registered at Companies House, although the other charges were. What is the order of priority?

The first fixed charge will be void against a liquidator, administrator or creditor (see below) as the priority rules are subject to registration. The second fixed charge, although granted after the floating charge, will take priority, unless the chargee had notice of a negative pledge clause in the floating charge.

It is possible for lenders to agree to a different arrangement as to their relative priority by entering into a *deed of priority*.

Registration of charges

Generally, all charges created by a company *may* be registered at Companies House (s 859A CA). Although registration is not compulsory, the potential consequences of non-registration for a secured lender are so serious that registration is routine.

Registration process

The process involves submitting the following to Companies House within 21 days of the creation of the charge (ss 859A(2) and (4) CA):

- form MR01
- a certified copy of the charge document
- the relevant fee.

The company will receive a certificate of registration (s 859I CA) and must also update its register of charges (if held - see **Chapter 3**).

Failure to register

A charge that is not registered in time is void against a liquidator, administrator or any creditor of the company (ss 859H(3) and (4) CA). The debt will be payable immediately but will be unsecured (s 859H(4)).

Clearly, there is potential for negligence on the part of solicitors who fail to register a charge.

Although there is provision for the court to extend the deadline, this is not guaranteed and priority will only be enjoyed from the date of registration (s 859F).

Fixed charges over land must also be registered at the Land Registry (see ***Revise SQE: Property Practice***).

A copy of the charge and MR01 should be made available for inspection and, when a charge is redeemed, form MR04 should be completed and sent to Companies House.

Remedies of debenture holders

If a company or LLP defaults on repayment of the loan, the debenture holder may:

- sue as a creditor
- petition for the winding-up (see **Chapter 6**) of the company
- utilise any powers in the debenture document (eg the appointment of a receiver - see **Chapter 6**).

A fixed charge holder will usually exercise their power to sell the charged assets.

Differences between debt (loan) finance and equity finance

Table 5.3 provides a summary of some of the key distinctions between debt finance and equity finance.

Table 5.3: Equity finance and debt finance compared

	Equity finance	Debt finance
Return on investment	Dividends *may* be paid if profit is available Capital value may decrease as well as increase Share issue may reduce both dividends and the value of shares, as the shareholding is diluted	Interest will be paid under contract terms Capital value will remain constant Security may be taken to protect the lender Other remedies may be available
Membership rights	Yes	No - a creditor
Investment repaid	Usually on sale or termination	Under terms of agreement
Transferability	May be restrictions on transfer (eg MA 26)	Usually transferable
Regulation	Heavy regulation - CA 2006	Contract law (less stringent)
Taxation	Dividends not deductible for corporation tax purposes	Debenture interest is deductible for corporation tax purposes

BUSINESS ACCOUNTS

Business accounts are summaries of financial information. For SQE1, it is important to understand how business accounts are constructed, the information they may give us about a business, and the relevant reporting requirements.

Preparation of accounts

Business accounts are based on the double-entry system (see ***Revise SQE: Solicitors' Accounts***), whereby every business transaction has two aspects (a debit and a credit). They begin with a *trial balance*, which involves obtaining all the credit and debit balances from the various accounts ledgers. This process is beyond the scope of this book, but it is important to appreciate that the figures are then used to prepare the final accounts of the **profit and loss account** and the **balance sheet**.

Key term: profit and loss account

The profit and loss account shows whether the business has made a profit or a loss *in the relevant period* (usually a financial year). The basic formula is **income**, less **expenses**, which gives *net profit*.

Key term: income

Income is usually recurring (see **Chapter 8**) and includes sales (for trading businesses), profit costs (for services businesses), interest received and rent received.

Key term: expenses

Expenses are usually incurred and exhausted over a short period of time. They are necessary to keep the business running. They include stock purchased (for trading businesses), wages, utilities, rent, interest paid, insurance, repairs, petrol and hire charges.

Key term: balance sheet

The balance sheet has two parts:

- The first part shows the value of a business *at a particular point in time*. The basic formula is **assets**, less **liabilities**. Current assets (see **Assets**), less current liabilities (see **Liabilities**) = net current assets. Total assets, less total liabilities = net assets.
- For an unincorporated business, the second part of the balance sheet shows what is owed to the owner (ie where the money the business has came from), *at a particular point in time*. The basic formula

is **capital**, plus net profit (from the profit and loss account), less **drawings**.

Key term: assets

Assets are also the result of expenditure, but their benefit is usually spread over a longer period of time. These include more permanent '*fixed assets*' (eg land, vehicles and machinery) and the more 'fluid' *current assets* (eg debtors and cash).

Key term: liabilities

Liabilities are sums owed by the business (eg loans and creditors). Those repayable within a year are *current liabilities* and those repayable beyond then are *long-term liabilities*.

Key term: capital

The sum invested in the business by the owner(s).

Key term: drawings

Money withdrawn by the owner(s) of an unincorporated business (see **Chapter 1**), on account of profits owed to them.

Revision tip

Candidates often get confused between expenses and liabilities. However, if you follow the definitions, it is quite straightforward. For example, a loan is a liability (over a period), but the interest paid would be an expense (usually recurrent).

Adjustments

Business accounts are usually based on the *accruals method of accounting*. This means that items within the accounts should properly relate to the relevant period (eg the financial year). Accordingly, it may be necessary to make adjustments to the accounts after the trial balance has been prepared, in order to ensure that they are an accurate reflection of the position. Entries are usually made to both the profit and loss account and balance sheet to reflect these. For SQE1, you should be aware of the main adjustments and how they may impact on the final accounts.

The main adjustments are **prepayments**, **accruals**, **closing stock/work in progress**, **opening stock/work in progress**, **depreciation**, **bad debts** and **doubtful debts**.

Key term: prepayments

These are payments that the business has made in advance, on account of a service or something that will not be used until the next financial year. *These are deducted as an expense in the profit and loss account and included as a current asset in the balance sheet* (see **Practice example 5.7**).

Practice example 5.7

Sergiu, Marina and Eugeniu are in partnership and have an accounting period that corresponds with the calendar year. They place an order for stationery on 15 December but will not receive and be able to use it until the following year. What will the impact of this be on the accounts?

This is a prepayment. It will be deducted as an expense in the profit and loss account and included as a current asset in the balance sheet.

Key term: accruals

These are payments the business will make in arrear, for services used in the financial year, but not yet paid for (the opposite of a prepayment). *These are included as an expense in the profit and loss account and a current liability in the balance sheet.*

Key term: closing stock/work in progress

This relates to stock (for trading businesses) and work in progress (for services businesses) that has not been used/billed in the current financial year. *It is included as income in the profit and loss account and a current asset in the balance sheet* (see **Practice example 5.8**).

Practice example 5.8

Sergiu, Marina and Eugeniu are in partnership as a firm of solicitors and have an accounting period that corresponds with the calendar year. At the close of business in the current year, they have unbilled work in progress of £10,000. What will the impact of this be on the accounts in the current year?

This is closing work in progress. It will be included as income in the profit and loss account and a current asset in the balance sheet.

Key term: opening stock/work in progress

This relates to closing stock/work in progress from the previous year. *It is deducted from income in the profit and loss account and there is no entry in the balance sheet.*

The value of assets may need to be recalculated over time. Assets that may increase in value need to be revalued, but many assets depreciate over time.

Key term: depreciation

Depreciation is a hidden expense and also has an impact on the value of the business. *The current year's depreciation is therefore included as an expense in the profit and loss account. The accumulated depreciation to date is deducted from the value of the asset in the balance sheet, to give its 'net book value' (its value at the current time).*

Practice example 5.9 provides an illustration of depreciation in practice.

Practice example 5.9

A business buys a car worth £10,000 and will own it for five years, when its estimated value will be £5,000. What is the annual depreciation and net book value of the car at the end of each year?

Each year, depreciation of £1,000 will be a hidden expense of the business, and the asset's net book value will decrease by £1,000 each year (see Table 5.4).

Table 5.4: Illustration of depreciation

Year	Value	Annual depreciation (expense - in profit and loss account)	Accumulated depreciation (reflect in asset value - in balance sheet)	Net book value
1	£10,000	£1,000	£1,000	£9,000
2	£10,000	£1,000	£2,000	£8,000
3	£10,000	£1,000	£3,000	£7,000
4	£10,000	£1,000	£4,000	£6,000
5	£10,000	£1,000	£5,000	£5,000

Key term: bad debts

A debt that the business resolves will *never* be paid, so it is written off. *It is included as an expense in the profit and loss account and deducted from the debtor's figure in the balance sheet.*

Key term: doubtful debts

A debt that the business decides is *unlikely* to be paid. *It is included as an expense in the profit and loss account and deducted from the debtor's figure as a separate entry.*

See **Practice example 5.10** for how bad and doubtful debts work in practice.

Practice example 5.10

Sergiu, Marina and Eugeniu are in partnership and have an accounting period that corresponds with the calendar year. In the current year, they agree to write off debts of £3,000 and provide for doubtful debts of £600. What will the impact of this be on the accounts?

As bad debts and doubtful debts are expenses in the profit and loss account, net profit will be reduced by £3,600. On the balance sheet, the figure for debtors will be reduced by £3,000 and the provision for doubtful debts will be shown as a separate entry/deduction of £600 from the debtors' figure.

Partnership accounts

The profit and loss account and the top part of the balance sheet for a partnership are the same as for a sole trader. However, an **appropriation account** is added to the bottom of the profit and loss account, and the second part of the balance sheet is adjusted to reflect that there is more than one owner of the business.

Key term: appropriation account

An extension of the profit and loss account, which shows the division of profits between the partners. Profit is divided into *salaries*, which are paid first, then *interest on capital* (see **Chapter 2**). Anything left (*residual profit*) is shared according to the agreed profit-sharing ratio (see **Practice example 5.11**).

Practice example 5.11

Tõni and Encarna are in partnership and make net profit of £200,000 in the current financial year. They each contributed £50,000 of capital and receive 5% interest on capital per annum. They each have a salary of £20,000 per annum and share the residual profits equally. What are their shares of the profits?

From the net profit, they each receive a salary of £20,000 and £2,500 interest on capital. The balance (£155,000 - ie £200,000 less £40,000, less £5,000) is split equally, so they receive £77,500 each.

The bottom half of the balance sheet for a partnership comprises the **capital account** and **current account** for each partner.

Key term: capital account

The amount of capital invested in the business by the partner. This is usually kept separate from the current account, so that the partner's investment can always be seen.

Key term: current account

The partner's share of the business, calculated as follows:
Opening balance (what remains undrawn) *plus* net profit share (from appropriation account) *less* drawings (see **Practice example 5.12**).

Practice example 5.12

The facts remain as in **Practice example 5.11**. Tõni has a current account opening balance of £10,000 and has made drawings of £30,000. What is the balance to which she is entitled?

£10,000 (opening balance) + £77,500 (appropriation of profits) - £30,000 (drawings) = £57,500.

Company accounts

Company accounts differ to those of unincorporated businesses, due to the separate legal personality of a company (see **Chapter 1**) and regulation concerning shares. The main difference is the need for a **share capital account** and a **share premium account**.

Key term: share capital account

This shows the funds contributed by shareholders in exchange for shares at their nominal/par value.

Key term: share premium account

This shows the funds contributed by shareholders in exchange for shares over their nominal/par value (ie where a premium has been paid).

Directors' salaries will be shown as an expense of the business, rather than an appropriation of the business, due to the company's separate legal personality.

Appropriation of profit

Profit is usually appropriated as follows:

- corporation tax – profits are shown before and after tax (see **Chapter 10**)
- dividends
- retained profit.

Company balance sheet

The second part of the balance sheet is usually headed 'Capital' (for **capital reserves**) and 'Reserves' (for **revenue reserves**), and shows what is owed to the shareholders.

Key term: capital reserves

Capital reserves (capital and share premium) are not usually distributable when a company is solvent, due to the principle of capital maintenance (see above).

Key term: revenue reserves

Revenue reserves are distributable and the most important one is the profit and loss reserve, which shows profit after tax and dividends.

Regulation of accounts

Directors must file annual accounts each year (see **Chapter 3**) and group companies must produce consolidated accounts, showing the financial position of the whole group.

Company accounts must comply with FRS102, a best practice guide produced by the accounting profession, and the International Financial Reporting Standards of the International Accounting Standards Board. The detail of the regulations is outside the scope of this book, but the purpose is to standardise accounts so that they are easier to interpret.

■ KEY POINT CHECKLIST

This chapter has covered the following key knowledge points. You can use these to structure your revision, ensuring you recall the key details for each point, as covered in this chapter.

- Equity finance concerns the company issuing shares to finance the company. When issuing shares, it is important to consider the issues of authority and pre-emption.
- Share transfer involves dealing with existing shares – no new money or assets are generated for the company.
- Shareholders may be entitled to dividends if the company has available profits.

- The company must usually maintain its capital, although in some circumstances a company may buy back its own shares.
- Companies may grant fixed and floating charges over their assets. Subject to registration, charges of the same type rank in order of creation and fixed charges usually have priority over floating charges.
- Accounts show a business' profit/loss over a period and the value of a business at a particular time. Accounts vary according to the nature of the business entity.

KEY TERMS AND CONCEPTS

- equity finance (**page 90**)
- debt finance (**page 91**)
- share issue (**page 91**)
- pre-emption rights (**page 93**)
- share transfer (**page 95**)
- share transmission (**page 95**)
- dividend (**page 98**)
- buyback of shares (**page 99**)
- capital maintenance (**page 99**)
- buyback from profits (**page 99**)
- buyback from capital (**page 100**)
- revolving credit facility (**page 103**)
- security (**page 103**)
- due diligence (**page 103**)
- mortgage (**page 104**)
- charge (**page 104**)
- fixed charge (**page 104**)
- floating charge (**page 104**)
- crystallisation (**page 104**)
- debenture (**page 105**)
- negative pledge clause (**page 105**)
- profit and loss account (**page 108**)
- income (**page 108**)
- expenses (**page 108**)
- balance sheet (**page 108**)
- assets (**page 109**)
- liabilities (**page 109**)
- capital (**page 109**)
- drawings (**page 109**)
- prepayments (**page 110**)
- accruals (**page 110**)
- closing stock/work in progress (**page 110**)
- opening stock/work in progress (**page 110**)
- depreciation (**page 111**)
- bad debts (**page 111**)
- doubtful debts (**page 112**)

- appropriation account (**page 112**)
- capital account (**page 113**)
- current account (**page 113**)
- share capital account (**page 113**)
- share premium account (**page 113**)
- capital reserves (**page 114**)
- revenue reserves (**page 114**)

■ SQE1-STYLE QUESTIONS

QUESTION 1

Five years ago, a company created a floating charge over its entire undertaking in favour of a bank. Three years later, the company completed a debenture in favour of a lender, which created a floating charge over all of its assets. The lender was aware of the prior charge, but it was not registered at Companies House. Both charges were duly executed by the parties and the lender's charge was registered at Companies House. The company is now in insolvent liquidation.

Which of the following best describes the position?

A. The lender's charge takes priority as the bank's charge is void against the liquidator and the lender.

B. The lender's charge takes priority as the bank's charge is void against the liquidator.

C. The bank's charge takes priority, because the lender had actual notice of the prior charge.

D. The bank's charge takes priority, because the date of creation determines the order of priority.

E. The bank's charge takes priority, because the date of creation determines the order of priority and registration is voluntary.

QUESTION 2

A company has a fixed charge over its freehold premises and a floating charge over its stock. Both charges were duly executed and registered and the fixed charge was granted first. The company is not in breach of either charge and is solvent.

Which of the following best describes the position as to dealing with the assets?

A. The company may sell the freehold premises and stock without recourse to the lender(s).

B. The company may sell the freehold premises but will need the bank's consent. It may sell the stock when the floating charge has crystallised.
C. The company may sell the freehold premises but will need the bank's consent. It may sell the stock without recourse to the bank.
D. The company may sell the freehold premises but the bank will need to be added as a party to the sale. It may sell the stock when the floating charge has crystallised.
E. The company may sell the freehold premises but will need the bank's consent. It may sell the stock without recourse to the bank unless and until crystallisation occurs.

QUESTION 3

A private limited company, formed in December 2010, with model articles of association and 100,000 ordinary shares, wishes to issue 50,000 new ordinary shares for cash. All of the shareholders are directors. Since incorporation, there have been no resolutions authorising the issue of shares.

Which of the following best describes the position?

A. The board can issue the shares without recourse to the members.
B. The members can issue the shares without reference to the board.
C. An ordinary resolution will be required to authorise the issue of shares and a special resolution will be required to disapply the statutory pre-emption rights.
D. An ordinary resolution will not be required to authorise the issue of shares, but a special resolution will be required to disapply the statutory pre-emption rights.
E. An ordinary resolution will not be required to authorise the issue of shares and a special resolution will not be required to disapply the statutory pre-emption rights.

QUESTION 4

A private limited company with unamended model articles of association wishes to authorise the purchase of some of its own shares for the sum of £50,000. Distributable profits are £200,000 and net assets are £1m.

Which of the following best describes the position?

A. A special resolution will be required to authorise the purchase out of capital.
B. The company may choose to purchase the shares out of profits, by way of ordinary resolution, or to purchase them out of capital, for which a special resolution will be required.

C. The company may only purchase the shares out of profits and an ordinary resolution will be required.
D. The company may only purchase the shares out of profits and a special resolution will be required.
E. An ordinary resolution will be required to authorise the purchase out of profits.

QUESTION 5

A business has fixed assets of £200,000, current assets of £40,000, current liabilities of £20,000 and long-term liabilities of £100,000.

Which of the following best describes the position?

A. Net assets are £20,000 and net current assets are £120,000.
B. Net assets are £120,000 and net current assets are £20,000.
C. Net assets are £100,000 and net current assets are £20,000.
D. Net assets are £20,000 and net current assets are £100,000.
E. Net assets are £300,000 and net current assets are £60,000.

ANSWERS TO QUESTIONS

Answers to 'What do you know already?' questions at the start of the chapter

1) False. The board may issue shares without recourse to the members only where the company will have one type/class of share, both before and after issue. Authority will be required, by ordinary resolution, or a provision in the articles if this is not the case. Pre-emption rights also need to be considered.
2) Pre-emption is the right for existing shareholders to have a right of first refusal on the issue of new shares, in proportion to their existing shareholding.
3) True. A fixed charge will usually have priority over a floating charge, unless a prior floating charge contains a negative pledge clause and the fixed chargee has notice of this. Only companies and LLPs may grant floating charges.
4) False. A charge against a company's assets *may* be registered at Companies House. Although registration is optional, the consequences of failing to do so are serious.
5) The profit and loss account sets out the profit or loss that a business has made *over a period* (income, less expenses). A balance sheet shows the

worth of a business *at a time* (assets less liabilities). The composition of accounts varies according to the nature of the business.

Answers to end-of-chapter SQE1-style questions

Question 1

The correct answer was A. The lender's charge takes priority as the bank's charge is void against the liquidator and the lender, due to non-registration. Option B is wrong as the charge is void against both the liquidator and the lender. Notice is not a factor in the priority between floating charges, so option C is wrong. Although the date of creation determines the order of priority, this is subject to registration, and although registration is voluntary, non-registration still has serious consequences. Therefore, options D and E are incorrect.

Question 2

The correct answer was E. This is because the lender's consent will be required for the sale of the premises, but the bank will not need to be added as a party to the sale as it does not have legal title to the property. Therefore, options A and D are wrong. It will be able to deal with the stock, freely, *until* crystallisation. Therefore options A, B, C and D are incorrect in this respect.

Question 3

The correct answer was D. This is because an ordinary resolution will not be required to authorise the issue as the company has only one class of shares. However, a special resolution will be required to disapply the statutory pre-emption rights as shares are being issued for cash. Therefore options A, C and E are incorrect. Option B is also incorrect as it is the directors who issue shares.

Question 4

The correct answer was C. This is because the company may not purchase shares out of capital, as profits are available, so option A is incorrect. An ordinary resolution will be required. The company does not have a choice in these circumstances, so option B is incorrect. Option E is technically correct, but the additional detail in option C makes the position clearer and thus option C is the better answer. Option D is incorrect as it says that a special resolution is required. For a purchase out of capital, an ordinary resolution is required to approve the contract, in addition to the special resolution to use capital.

Question 5

The correct answer was B. This is because current assets less current liabilities = net current assets. Total assets less total liabilities = net assets. Option A is incorrect as the figures are the wrong way around. Option C is incorrect as it deducted long-term liabilities from fixed assets. Option D used the same incorrect figures for net current assets and net assets. Option E is incorrect as it added together the incorrect figures.

■ KEY CASES, RULES, STATUTES AND INSTRUMENTS

The SQE1 Assessment Specification does not require you to know any statutory authorities or specific case names for this topic. However, you should be able to apply the key provisions relating to this chapter from a practical perspective. The references to the CA and the MAs are for information purposes only.

6

Termination and insolvency

■ MAKE SURE YOU KNOW

This chapter provides an overview of the termination of a solvent company, as well as individual and corporate insolvency (see **Chapter 2** for termination of a solvent partnership).

For the SQE1 assessments, you will need to understand the options available, and procedures concerning, termination of a business and insolvency. These include bankruptcy, individual voluntary arrangements (IVAs) and debt relief orders (DROs) for individuals and liquidation (compulsory and voluntary), company voluntary arrangements (CVAs), administration and receivership for companies. You will also need to understand the provisions relating to the clawback of assets by an insolvency practitioner for the benefit of creditors and the order of priority for distribution to creditors. Your understanding of these subjects will enable you to identify and apply the relevant legal rules and principles to SQE1-style single best answer MCQs.

■ SQE ASSESSMENT ADVICE

For SQE1, you are required to understand termination and insolvency of businesses from a practical perspective. It is likely that you will be required to know whether an individual or business is insolvent and what options will be available to them. You will also need to appreciate how the various insolvency procedures operate, which assets may be clawed back by a trustee in bankruptcy/insolvency practitioner and how the assets will be distributed.

As you work through this chapter, remember to pay particular attention in your revision to:

- the bankruptcy process and the implications of bankruptcy
- alternatives to bankruptcy - IVAs and DROs
- clawback of assets on bankruptcy and the order of distribution
- the liquidation process (compulsory and voluntary)
- alternatives to liquidation - CVA, administration and receivership
- clawback of assets on liquidation and the order of distribution.

WHAT DO YOU KNOW ALREADY?

Attempt these questions before reading this chapter. If you find some difficult or cannot remember the answers, remember to look more closely at that area during your revision.

1) What are the thresholds for both bankruptcy and winding-up proceedings?

   [Individual (personal) insolvency and bankruptcy, page 122, and Corporate insolvency, page 132]

2) True or false? A court order will always be required to sell the bankrupt's home.

   [Bankrupt's home, page 125]

3) True or false? Paying off one creditor prior to a bankruptcy or winding-up order is a potential transaction at an undervalue.

   [Investigating past transactions, page 125]

4) What are preferential creditors?

   [Order of distribution, page 129]

5) True or false? A company must be solvent to enter into a members' voluntary liquidation.

   [Liquidation (winding-up), page 132]

INDIVIDUAL (PERSONAL) INSOLVENCY AND BANKRUPTCY

This section deals with the concept of individual insolvency, as well as the bankruptcy process and procedures.

Insolvency

Individual insolvency concerns an individual who is **insolvent** and has an **inability to pay** their debts.

Key term: insolvent

An individual may be insolvent when:

a) a debt is payable immediately or at some certain time in the future; and
b) the debtor appears either unable to pay it, or to have no reasonable prospect of being able to pay it (s 267 Insolvency Act 1986 (IA)).

Key term: inability to pay - individual insolvency

There are three ways to show inability to pay under ss 267 and 268 IA:

1) A **statutory demand** has been served for a **liquidated and unsecured sum** of at least £5,000 or more, *payable immediately*, and after three weeks it remains unsatisfied (ie unpaid)/there is no application to set it aside.

2) A statutory demand has been served for a liquidated and unsecured *future* liability of at least £5,000, and three weeks have passed without reasonable prospect of payment being shown or an application to set it aside.
3) Attempt has been made to enforce a **judgment debt** of at least £5,000, but it remains unsatisfied (eg bailiffs or sheriffs have been sent in to recover cash or items to satisfy the debt, but have been unsuccessful).

Key term: statutory demand

A formal written demand for payment.

Key term: liquidated and unsecured sum

An exact sum, rather than one that needs to be calculated or assessed, that is not secured (see **Chapter 5**).

Key term: judgment debt

A debt that is deemed due following a judgment of the court (see ***Revise SQE: Dispute Resolution***).

The bankruptcy process

For SQE1, you should have a good working knowledge of the **bankruptcy** process that may apply when an individual is unable to pay their debts.

Key term: bankruptcy

Bankruptcy is a judicial process whereby *most of the bankrupt's assets* pass to a **trustee in bankruptcy** and the bankrupt becomes subject to restrictions. The majority of bankrupts are usually discharged and free of restrictions after one year (see **Restrictions on bankrupts** and **Discharge**, below).

Key term: trustee in bankruptcy

A trustee in bankruptcy (a qualified insolvency practitioner) takes control of most of the bankrupt's property (see **Bankrupt's property**). They are under a duty to maximise the funds that will be available to the creditors (see **Investigating past transactions**) and to distribute the bankrupt's property (see **Order of distribution**, below).

Creditor's petition or debtor's application

The bankruptcy process usually starts with a **creditor's petition**, although the debtor may seek to make a **debtor's application**.

Key term: creditor's petition

A creditor owed a liquidated and unsecured sum of £5,000 or more may present a bankruptcy petition if a debtor is unable to pay their debts. The creditor will need to prove this by having followed one of the three methods to show inability to pay debts (see the key term **inability to pay - individual insolvency** above).

If the creditor has a secured sum owed to them, they must relinquish their security to pursue the bankruptcy process. They will usually rely on their security, as it should give them priority over other creditors (see **Chapter 5**).

Joint petitions are possible if a creditor is owed less than £5,000 (see **Practice example 6.1**). The court fee and a deposit to cover the costs of the trustee in bankruptcy must be paid, and the petition must usually be filed at the debtor's local county court with bankruptcy jurisdiction, and then served on the debtor.

Practice example 6.1

Eric owes Tix £700 and Vikki £4,500 (the debts are unsecured). Can they petition for Eric's bankruptcy?

They can present a joint petition for the combined sum, as it is £5,000 or more, but first they will need to prove inability to pay.

Key term: debtor's application

If a debtor is unable to pay their debts, an online application for bankruptcy may be made and will be decided upon by an adjudicator (an official acting for the Insolvency Service).

The application fee and a deposit to cover the costs of the adjudicator/official receiver must be paid. A bankruptcy order must usually be made within 28 days.

An individual will usually make a debtor's application as a self-help measure, to avoid pressure from creditors where a creditor's petition is inevitable.

Bankruptcy order

When the bankruptcy order has been made, the official receiver (an officer of the court) takes control of most of the bankrupt's assets and acts as trustee in bankruptcy. The bankrupt must produce a statement of affairs, setting out their financial position, to assist the trustee.

The trustee has wide powers to realise assets (ie convert a bankrupt's assets into cash and sell them) and may also investigate and unwind certain transactions to maximise the available funds to creditors (see **Investigating past transactions**, below).

Bankrupt's property

Title to the bankrupt's property vests in (is transferred to) the trustee, with the exception of tools of the trade (eg tools and vehicles) and everyday items such as clothing and furniture. If these items are of high value, the trustee may insist that they be sold and substituted with cheaper items, in order to increase funds available to creditors.

If the bankrupt's salary is more than is needed for reasonable needs, an income payments agreement may be agreed, or an income payments order made. Under such an agreement/order, the bankrupt must make contributions to funds available to creditors for any period of up to three years.

Bankrupt's home

The bankrupt's interest in his home will pass to the trustee. Where the bankrupt has sole legal and beneficial interest in the home and no one else has an interest or a right of occupation, a court order will not be required to sell it. However, in other cases, a court order will be required.

The court will consider the circumstances set out in s 335A IA in deciding whether to order sale. These include the interests of creditors, spouses/civil partners and children. However, after one year, the creditors' interests are paramount, unless there are exceptional circumstances.

Three years after the bankruptcy order, ownership reverts to the bankrupt, unless alternative arrangements have been made (eg the property has been sold).

Investigating past transactions

The trustee in bankruptcy may investigate past transactions. These include the following:

- disclaiming onerous property
- transactions at an undervalue
- preferences
- transactions defrauding creditors
- extortionate credit transactions.

> **Revision tip**
>
> Candidates usually have a better appreciation of these powers when they understand the rationale behind them. They involve the trustee minimising liability or unwinding/undoing past transactions (ie clawing back the money or property) with the aim of increasing the amount available in the bankrupt's estate to pay as many creditors as possible.

Disclaiming onerous property (s 315 IA)

The trustee may disclaim **onerous property** in order to reduce liability.

> **Key term: onerous property**
>
> Onerous property is any property of the bankrupt that is essentially a liability/drain on resources, rather than an asset. The most common example is a lease with no premium/capital value (ie realisable sale value) whereby liability to pay rent will build up over time to increase the bankrupt's liability to creditors. Other examples include contracts that are making a loss and land that is heavily polluted, such that it would cost more to return to a usable condition than it is worth.

Disclaimer means that liabilities will cease. However, anyone who suffers as a result of such disclaimer (eg a landlord of a lease) may claim as an unsecured creditor for what is owed to them. They can also push the trustee into making a decision to disclaim (eg so that a landlord may re-let the property, in a rising market). The procedure here is to ask the trustee to disclaim within 28 days (s 316), after which it will no longer be possible for the trustee to do so.

Transactions at an undervalue (s 339 IA)

The trustee may investigate and set aside a **transaction at an undervalue**.

> **Key term: transaction at an undervalue**
>
> A gift, or sale of a property where the consideration received is significantly less than the value of the property.

The trustee can set aside undervalue transactions going back up to five years from the date of presentation of the petition (the 'relevant date'). If the transaction was in the first two years from the relevant date, there are no additional pre-conditions. However, if the transaction took place more than two years prior to the relevant date, it must be proved that the bankrupt was either insolvent at the time or became insolvent because of the transaction.

If the undervalue is in favour of an **associate**, there is a rebuttable presumption that the bankrupt was insolvent at the time of the transaction (see **Practice example 6.2**). Transactions at an undervalue are best illustrated with a timeline (see **Figure 6.1**).

> **Key term: associate (s 435 IA)**
>
> The key individuals included within the definition are as follows:
>
> - *relatives* (includes brother, sister, uncle, aunt, nephew, niece, lineal ancestor or lineal descendant – eg parents, grandparents, children)
> - spouse/civil partner and their relatives
> - spouses/civil partners of relatives or of spouse/civil partner's relatives

- business partners and employees/employers
- a company controlled by a person either alone or together with their associates (ie able to exercise at least one-third of the voting power).

Revision tip

It is important to have a good working knowledge of the definition of 'associate' when considering undervalue transactions and preferences.

Revision tip

Figure 6.1 and the other timelines in this chapter are really useful once you have identified the nature of the transaction. First, ascertain the relevant date and use it to identify any relevant pre-conditions.

Insolvency needs to be proved			No additional pre-conditions		
Insolvency presumed if in favour of an associate					
5 years	4 years	3 years	2 years	1 year	Date of insolvency

Figure 6.1: Undervalue transactions – individual insolvency

Practice example 6.2 provides an example of a potential undervalue in practice.

Practice example 6.2

Lesley, a sole trader, owned a second home worth £400,000. She was concerned that if her business became insolvent, she would lose the property, so she transferred it to her daughter, Destiny, for £200,000. Four years later, a bankruptcy petition was presented against Lesley and a bankruptcy order was made. Is this a potential undervalue transaction?

The sale was within five years of the relevant date. If it can be proved that Lesley was insolvent at the time, or because of the transaction, the sale may be set aside, and the property may be reclaimed. Insolvency will be presumed, as Destiny is Lesley's associate, and the burden is on Lesley and Destiny to rebut this. The impact of reclaiming the property will be to increase the pool of funds that may be available to pay creditors (see Order of distribution, below).

Preferences (s 340 IA)

The trustee may investigate and set aside voidable **preferences**.

Key term: preferences

A preference is an arrangement that places a creditor or guarantor in a better position than they would otherwise have been in the event of an individual's bankruptcy (eg by repaying them as a priority, or giving them security over other creditors).

A desire to prefer the particular creditor must be shown and this is presumed if the preference is in favour of an associate (see the key term **associate** above and **Practice example 6.3**).

The trustee in bankruptcy can investigate and set aside preferences going back six months for any preference, or up to two years from the relevant date (as for undervalues, the date of presentation of the petition), if in favour of an associate. For all preferences, it must be shown that the bankrupt was insolvent at the time or became insolvent because of entering into the transaction (see **Figure 6.2** for a timeline).

<table>
<tr><td colspan="3">Must be in favour of an associate</td><td colspan="2"></td></tr>
<tr><td colspan="4">Insolvency needs to be proved</td><td rowspan="3"></td></tr>
<tr><td colspan="4">Desire to prefer must be proved</td></tr>
<tr><td colspan="4">Desire to prefer presumed if in favour of an associate</td></tr>
<tr><td>2 years</td><td>18 months</td><td>1 year</td><td>6 months</td><td>Date of insolvency</td></tr>
</table>

Figure 6.2: Preferences – individual insolvency

Revision tip

Candidates often conflate the concepts of preferences and undervalues. The key distinguishing feature of a preference is that it usually involves a *creditor or guarantor.*

Practice example 6.3 provides an example of a potential preference in practice.

Practice example 6.3

Sakis owes his bank £20,000 and owes his brother, Deen, £20,000. He repays his brother. A bankruptcy petition is presented against Sakis one year later and a bankruptcy order is subsequently made. Is Sakis' repayment to Deen a potential preference?

It is a potential preference as Deen is an associate. It would need to be proved that Sakis was insolvent at the time or became insolvent as a result of the transaction. Desire to prefer is likely in the circumstances

and will be presumed (it would be for Sakis and Deen to rebut this). By clawing back the money, it will increase the pool of funds that may be available to pay creditors (see Order of distribution, below).

Transactions defrauding creditors (s 423 IA)

The trustee may investigate and set aside **transactions defrauding creditors**.

Key term: transactions defrauding creditors

An *undervalue* transaction where there is an intention to put assets beyond the reach of someone or prejudice their interests in relation to a potential claim.

There is no time limit in these circumstances, so the section is often used where the relevant time for undervalue transactions has expired. It is harder to prove than a simple undervalue, due to the intention required.

Extortionate credit transactions (s 343 IA)

The trustee may investigate and set aside or vary the terms of **extortionate credit transactions**.

Key term: extortionate credit transactions

A credit transaction entered into within three years of the relevant date (as for undervalues) that involves *grossly exorbitant payments* or *grossly contravenes ordinary principles of fair dealing*.

This provision is seldom used and there is a lack of case law on the requirements.

Order of distribution

The IA sets out a clear order of distribution of the bankrupt's assets:

- secured creditors (see **Chapter 5**). These are paid first, and they will often sell the charged asset(s) themselves. If the sum realised exceeds the secured debt, they must pay any surplus to the trustee. If there is a deficit (ie the sum realised for the charged assets is less than the secured debt), they may claim the balance as an unsecured creditor
- costs of bankruptcy
- preferential debts
- unsecured creditors
- postponed creditors (spouse/civil partner of the bankrupt).

If there are insufficient funds to settle **preferential debts** or unsecured creditors, those within the category receive a proportionate sum of what is left (see **Practice example 6.4**).

Key term: preferential debts

There are two categories of preferential creditors.
Primary preferential debts are:
- wages for work carried out in the four months preceding the bankruptcy order (up to a maximum of £800)
- accrued holiday pay.

Secondary preferential debts are sums owed to HMRC for PAYE and VAT (see **Chapters 7 and 8**).

Practice example 6.4

On Ruslana's bankruptcy, £1,000 remains owed to ordinary unsecured creditors and £500 is left after preferential debts have been paid. How much will the creditors receive?

They will receive 50p for every £1 owed to them (ie half of what is owed to them, as that is all that is available).

Restrictions on bankrupts

Bankrupts are subject to a number of restrictions on their activities until discharged from bankruptcy (see **Discharge**, below) and may face criminal liability in the event of breach. The restrictions stipulate:
- they must disclose their bankruptcy if obtaining credit of more than £500
- they cannot act as a director (CDDA 1986 - see **Chapter 4**)
- they must disclose their bankruptcy if trading under a different name
- they cannot be a partner (unless s 33 Partnership Act 1890 is varied - see **Chapter 2**)
- they cannot be involved in company management, promotion or formation without leave of the court (CDDA - see **Chapter 4**)
- they require the leave of the SRA to practise as a solicitor.

Discharge

Most bankrupts are automatically discharged after one year. However, **bankruptcy restriction orders (BROs)** or **bankruptcy restriction undertakings (BRUs)** may continue to apply. Liability to repay student loans will continue (s 42 Higher Education Act 2004).

Key term: bankruptcy restriction orders (BROs) and bankruptcy restriction undertakings (BRUs)

These provide additional restrictions for particularly 'culpable' bankrupts for any period between 2 and 15 years. The aim is to protect the public from the financially reckless. BRUs are entered into by agreement, whereas BROs are issued by the court.

PERSONAL INSOLVENCY: ALTERNATIVES TO BANKRUPTCY

A number of alternatives to bankruptcy may be available. For SQE1, you should know when they are available, how they operate and their advantages/disadvantages.

Individual voluntary arrangement (IVA)

An **IVA** is the main alternative to bankruptcy for an individual.

Key term: individual voluntary arrangement (IVA)

A binding agreement to settle between debtor and unsecured creditors. It avoids the stigma of bankruptcy and may give the creditors a better result than on bankruptcy.

The debtor appoints a nominee (an insolvency practitioner) to become supervisor of the IVA. The debtor then produces a statement of affairs (details of their financial circumstances) and applies to the court to obtain a *moratorium* (a stay on further proceedings/enforcement, of usually 14 days).

In order for the IVA to be approved, 75% or more of the creditors in value must agree to the proposals, of which at least 50% in value are not associates of the debtor (see key term associate above). If approved, it is binding on every ordinary, unsecured creditor.

If the debtor defaults, petition may be made for their bankruptcy. It is preferable to an informal agreement with a creditor(s), which could be viewed as a voidable preference (see above). The IVA Protocol provides a voluntary framework for creditors when dealing with straightforward consumer IVAs. The detail of the Protocol is beyond the scope of this book, although it is important to be aware of its existence.

Debt relief order (DRO)

Another alternative to bankruptcy is an online application for a **DRO**.

Key term: debt relief order (DRO)

A DRO involves the write-off of debts and is only available where assets and liabilities are low:

- unsecured liabilities cannot exceed £50,000
- gross assets cannot exceed £2,000
- cannot have car worth £4,000 or more (unless adapted due to disability)
- cannot have disposable income of more than £75 per month
- cannot have had a DRO in the preceding six years
- cannot be subject to other insolvency proceedings.

The debtor is usually discharged and free of debt after one year.

Debt respite scheme (DRS)

The **debt respite scheme (DRS)** is a relatively new regime which commenced in May 2021.

Key term: debt respite scheme (DRS)

The DRS provides 'breathing space' for up to 60 days (generally) or 30 days plus any treatment period (for a mental health crisis). It provides time during which no further action can be taken against the debtor.

CORPORATE INSOLVENCY

For SQE1, you need to understand the process of **corporate insolvency**, which is when a company has an **inability to pay** its debts.

Key term: inability to pay - corporate insolvency

There are four ways to show inability of a company to pay its debts under s 123 IA:

1) A statutory demand has been served for a liquidated sum of £750 or more and has been unsatisfied after 21 days.
2) Attempt has been made to enforce a judgment debt against the company, but it remains unsatisfied.
3) The company is unable to pay its debts as they fall due.
4) The company's liabilities are more than its assets.

An insolvent company may go into **liquidation (winding-up)** and the two main alternatives are **administration** and a **company voluntary arrangement (CVA)** (see below).

Secured creditors may have additional options (see **Secured creditors**, below).

Liquidation (winding-up)

Liquidation (winding-up) is the most drastic insolvency procedure for companies.

Key term: liquidation (winding-up)

Liquidation involves the company ceasing to trade and a liquidator (an insolvency practitioner) taking control to review past transactions, sell its assets, and distribute the proceeds to the creditors. The company is then dissolved.

There are three types of liquidation - **compulsory liquidation**, **creditors' voluntary liquidation** and **members' voluntary liquidation**.

Compulsory liquidation

Key term: compulsory liquidation

Liquidation commenced by a creditor presenting a 'winding-up petition' when a company is insolvent. *It is the corporate equivalent of a bankruptcy petition.*

A creditor will usually prove inability to pay by showing that a statutory demand has been unsatisfied for 21 days.

If the debt is disputed, the petition will be unable to proceed and the court may adjourn the hearing if the company says it will be able to pay the sum due within a reasonable period.

When a winding-up order is made by the court, the official receiver (an officer of the court) becomes the liquidator.

Creditors' voluntary liquidation (CVL)

Key term: creditors' voluntary liquidation (CVL)

The corporate equivalent of a debtor's application for bankruptcy. A CVL is commenced by an *insolvent* company, usually as a response to creditor pressure and/or concern of the directors as to personal liability (see **Chapter 4**, **Personal liability of directors**). A special resolution is required (see **Chapter 3**).

Members' voluntary liquidation (MVL)

Key term: members' voluntary liquidation (MVL)

MVL is commenced by a *solvent* company (it is only an option for a solvent company). It is often used for corporate restructuring or for closing down a company that is no longer needed. A special resolution is required, as is a statutory declaration from the directors that the company is solvent.

Effect of liquidation

The liquidator takes over the company and the directors' powers cease.

The liquidator has wide powers to manage and wind up the company. These powers include the ability to investigate and unwind past transactions where permitted under the IA (see **Investigating past transactions**, below).

After submission of final accounts, the liquidator may apply to be released and the company will be dissolved three months later.

Investigating past transactions

In a similar way to bankruptcy, the liquidator may investigate and unwind certain transactions in order to increase the funds available to creditors.

The liquidator may also seek to impose personal liability on the directors for misfeasance, wrongful trading or fraudulent trading (see **Chapter 4**).

Floating charges (s 245 IA)

A floating charge (see **Chapter 5**) will automatically be void if it is granted at the 'relevant time' before insolvency (s 245(5) – the presentation of the winding-up petition), without the company receiving fresh consideration.

The relevant time is two years if the charge is in favour of a connected person or 12 months if the charge is in favour of an unconnected person.

Insolvency is a prerequisite if the charge was in favour of an unconnected person (ie the company was insolvent at the time or as a result of the transaction) (see **Figure 6.3** for a timeline).

Must be in favour of a connected person		May be in favour of a connected or unconnected person		
		Insolvency must be proved if in favour of an unconnected person		
2 years	18 months	1 year	6 months	Date of insolvency

Figure 6.3: Avoidance of floating charges

The definition of 'connected person' is in ss 249 and 435 IA. This includes a director and his associates or an associate of the company (see **Transactions at an undervalue**, above).

Practice example 6.5 demonstrates how this works in practice.

Practice example 6.5

Embers Limited owes money to its main supplier on an unsecured basis. Concerned as to the financial position of the company, the supplier insists that the existing debt be secured by way of floating charge. Eight months later, a winding-up petition is presented, and the company goes into liquidation. What is the position with the charge?

The charge will automatically be invalid as no fresh consideration was received. The supplier's debt will be unsecured.

Preferences (s 239 IA)

Preferences work in a similar way to individual insolvency (see **Figure 6.4** for a timeline and **Preferences**, above, for an outline of the principles).

Must be in favour of a connected person				
Insolvency needs to be proved				
Desire to prefer must be proved				
Desire to prefer presumed if in favour of a connected person				
2 years	18 months	1 year	6 months	Date of insolvency

Figure 6.4: Preferences - corporate insolvency

Transactions at an undervalue (s 238 IA)

Transactions at an undervalue work in a similar way to individual insolvency, although the time limits do differ (see **Figure 6.5** for a timeline and **Transactions at an undervalue**, above, for an outline of the principles).

There is also a possible defence if the transaction was entered into in good faith for the purpose of carrying on business and there were reasonable grounds for believing it would benefit the company.

Insolvency needs to be proved				
Insolvency presumed if in favour of a connected person				
Potential defence may be available				
2 years	18 months	1 year	6 months	Date of insolvency

Figure 6.5: Undervalue transactions - corporate insolvency

Extortionate credit transactions (s 244 IA)

See **Extortionate credit transactions** for personal insolvency above.

Transactions defrauding creditors (s 423 IA)

See **Transactions defrauding creditors** for personal insolvency above.

Order of distribution

The IA sets out a clear order of distribution of the insolvent company's assets:

- fixed charge holders - any surplus (see **Order of distribution** for individual insolvency, above) goes to the liquidator and if there is a deficit, this can be claimed as an unsecured creditor

- winding-up expenses
- preferential debts (see **Order of distribution** for individual insolvency, above)
- floating charge holders (according to priority, see **Chapter 5**)
- unsecured creditors.

Unsecured creditors must usually complete a form in order to prove their debt.

If there are insufficient funds to settle preferential debts or unsecured creditors, those within the category receive a proportionate sum of what is left (see **Practice example 6.4**, above).

Ring fencing

Fifty per cent of the first £10,000 and 20% of the balance owed to floating charge holders is set aside for unsecured creditors. This is subject to a statutory limit (eg £800,000 for charges granted from 6 April 2020 or £600,000 for charges created before).

Alternatives to liquidation

The two main alternatives to liquidation are administration and a company voluntary arrangement (CVA). Secured creditors may appoint an LPA receiver or administrative receiver (see **Secured creditors** below).

Administration

Key term: administration

Administration involves an administrator (an insolvency practitioner) running the company to rescue it and/or enable it to be sold as a going concern (ie as a business that is still running). They must act in the interests of the creditors and their general priority is to achieve a better result than on winding-up.

Administration creates a moratorium, which prevents proceedings or the continuance of proceedings against the company: in essence, this provides 'breathing space' for the administrator to do their work.

The administrator can be appointed through the court or out of court.

Court appointment

Available if the company is likely to be unable to pay its debts and the administration is likely to achieve its purpose. **Qualifying floating charge** holders as well as those entitled to appoint an administrative receiver (see below) must be notified.

Key term: qualifying floating charge (QFC)

A QFC is a floating charge which (a) states para 14 of Schedule B1 IA (the statutory power to appoint) applies, (b) relates to whole/substantially the whole of the company's property and (c) purports to empower the QFC holder to appoint an administrator *or* administrative receiver.

Out of court appointment: made by company/directors

The court, QFC holders, as well as those entitled to appoint an administrative receiver (see below) must be notified.

A statutory declaration must be filed that the company is unable to pay its debts and is not in liquidation.

Out of court appointment: made by QFC holder

QFC holder must notify other QFC holders with priority (see **Chapter 5**) and the charge must be enforceable. They must then file notice of appointment at court along with a statutory declaration confirming the lender is a QFC holder, the charge is enforceable and the appointment complies with Schedule B1 IA.

Conduct of administration

The administrator has a duty to all of the creditors and the moratorium will continue whilst they act.

A majority in value of the creditors, present and voting at a meeting convened by the administrator, must vote in favour of the proposals. However, the resolution will not be passed if those against are more than 50% in value of the creditors who are unconnected to the company.

The administrator manages the company, and the moratorium continues. Directors' powers cease and the administrator has wide powers to manage the company.

Administration ends after one year (unless extended, or ended earlier by the administrator or a creditor). It is also important to be aware of a specific use of the administration procedure known as a **pre-pack administration**.

Key term: pre-pack administration

A pre-pack (short for 'pre-packaged') administration involves the use of the administration procedure for the specific purpose of selling the business as a going concern, often to the existing management team.

It is pre-packaged in the sense that it is pre-arranged for the specific purpose. The detail of pre-pack administration is beyond the scope of this book.

Company voluntary arrangements (CVAs)

A CVA is the corporate equivalent of an IVA.

Key term: company voluntary arrangement (CVA)

A CVA is a binding agreement between the company and the creditors. It is essentially a formal compromise arrangement, whereby creditors accept part payment and/or a delay in payment. The outcome for creditors can be better than on winding-up. It is usually cheaper than administration.

The CVA proposals must be approved by:

- 75% or more in value of the company's creditors; and
- 50% or more of unconnected creditors.

If approved, the proposal is binding on all unsecured creditors in respect of past debts.

Corporate Insolvency and Governance Act 2020 (CIGA 2020) moratorium

This is a relatively new process introduced by the CIGA 2020. It permits a company to enjoy a moratorium of 20 business days to give it breathing space. The full detail of the scheme is beyond the scope of this book.

CIGA 2020 restructuring plan

This is another relatively new process introduced by the CIGA 2020. It provides an alternative mechanism for a company in financial difficulty or prospective financial difficulty to achieve a court-sanctioned restructuring plan. The full detail of the process is beyond the scope of this book.

Secured creditors

Secured creditors (see **Chapter 5**) may also appoint an **LPA (Law of Property Act 1925) receiver** or an **administrative receiver**.

Key term: LPA receiver

A *fixed charge* holder may appoint an LPA receiver, usually to sell the property. Their power to appoint is usually in the charge document.

Key term: administrative receiver

An administrative receiver is appointed by a *floating charge holder* for charges created before 15 September 2003. Their power to appoint is usually in the charge document and they usually run the company and sell the charged assets.

KEY POINT CHECKLIST

This chapter has covered the following key knowledge points. You can use these to structure your revision, ensuring you recall the key details for each point, as covered in this chapter.

- Individuals may be made bankrupt if they fail to satisfy a statutory demand for an unsecured sum of at least £5,000. They may also make an online application for their own bankruptcy if they are unable to pay their debts.
- Most of the bankrupt's property vests in the trustee in bankruptcy. The trustee in bankruptcy may investigate and unwind prior transactions and there is a clear order of payment under the IA. The bankrupt is usually discharged after one year.
- Alternatives to bankruptcy include an IVA and DRO.
- A company may be subject to winding-up proceedings if it is unable to pay its debts. This can include failing to satisfy a statutory demand for a sum of at least £750. A company may also petition for its own winding-up, whether it is solvent or insolvent.
- The liquidator may investigate and unwind prior transactions and there is a clear order of payment under the IA.
- Alternatives to liquidation include administration or a CVA. Secured creditors may have the option of LPA or administrative receivership.

KEY TERMS AND CONCEPTS

- insolvent (**page 122**)
- inability to pay - individual insolvency (**page 122**)
- statutory demand (**page 123**)
- liquidated and unsecured sum (**page 123**)
- judgment debt (**page 123**)
- bankruptcy (**page 123**)
- trustee in bankruptcy (**page 123**)
- creditor's petition (**page 124**)
- debtor's application (**page 124**)
- onerous property (**page 126**)
- transaction at an undervalue (**page 126**)
- associate (**page 126**)

- preferences (**page 128**)
- transactions defrauding creditors (**page 129**)
- extortionate credit transactions (**page 129**)
- preferential debts (**page 130**)
- bankruptcy restriction orders and bankruptcy restriction undertakings (**page 130**)
- individual voluntary arrangement (**page 131**)
- debt relief order (**page 131**)
- debt respite scheme (**page 132**)
- inability to pay - corporate insolvency (**page 132**)
- liquidation (winding-up) (**page 132**)
- compulsory liquidation (**page 133**)
- creditors' voluntary liquidation (**page 133**)
- members' voluntary liquidation (**page 133**)
- administration (**page 136**)
- qualifying floating charge (**page 137**)
- pre-pack administration (**page 137**)
- company voluntary arrangement (**page 138**)
- LPA receiver (**page 138**)
- administrative receiver (**page 139**)

■ SQE1-STYLE QUESTIONS

QUESTION 1

A bankruptcy order is made against a client, who is a sole trader. They have no secured debt, but owe money to an employee, trade supplier, HMRC and their civil partner.

Which of the following are potentially preferential creditors?

A. The employee only.

B. The employee, trade supplier and civil partner.

C. The employee, HMRC and trade supplier.

D. The employee and HMRC.

E. HMRC and the trade supplier.

QUESTION 2

A bankruptcy order is made against a man this month, following presentation of a bankruptcy petition in the previous month.

Which of the following most accurately describes a potential preference(s)?

A. A gift of £10,000, made to the man's friend, 12 months ago.

B. Repayment of a loan of £5,000 to the man's sister, 18 months ago.

C. The sale of a property, for £120,000 less than its then market value, to the man's son, four years ago.

D. Full repayment of his credit card balance, one year ago.

E. Repayment of a loan of £5,000 to the man's sister, 18 months ago and full repayment of his credit card balance, one year ago.

QUESTION 3

A company's assets exceed its liabilities, and it is generally able to pay its debts as they fall due. However, a statutory demand for an unsecured debt of £6,000 was served four weeks ago by a creditor and has not been complied with. The company has also not made an application to set it aside.

Which of the following best describes the position?

A. The creditor may petition for the winding-up of the company.

B. The company is able to pay its debts under insolvency legislation.

C. The company is unable to pay its debts under insolvency legislation and the creditor may petition for the winding-up of the company.

D. The company is unable to pay its debts under insolvency legislation, so the company will be wound up.

E. The company is able to pay its debts under insolvency legislation as assets exceed liabilities and technically it can pay its debts as they fall due.

QUESTION 4

A company in liquidation has assets of £200,000 and liabilities of £400,000 after payment of fixed charge holders and winding-up expenses. Of the liabilities, £50,000 is owed to preferential creditors and there are no floating charge holders. The client is owed £50,000 as an unsecured creditor.

Which of the following best sets out what the client will receive?

A. £25,000.00.

B. £28,571.43.

C. £0.50 for every £1.

D. £18,750.00.

E. £21,428.57.

QUESTION 5

A bankruptcy order is made against a client, who is the joint owner of the matrimonial home.

Which of the following best describes the position?

A. All of the client's property will vest in the trustee in bankruptcy. A court order will be required to sell the home.

B. All of the client's property will vest in the trustee in bankruptcy except for tools of the trade and most items essential for day-to-day living. A court order will not be required to sell the home.

C. All of the client's property will vest in the trustee in bankruptcy except for tools of the trade, their interest in the home, and most items essential for day-to-day living. A court order will be required to sell the home.

D. All of the client's property will vest in the trustee in bankruptcy except for tools of the trade, their interest in the home, and most items essential for day-to-day living. A court order will not be required to sell the home.

E. All of the client's property will vest in the trustee in bankruptcy except for tools of the trade and most items essential for day-to-day living. A court order will be required to sell the home.

■ ANSWERS TO QUESTIONS

Answers to 'What do you know already?' questions at the start of the chapter

1) The thresholds are £5,000 for individual insolvency and £750 for corporate insolvency (although inability of a company to pay may be proved in other ways).
2) False. A court order will not be required where the bankrupt has sole legal and beneficial ownership of the property and is the only person living or entitled to live at the property.
3) False. This describes a potential preference.
4) Preferential creditors are entitled to be paid after fixed charge holders and the costs of the insolvency procedure.
5) True. Solvency is a prerequisite of a members' voluntary liquidation.

Answers to end-of-chapter SQE1-style questions

Question 1

The correct answer was D. The employee is primary preferential creditor and HMRC is secondary preferential creditor. The trade supplier will be an ordinary creditor and the civil partner will be a postponed creditor (so options B, C and E are incorrect). Option A also omits HMRC and option E omits the employee.

Question 2

The correct answer was B. The man's sister is his associate. Provided that he was insolvent at the time or because of the transaction and had a desire to prefer, it will be voidable. Desire to prefer will be presumed in the circumstances. Options A and C are potential undervalues. Although a potential preference, option D is out of time as it is to an unconnected person (also making option E incorrect).

Question 3

The correct answer was C. Option A is partially correct, but omitted reference to insolvency legislation. Options B and E are incorrect as even though the company appears solvent, non-compliance with the statutory demand deems the company unable to pay its debts. Option D is incorrect as it omits the need for a winding-up petition.

Question 4

The correct answer was E. Preferential creditors are paid first, which reduces assets and liabilities by £50,000. 150,000/350,000 = 0.42857143 x £50,000 = £21,428.57. Options A and C are incorrect as they do not take into account the preferential creditors. Options B and D are incorrect as they reduced only the liabilities and assets figures respectively by £50,000.

Question 5

The correct answer was E. Option A is incorrect as it did not exclude tools of the trade and day-to-day items. Options B and D are incorrect as a court order will be required. Options C and D are also incorrect as they suggest that the bankrupt's share of the home will not pass to the trustee in bankruptcy.

■ KEY CASES, RULES, STATUTES AND INSTRUMENTS

The SQE1 Assessment Specification does not require you to know any statutory authorities or specific case names for this topic. However, you should be able to apply the key provisions relating to insolvency from a practical perspective. The references to the CA, IA and MAs are for information purposes only.

Trading profits and VAT

■ MAKE SURE YOU KNOW

This chapter provides an overview of the calculation of trading profits and value added tax (VAT). For SQE1, you will need to have an understanding of both of these areas.

Trading profits are crucially important to the calculation of income tax (for individuals and individual partners - see **Chapter 8**) and corporation tax (for companies - see **Chapter 10**). As such, the calculation of trading profits provides the basis for a business' financial record-keeping and accounting, and the associated statutory filing and disclosure requirements. The chapter will also consider reliefs that may apply for trading losses for unincorporated businesses (see **Chapter 10** for incorporated businesses).

VAT is vitally important for most businesses, so it is necessary to appreciate how it applies in the context of trading. This chapter will consider the scope of VAT, registration, VAT invoices, returns/payment and record-keeping requirements. Again, VAT forms a key record-keeping and disclosure requirement for most businesses.

Your understanding of these subjects will enable you to identify and apply the relevant legal rules and principles to SQE1-style single best answer MCQs.

■ SQE ASSESSMENT ADVICE

For SQE1, you are required to understand the calculation of trading profits and VAT from a practical perspective. It is likely that you will be required to know how trading profits are calculated, what reliefs may be available for trading losses and apply the rules to problem-based, single best answer MCQs. You will also need to be aware of the key principles and practical requirements of VAT and its operation in England and Wales.

As you work through this chapter, remember to pay particular attention in your revision to:

- how trading profits are calculated (including the availability of capital allowances)

- reliefs for trading losses
- the scope of VAT (key principles of supply, input and output tax)
- registration requirements and the issue of VAT invoices
- returns/payment of VAT and record-keeping.

■ WHAT DO YOU KNOW ALREADY?

Attempt these questions before reading this chapter. If you find some difficult or cannot remember the answers, remember to look more closely at that area during your revision.

1) True or false? The basic calculation of trading profits is chargeable receipts, less deductible expenses.
   [Calculation of trading profits, page 145]
2) True or false? The cost of purchasing new plant and machinery will be a deductible expense when calculating a business' trading profit.
   [Calculation of trading profits, page 145]
3) Explain the purpose of capital allowances.
   [Calculation of trading profits, page 145]
4) True or false? If an unincorporated business makes a trading loss during an accounting period, there will be a nil liability to tax. In addition, tax relief may be available in respect of the loss.
   [Relief for trading losses, page 149]
5) Explain when VAT registration is compulsory.
   [Taxable persons, registration, supply, input and output tax, page 153]

CALCULATION OF TRADING PROFITS

For SQE1, you need to understand how trading profits are calculated and how capital allowances work within this context.

A business will usually prepare accounts for a 12-month accounting period in order to show whether a profit or loss has been made (see **Chapter 5**). Income can include things like trading profits, interest received and rent received (see **Chapter 8**). The principles of calculation are common to both incorporated and unincorporated businesses (see **Chapter 1**) and the basic formula is as follows:

Chargeable receipts

LESS

Deductible expenses

LESS

Capital allowances

EQUALS

Trading profit or loss

We will now look at this in a bit more detail.

Key term: chargeable receipts

A chargeable receipt means something of an income nature (see **Chapter 8**) rather than a capital nature (see **Chapter 9**) that is in respect of/derived from the trade. The most common examples are income from the sale of goods (sales) or services (profit costs).

Deductible expenses are then deducted from chargeable receipts.

Key term: deductible expenses

To be a deductible expense the sum must:

- *not be prohibited by statute* (eg business entertainment expenses are prohibited - the full extent of the statutory prohibitions is beyond the scope of this book)
- *be of an income nature* (not of a capital nature) - for example, goods purchased to sell at a profit (stock) and expenses such as rent, utility bills, business rates and salaries (essentially, expenses that are necessary to facilitate the making of a profit). The hallmark of income is that it usually has an element of recurrence (see **Chapter 8**). On the other hand, although capital items also help facilitate trade, their benefit usually spreads over a longer period of time (eg freehold premises, machinery or cars - see **Chapters 5 and 8**)
- *be incurred wholly and exclusively for the purposes of the trade* - for example, the cost of eating out when away from home on business would not be included, as people need to eat in any event. In some circumstances, expenses can be apportioned (eg utility bills when working from home).

Capital allowances are then deducted, to give the trading profit or loss.

Key term: capital allowances

Capital allowances allow businesses to deduct some of the cost of **plant and machinery** from chargeable receipts, to reduce tax liability.

Capital allowances serve to encourage investment, as without them, the cost of plant and machinery would not be deductible, as they are not income in nature. This would be unfair to many businesses and could discourage investment, particularly as these assets (see **Chapters 5 and 8**) can be very expensive and usually depreciate (ie lose value) over time.

Key term: plant and machinery

Plant and machinery include assets used to help carry on business (eg machines, office equipment and tools), but not items that are bought to be sold as part of the business.

There are three types of capital allowance that may be claimed – the **writing down allowance** (which we will look at first), followed by the **annual investment allowance**, and the **first year allowance**.

Key term: writing down allowance (WDA)

The WDA allows 14% (reduced from 18% in April 2026) of the total value of plant and machinery in each financial year to be deducted from chargeable receipts. The 14% is then deducted from the total value of the plant and machinery, to give the written down value (WDV).

See **Practice example 7.1** for an illustration of the WDA in practice.

Practice example 7.1

Chiara (Islington) Properties Limited buys plant and machinery for £200,000 in the first year of trade. Disregarding other capital allowances, what will the WDVs be in the first and second years of trade?

Year one – £200,000 (total value) x 14% = £28,000 WDA (to be deducted from chargeable receipts). The plant and machinery now has a WDV of £172,000 (ie £200,000 minus £28,000).

Year two – £172,000 (WDV) x 14% = £24,080 WDA (to be deducted from chargeable receipts). The plant and machinery now has a WDV of £147,920 (ie £172,000 minus £24,080).

As businesses often have more than one item of plant and machinery, the items are usually **pooled**.

Key term: pooling

Pooling means that the WDA each year is usually calculated on the value of all of the assets 'pooled together'. This makes it much simpler when assets are disposed of individually, as the proceeds are deducted from the total value of the pool. If, on sale of all of the assets, the sale price exceeds the WDV, the balance will be included as a chargeable receipt.

See **Practice example 7.2** for how pooling applies in practice.

Practice example 7.2

Cliff, a sole trader, owns plant and machinery with a pooled WDV of £200,000 at the start of the accounting period. He sells an item of machinery for £40,000. What will the WDV be?

Pooled WDV - £200,000

Less disposal - £40,000

= £160,000

WDA of 14% = £22,400

WDV of £137,600 (ie £160,000 less £22,400)

If all of the remaining assets were then sold for £138,600, £1,000 would be added as a chargeable receipt of the business.

The second type of capital allowance is the annual investment allowance.

Key term: annual investment allowance (AIA)

Under the AIA, a business can deduct the *entire cost* of newly purchased plant and machinery in that accounting period from chargeable receipts (subject to a cap of £1m each year). Group companies have one AIA between them. If the cost of new machinery exceeds the AIA, the first year allowance (FYA) or writing down allowance (WDA) can be claimed on the balance over the cap (see **Practice example 7.3**).

Revision tip

The cap on AIA has been subject to many changes since it was introduced. Make sure you check the current limit at the time you sit SQE1. It can be found on www.gov.uk. A temporary 'super deduction' of 130% applied for assets purchased between 1 April 2021 and 31 March 2023, as an alternative to the AIA and WDA. The 'super deduction' came to an end on 1 April 2023 and was replaced with **full expensing**.

Key term: full expensing (FE)

Full expensing applies to companies only and not unincorporated businesses. It allows companies to deduct 100% of the cost of plant and machinery purchased in the relevant accounting period from chargeable receipts. Unlike the AIA, it is uncapped.

The third type of capital allowance is the first year allowance.

Key term: first year allowance (FYA)

The FYA is a new relief (from 1 January 2026) set at 40% applying to assets beyond the current availability of full expensing (see above) and the AIA. It applies to all businesses (incorporated and unincorporated) although second-hand assets and cars are specifically excluded.

Practice example 7.3

Dragana, a sole trader, has a pool of assets with a WDV of £500,000. In the next financial year, she buys new machinery for £2m. What capital allowances will be available?

The WDV of the existing pool will be £430,000 (£500,000 less WDA of £70,000 - ie 14% of £500,000)

The full AIA will be £1m (ie the cost of the new machinery, up to the limit of £1m)

The FYA will be available on the remaining £1m, at a rate of 40% (ie £400,000) - WDV of £600,000

Total capital allowances = £1m AIA plus £400,000 FYA and WDA of £70,000

The WDV for the pool in the next financial year will be:
£1,030,000 (ie £430,000 plus £600,000) - 14% (£144,200) = £885,800 (WDA of £144,200 - ie 14% of £1,030,000)

Revision tip

It is important to be aware of the crucial differences between the AIA, FE and the FYA. FE is uncapped and applies to companies and to brand-new assets only. AIA is capped, applies to unincorporated businesses as well as companies and to assets in any condition (new, second-hand and refurbished). FYA applies to all businesses, and new assets, and can include assets bought for leasing.

Relief for trading losses

If an unincorporated business makes a trading loss during an accounting period, there will be a nil liability to tax (ie no tax will be payable). In addition, tax relief may be available in respect of the loss.

The reliefs are as follows:

- **start-up loss relief/early trade losses relief**
- **carry-across/back one year relief/trade loss relief against general income**
- **carry-forward relief**
- **terminal loss relief**
- **carry-forward relief on incorporation of business.**

Practice example 7.4 on **page 152** illustrates how the reliefs apply in practice.

The owner of a business may have a choice of reliefs, although the same loss cannot be claimed for twice. Some may be preferable to others, based on particular circumstances. Each individual partner in a partnership will choose their own relief(s).

Key term: start-up loss relief/early trade losses relief (SULR) (ss 72-81 Income Tax Act 2007 (ITA))

Losses made during the *first four years of trade* may be set off against *any other income* in the three tax years before the loss.

- can be used against any other income
- involves claim-back of tax paid (eg from a previous job or business)
- set against earlier years first
- time limit - must be claimed on or before the first anniversary of 31 January following the end of the loss-making tax year (eg 31 January 2028 if the loss occurred in 2025/26)
- cap applies (see **Cap on reliefs**, below).

Key term: carry-across/back one year relief/trade loss relief against general income (CA and CB) (ss 64-71 ITA)

The amount of the loss may be deducted from *any other income* taxable in that tax year (carry across) and/or the preceding tax year (carry back).

- can be used against any other income
- carry across can be used against chargeable gains in the same tax year if the loss is not absorbed
- time limit - must be claimed on or before the first anniversary of 31 January following the end of the loss-making tax year
- cap applies (see **Cap on reliefs**, below).

Exam warning

It is important to be aware of any temporary changes to these rules. Under an extension to CB relief, losses in accounting periods ending in the tax years 2020/21 and 2021/22 could be carried back for three years. This extension has now ended.

Key term: carry-forward relief (CF) (ss 83-85 ITA)

The amount of the loss may be deducted from *future income profits of the same trade.*

- set against earlier years first
- can only be used against trading profits from the same trade
- can be carried forward indefinitely
- taxpayer is required to notify HMRC no more than four years after the end of the loss-making tax year
- no cap applies.

Key term: terminal loss relief (TLR) (ss 89-94 ITA)

A loss made during the last year of trade may be set off against *trading profits connected to the same trade* in the *final year and in the three tax years prior to the final tax year.*

- set against later years first
- can only be used against income profits from the same trade
- time limit - claim must be made no more than four years after the end of the loss-making tax year
- involves claiming a rebate on tax paid (ie repayment of tax already paid)
- no cap applies.

Key term: carry-forward relief on incorporation of business (CFIB)

Allows trading losses to be set off against any income received from the company (eg dividends or directors' fees - see **Chapter 8**) when an unincorporated business is transferred to a company wholly or mainly in return for shares (shares must be at least 80% of the consideration).

- can be carried forward indefinitely
- time limit - claim must be made no more than four years after the end of the loss-making tax year
- no cap applies.

Cap on reliefs

The greater of £50,000 or 25% of the taxpayer's income from other sources in the tax year in relation to which the relief is claimed.

A summary of these reliefs and the key points is set out in **Table 7.1**.

Table 7.1: Reliefs for trading losses

	Loss period	Claim period	Set against total income	Final year losses only	Cap
SULR	First four tax years	Three tax years before the loss	Yes	No	Yes
CA/ CB	Any year	Loss-making year and previous year	Yes, and chargeable gains if loss not absorbed	No	Yes
CF	Any year	Subsequent periods	Same trade only	No	No
TLR	Final tax year	Final tax year and three preceding tax years	Same trade only	Yes	No
CFIB	Losses up to incorporation	Subsequent periods	Income received from the company	No	No

Practice example 7.4

Melovin started up business as a sole trader on 6 April 2013.

The recent profits and losses of the business are as follows and Melovin has no intention to cease trading:

y/e 05.04.2023 - £5,000
y/e 05.04.2024 - (£25,000) loss
y/e 05.04.2025 - £4,000
y/e 05.04.2026 - £7,000

In addition to his business income, Melovin has other income of £5,000 pa throughout this period. What reliefs are available to Melovin in relation to the £25,000 loss which the business has incurred?

	2022/23	2023/24	2024/25	2025/26
Business income	5,000	Loss of 25,000	4,000	7,000
Other income	5,000	5,000	5,000	5,000
Total income	10,000	5,000	9,000	12,000
Loss relief	(10,000) CB	(5,000) CA	(4,000) CF	(6,000) CF
Final income	Nil	Nil	5,000	6,000

SULR does not apply as he started trading in 2013. CFIB does not apply as the business has not been incorporated and TLR does not apply as he is not in the last year of business. CA can be applied against the other income in the loss-making year and CB can be applied against the total income in the previous year. This leaves £10,000 where CF can be applied. It can only be claimed against profits from the same trade and it must be claimed against earlier years first.

VAT

This section deals with the nature and scope of **VAT** and how it applies in practice.

Scope of VAT

For SQE1, it is important to have a good general appreciation of how the VAT system in England and Wales works, in the context of trading.

VAT is charged when a business supplies goods or services. The main charging statute is the Value Added Tax Act 1994 (VATA).

Key term: VAT

VAT is 'charged on any *supply of goods or services* made in the United Kingdom, where it is a **taxable supply** made by a **taxable person** in the *course or furtherance of any business* carried on by him' (s 4 VATA).

Key term: taxable supply

A supply is taxable unless it is exempt. The main exempt supplies are education and health services, residential land and insurance.

Taxable persons, registration, supply, input and output tax

A taxable person charges VAT on the *value of the supply* of goods (eg items sold) or services (eg profit costs) (ie the value without VAT).

Key term: taxable person

A taxable person is someone who makes *taxable supplies*. They must register for VAT with HMRC if the value of their taxable supplies exceeded £90,000 in the previous year. Otherwise, registration is voluntary. It is not possible to register if the business only makes exempt supplies.

Upon registration, a VAT number is assigned to the business.

Businesses charge VAT on the value of goods and services provided (output tax). It can deduct any VAT paid on the goods and services it uses (input tax) and must account to HMRC for any difference (see **Practice example 7.5**).

The current normal rate of VAT is 20%.

Practice example 7.5

Sertab is a sole trader. She buys goods for £100 plus VAT and sells them for £200 plus VAT. What will be her VAT liability?

Sertab has paid input tax of £20 (£100 x 20%), which she can deduct from the output tax received of £40 (£200 x 20%). The total due to HMRC here will be £20 (£40 - £20).

There is a rate of 0% for so-called 'zero-rated supplies' (eg non-catering food, books and water) and a reduced rate of 5% for some supplies (eg domestic fuel).

Revision tip

VAT for hospitality, leisure and entertainment businesses was set at 12.5% between October 2021 and March 2022. It is therefore important to check the prevailing rates on www.gov.uk at the time you sit SQE1.

Exam warning

It is important to appreciate the difference between exempt supplies and zero-rated supplies. A person who makes only exempt supplies cannot register for VAT and cannot recover input tax paid. However, a person who makes only zero-rated supplies can register for VAT and recover input tax paid.

Returns/payment, VAT invoices and record-keeping

A VAT return must usually be submitted to HMRC and VAT paid within one month from the end of each quarter. A rebate will be payable if input tax exceeds output tax, and full records must be kept.

VAT invoices (including VAT number, value of supply and rate of tax) must be provided for a taxable supply to a taxable person. These are important as they are required to deduct input tax.

Penalties for failing to adhere to the legislation include the following:

- repayment with interest
- unlimited fine and imprisonment for up to seven years for tax evasion
- fixed financial penalties for failing to keep records
- the 'default surcharge' of 15% of the tax for persistent default in filing returns.

■ KEY POINT CHECKLIST

This chapter has covered the following key knowledge points. You can use these to structure your revision, ensuring you recall the key details for each point, as covered in this chapter.

- The method of calculation of income profits of a business is common to incorporated and unincorporated businesses. The basic formula is chargeable receipts, less deductible expenses and capital allowances.
- There are two types of capital allowance that may be claimed - the writing down allowance and the annual investment allowance.
- If an unincorporated business makes a trading loss during an accounting period, there will be a nil liability to tax. In addition, tax relief may be available in respect of the loss. There will often be a choice of reliefs and different conditions apply to them. The same loss cannot be claimed for twice.
- VAT is charged when a taxable business supplies goods or services. The basic formula allows input tax to be deducted from output tax. Registration is only possible for an individual who makes taxable supplies and is compulsory for those over a set income of £90,000. There are a range of criminal and civil penalties for failure to comply with the legislation.

■ KEY TERMS AND CONCEPTS

- chargeable receipts (**page 146**)
- deductible expenses (**page 146**)
- capital allowances (**page 146**)
- plant and machinery (**page 147**)
- writing down allowance (**page 147**)
- pooling (**page 147**)
- annual investment allowance (**page 148**)
- full expensing (**page 148**)
- first year allowance (**page 149**)
- start-up loss relief/early trade losses relief (**page 150**)
- carry-across/back one year relief/trade loss relief against general income (**page 150**)
- carry-forward relief (**page 151**)
- terminal loss relief (**page 151**)
- carry-forward relief on incorporation of business (**page 151**)

- VAT (**page 153**)
- taxable supply (**page 153**)
- taxable person (**page 153**)

■ SQE1-STYLE QUESTIONS

QUESTION 1

In an accounting period, a company buys stock totalling £750,000, which it sells for £2m. It pays wages of £100,000 and other bills of £80,000 and buys new freehold premises and cars for £200,000 and £50,000 respectively.

Ignoring any capital allowances, what are the company's trading profits?

A. £820,000.
B. £1,070,000.
C. £1,250,000.
D. £1,020,000.
E. £870,000.

QUESTION 2

A sole trader buys new plant and machinery costing £2m and has an existing pool of plant and machinery with a written down value of £1m in the previous financial year.

Which of the following best describes the capital allowances the sole trader will be able to claim?

A. The sole trader will be able to claim 14% of the cost of the new plant and machinery and 14% of the written down value of the existing pool.
B. The sole trader will be able to claim the cost of the new plant and machinery and 14% of the written down value of the existing pool.
C. The sole trader will be able to claim the cost of the new plant and machinery up to £1m and 14% of the written down value of the existing pool.
D. The sole trader will be able to claim the cost of the new plant and machinery up to £1m, 40% relief on the balance of £1m, and 14% of the written down value of the existing pool.
E. The sole trader will be able to claim the cost of the new plant and machinery up to £1m and 40% relief on the balance of £1m.

QUESTION 3

A sole trader makes a trading loss in the first year of trade, a profit in their second year of trade and a loss in their final year of trade. Prior to setting up the business, they had salary income for several years and they continue to receive a salary of £10,000 per annum for consultancy work.

Which of the following best describes the reliefs that may be available for the trading losses?

A. Start-up loss relief, carry-across relief, carry-back relief and carry-forward relief.
B. Start-up loss relief and terminal loss relief.
C. Start-up loss relief, terminal loss relief and carry-forward relief on incorporation.
D. Carry-across relief, carry-back relief and carry-forward relief.
E. Start-up loss relief, carry-across relief, carry-back relief, carry-forward relief and terminal loss relief.

QUESTION 4

A client sets up business as a private medical doctor and works exclusively in providing medical diagnosis and treatment. In their first year of business, the client made trading profits of £100,000.

Which of the following best describes the client's VAT position in their second year of business?

A. The client must register for VAT as their taxable profits in the previous year exceeded £90,000.
B. The client does not need to register for VAT as they make only exempt supplies. The client will be unable to recover any input tax paid.
C. The client does not need to register for VAT as they make only zero-rated supplies.
D. The client does not need to register for VAT as they make only exempt supplies. The client will be able to recover any input tax paid.
E. The client must register for VAT as their taxable profits in the previous year exceeded £90,000. The client will be able to recover any input tax paid.

QUESTION 5

A client, who is a taxable person and registered for VAT, buys raw materials for £100 plus VAT and sells the finished products for £300 plus VAT.

Assuming VAT is chargeable at the standard rate, which of the following best describes the client's VAT liability?

A. £40.
B. £60.
C. £80.
D. £35.
E. £25.

ANSWERS TO QUESTIONS

Answers to 'What do you know already?' questions at the start of the chapter

1) False. The basic calculation of trading profits is chargeable receipts, less deductible expenses, *less capital allowances*.
2) False. The cost of purchasing new plant and machinery will not be a deductible expense when calculating a business' trading profit as it is of a capital nature, rather than an income nature. However, capital allowances may be available.
3) Capital allowances allow businesses to deduct some of the cost of plant and machinery from chargeable receipts, to reduce tax liability. The aim is to encourage investment in items that are not deductible expenses as they are of a capital nature, rather than an income nature.
4) True. If an unincorporated business makes a trading loss during an accounting period, there will be a nil liability to tax. In addition, tax relief may be available in respect of the loss.
5) Registration for VAT is only possible if a person makes taxable supplies. They must register for VAT with HMRC if the value of their taxable supplies exceeded £90,000 in the previous year.

Answers to end-of-chapter SQE1-style questions

Question 1

The correct answer was B. The cars and freehold premises are not deductible expenses as they are of a capital nature, rather than an income nature. Option A is incorrect as it deducted all figures from the sales. Option C is incorrect as it did not deduct any expenses other than the purchases. Option D is incorrect as it deducted everything except the premises (incorrectly deducting the cars as an expense) and option E is incorrect as it deducted everything except the cars (incorrectly deducting the premises as an expense).

Question 2

The correct answer was D. Option B is incorrect due to the cap of £1m on the annual investment allowance and the limit on the first year allowance. Option E is incorrect as it fails to take into account the writing down allowance on the existing plant and machinery. Option C is incorrect as it fails to take into account the first year allowance on the remaining cost of the new plant and machinery. Option A is incorrect as it fails to take into account the annual investment allowance and first year allowance.

Question 3

The correct answer was E. All of the other options omit at least one of these reliefs. Option C is also incorrect as carry-forward relief on incorporation is irrelevant to the facts.

Question 4

The correct answer was B. The client does not need to register as they make only exempt supplies, so options A and E are incorrect. They do not make zero-rated supplies, so option C is incorrect. Businesses that make only zero-rated supplies may apply for registration for VAT and may recover input tax paid. The client will be unable to recover any input tax paid, so options D and E are also incorrect on this point.

Question 5

The correct answer was A. Input tax at 20% of £100 (£20) may be deducted from output tax of 20% of £300 (£60). Option B is incorrect as it did not deduct the input tax and option C is incorrect as it added the input tax to the output tax. Options D and E are incorrect as they applied the rates of 17.5% and 12.5% respectively.

■ KEY CASES, RULES, STATUTES AND INSTRUMENTS

The SQE1 Assessment Specification does not require you to know any statutory authorities or specific case names for this topic. However, you should be able to apply the key provisions relating to calculation of trading profits and VAT from a practical perspective. Remember that, like all taxes, rates etc can change annually, so you should be aware of the prevailing rates, thresholds, reliefs and exemptions at the time you sit SQE1.

8

Income tax

MAKE SURE YOU KNOW

This chapter provides an overview of income tax (IT). For the SQE1 assessments, you will need to understand who is liable to pay IT (chargeable persons/entities) and the basis of the charge for IT (types of income). You will also need to know how IT is calculated and collected (including the main reliefs, exemptions and allowances) and have knowledge of the scope of the anti-avoidance provisions. Your understanding of these subjects will enable you to identify and apply the relevant legal rules and principles to SQE1-style single best answer MCQs. For the latest income tax rates, please check https://www.gov.uk/browse/tax.

SQE ASSESSMENT ADVICE

For SQE1, you are required to understand IT from a practical perspective. It is likely that you will be required to identify whether someone will be liable for IT, how it will be calculated (for individuals, unincorporated businesses and partners), and apply the rules to problem-based, single best answer MCQs. You may also be required to advise on liability under the anti-avoidance provisions.

As you work through this chapter, remember to pay particular attention in your revision to:

- who is liable to pay IT (chargeable persons/entities)
- what IT is charged on (the basis of the charge)
- how IT is calculated in England and Wales (including the main reliefs, exemptions and allowances)
- collection of IT
- liability under the anti-avoidance provisions.

WHAT DO YOU KNOW ALREADY?

Attempt these questions before reading this chapter. If you find some difficult or cannot remember the answers, remember to look more closely at that area during your revision.

1) Who pays IT and what does income include?
   [Chargeable persons/entities, page 161]

2) When does the IT year begin and end?
   [Basis of charge to IT, page 161]
3) Explain what is meant by the term 'taxable income'.
   [Calculation of IT: individuals, page 162]
4) True or false? A higher rate taxpayer will pay IT at the higher rate on all of their taxable income.
   [Calculation of IT: individuals, page 162]
5) True or false? When a new partner joins a firm, a special rule, known as the opening year rule, will apply to them, but the existing partners will be assessed for IT on what is known as the current year basis.
   [Calculation of IT: partners, page 172]

CHARGEABLE PERSONS/ENTITIES

The starting point is to be able to identify who are **chargeable persons** for IT purposes.

Key term: chargeable persons

Chargeable persons are the following, who are liable to pay IT:

- individuals (including sole traders) (see **Chapter 1**)
- individual partners (see **Chapter 2**)
- trustees (see ***Revise SQE: Trusts Law***)
- personal representatives (see ***Revise SQE: Trusts Law***).

Companies and corporate partners pay corporation tax on their income profits and capital gains (see **Chapter 10**).

BASIS OF CHARGE TO IT

For the purposes of SQE1, you need to know the basis of the charge to **income tax (IT)**.

Key term: income tax (IT)

IT is a tax levied on a chargeable person's **income**.

Key term: income

Income includes the following:

- salary
- dividends (a shareholder's return on their investment (see **Chapter 5**))
- interest received (eg on a savings account, also termed 'savings income')

- trading profit (for sole traders and partners)
- the profit element of rent received (eg for renting out a property).

The hallmark of income is that it is usually recurring in nature, unlike a capital gain, which accumulates over time, because of an increase in an asset's value (see **Chapter 9**).

The key charging statutes are as follows:

- Income Tax Act 2007 (ITA)
- Income Tax (Trading and Other Income) Act 2005 (ITTOIA)
- Income Tax (Earnings and Pensions) Act 2003 (ITEPA).

Chargeable persons pay IT on income earned/profits made during the **income tax year**.

Key term: income tax year

The IT year runs from 6 April in one year to 5 April in the next year. It is named after the two years that it straddles. For example, in October 2025, the tax year was 2025/26 (see also **Practice example 8.1**).

Practice example 8.1

Verka started business on 1 August 2025 and Bonnie started business on 10 March 2026. What will be their first tax years?

Both Verka and Bonnie's first tax years will be 2025/26. The businesses started during the tax year that started on 6 April 2025 and ended on 5 April 2026.

Exam warning

IT is renewed annually, so rates, thresholds, exemptions and reliefs can change from year to year. For the purposes of SQE1, it is important that you know the personal allowance for the current tax year, the basic and higher rate thresholds and the key rates of IT (see **Calculation of IT: individuals**, below). These can be found on www.gov.uk.

CALCULATION OF IT: INDIVIDUALS

IT is a progressive tax, which means that the rate increases as income increases. Individuals may make use of the lower rate(s) first, but pay IT at the higher rate(s) as their income increases (see **Practice example 8.2, page 165**).

The basic five-step calculation for IT is as follows:

Step one: Calculate **total income** (see **Total income** below)

Step two: Deduct **allowable reliefs** (gives **net income**) (see **Allowable reliefs** below)

Step three: Deduct personal allowances (see **Personal allowances** below) = **taxable income**

Revision tip

When revising for SQE1, it is important to understand the terminology in the steps above, as it will help you to approach questions with confidence. For example, if someone has 'total income' of £50,000, allowable reliefs and personal allowances must be deducted before the tax is calculated. The definition of taxable income is particularly important.

Key term: taxable income

Income *after* deduction of allowable reliefs and personal allowances. From this figure, we can automatically tell whether someone is a **basic rate**, **higher rate** or **additional rate taxpayer**.

Key term: basic rate taxpayer (BRT)

A person whose taxable income does not exceed the basic rate threshold (£37,700 in 2026/27).

Key term: higher rate taxpayer (HRT)

A person whose taxable income exceeds the basic rate threshold, but does not exceed the additional rate threshold (£125,140 in 2026/27).

Key term: additional rate taxpayer (ART)

A person whose taxable income exceeds the additional rate threshold.

Step four: Calculate the tax for each source of income

An individual's taxable income is then charged at the appropriate rate(s). There are different rates for different categories of income. Therefore, it is necessary to separate savings and dividend income from taxable non-savings/non-dividend income (**NSNDI**).

Key term: NSNDI

Taxable income, after deduction of savings income and dividend income.
Taxable income – savings income – dividend income = taxable NSNDI

The income is then taxed at the following rates, in the following order:

Step four (a): First – NSNDI (see **Table 8.1**)

Table 8.1: Income tax main rates – 2026/27 for NSNDI

Rate	Charge	Taxable income
Basic rate	20%	1–37,700
Higher rate	40%	37,701–125,140
Additional rate	45%	125,141 & above

Step four (b): Second – savings income (see **Table 8.2**)

Table 8.2: Income tax rates – 2026/27 for savings income

Rate	Charge	Taxable income
Starting rate	0%	5,000
Basic rate	20%	5,001–37,700
Higher rate	40%	37,701–125,140
Additional rate	45%	125,141 & above

Step four (c): Finally – dividend income (see **Table 8.3**)

Table 8.3: Income tax rates – 2026/27 for dividend income

Rate	Charge	Taxable income
Ordinary rate	10.75%	1–37,700
Upper rate	35.75%	37,701–125,140
Additional rate	39.35%	125,141 & above

Step five: Add together the tax for each source of income and deduct any tax previously paid/deducted at source (see **Total income**, below), to give IT liability.

Practice example 8.2 shows the progressive nature of IT in practice.

Practice example 8.2

In 2026/27, Céline has taxable NSNDI of £20,000, Sandra has taxable NSNDI of £52,000 and Gali has taxable NSNDI of £200,000. Remember, 'taxable income' means the allowable reliefs and personal allowances have already been deducted. What rate(s) of IT will they pay?

Céline is a BRT. She will pay IT at 20%.

Sandra is an HRT. She will pay IT at 20% on the first £37,700 and 40% on the balance.

Gali is an ART. She will pay IT at 20% on the first £37,700, 40% on the balance up to £125,140 and 45% on the 'top slice' of £74,860.

Exam warning

It is proposed that separate rates for property and savings income will be introduced from April 2027 for the tax year 2027/28: 22% (basic rate), 42% (higher rate) and 47% (additional rate), with NSNDI other than property income being taxed first.

Total income

Step one of a full IT calculation is to calculate total income.

Key term: total income

Total income is the aggregate gross income from each source (ie without any IT deducted).

Income is taxable if it comes from a source specified in the relevant legislation:

- Part 3 ITTOIA (property income)
- Part 2 ITTOIA (profits of a trade or profession)
- Part 4 ITTOIA (savings income)
- ITEPA (employment and pensions income).

Certain income is exempt (eg child benefit, interest paid on national savings certificates, interest from individual savings accounts (ISAs) and interest on damages for personal injuries or death).

Most types of income are paid gross, including the following:

- interest paid by banks and building societies
- dividends paid to shareholders (see **Chapter 5**)
- property (rental) income.

Some types of income will be received net by the taxpayer (ie IT will already have been deducted at source). The main source of income here is employment income, where tax is deducted as part of the PAYE (Pay as you earn) scheme. The gross amount (ie the net amount received, plus the IT already deducted at source) must, however, be included in the full IT calculation.

Employees and directors

The charge to IT on directors and employees is under ITEPA and includes a charge on all 'earnings' (ie all benefits received as a reward for services provided, for example, salary).

A distinction is made between the receipt of a cash and a non-cash benefit, and, generally, all benefits that derive from the office or employment are liable to tax.

Employees are usually taxed on the cost to the employer of providing the benefit, and directors are generally liable to tax on the benefits of rent-free and low-rent accommodation.

A lump sum payment that is made to compensate a director/employee for an early termination of their contract will be taxable if they are contractually entitled to it. Any payment on retirement/removal from office that is not otherwise chargeable to tax may be taxable, although the first £30,000 of any such sum is usually exempt.

Allowable reliefs

Step two is to deduct allowable reliefs.

Key term: allowable reliefs (ARs)

The most important AR to remember is interest payments on 'qualifying loans'. This includes interest paid on (a) a loan to buy a share in a partnership, or (b) a loan to invest in a close trading company (see **Chapter 10**).

The figure after ARs have been deducted from total income is known as net income.

Key term: net income

Total income *after* deduction of ARs, but before deduction of personal allowances.

Personal allowances

Step three is to deduct **personal allowance(s)** from net income to give taxable income.

Key term: personal allowance (PA)

The amount an individual can earn each year before paying IT (£12,570 for 2026/27, subject to an income limit of £100,000). It cannot be carried forward to a new tax year.

The PA is reduced by 50% (ie by £1 for every £2) to the extent that income exceeds £100,000.

To arrive at the revised PA for those over the income limit, you take the net income figure, minus £100,000 and divide it by two. You then deduct the resulting figure from the current PA (see **Practice example 8.3**).

Practice example 8.3

Rafał has net income of £110,000 in 2026/27. What will his PA be?

£110,000 - £100,000 = £10,000 ÷ 2 = £5,000

£12,570 - £5,000 = £7,570

Depending on circumstances, two other PAs may be applicable.

Marriage allowance and blind person's allowance

Up to £1,260 of an individual's unused PA may be transferred to a spouse or civil partner (the spouse/civil partner must be a BRT). People who are registered blind receive an additional £3,250 PA.

Property and trading allowances

Up to £1,000 of gross property income and £1,000 of gross trading income will not be subject to IT. For amounts over the £1,000 limit, the allowance may be deducted from the gross figure as an alternative to deducting actual expenses (see **Chapter 5, Business accounts** and **Chapter 7**).

Slices of taxable income

Step four is to separate the different types of income and calculate the tax for each source in the order set out in **Figure 8.1**.

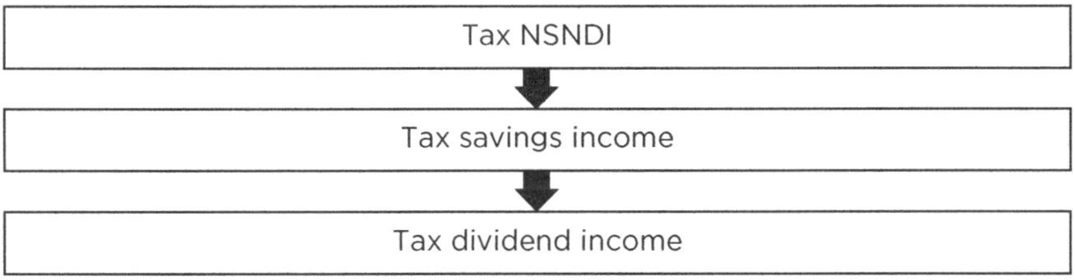

Figure 8.1: Slices of taxable income

As IT is a progressive tax and there is a clear order of calculation, it is important to know how far a taxpayer is away from hitting the next threshold (eg higher rate) at each stage of the calculation (ie the cumulative total). See **Practice example 8.4** for an illustration of this.

Practice example 8.4

Annie has taxable NSNDI of £30,000 in 2026/27. How far away is she from moving up to the higher rate?

£37,700 - £30,000 = £7,700

Savings income

When taxing savings, the **personal savings allowance** needs to be considered and, for SQE1, you need to appreciate how it operates.

Key term: personal savings allowance (PSA)

Under the PSA, *up to* the first £1,000 of savings income will be tax-free. The PSA varies according to an individual's taxable income (see **Table 8.4**).

Table 8.4: Personal savings allowance

Tax rate	Taxable income	PSA
BRT	£0–37,700	£1,000 tax-free
HRT	£37,701–125,140	£500 tax-free
ART	£125,141 and above	No allowance

The available PSA is added to the taxable NSNDI figure, and then taxed at 0%. However, basic rate taxpayers with taxable NSNDI under £5,000 may use up the starting rate first before the PSA is applied.

The tax-free amount still counts towards the cumulative total in moving from one threshold to the next. Any savings income over the PSA is taxed at the appropriate rate(s) for savings income (see **Table 8.2**), based on the cumulative income taxed so far. See **Practice example 8.5** for an illustration of this.

Practice example 8.5

Jamala has taxable NSNDI of £5,000 and receives gross interest of £2,000. She has no other income in 2026/27. What rate(s) of IT will she pay?

Jamala is a BRT. She will pay IT at 20% on her NSNDI. The PSA will mean that no IT will be payable on the first £1,000 of the interest. She will pay IT at 20% on the remaining £1,000.

Måns has taxable NSNDI of £38,000 and receives gross interest of £1,000. He has no other income in 2026/27. What rate(s) of IT will he pay?

Måns is an HRT. His basic rate band has already been used up (and exceeded) with his NSNDI. He will be entitled to a PSA of £500 and will pay IT at 40% on the balance.

Remember to keep a note of how far the taxpayer is from moving on to the next succeeding rate increase at each stage, as it will make it easier to identify when a rate change will apply (see **Practice example 8.6**).

Practice example 8.6

Colin has taxable NSNDI, PSA and remaining savings income of £34,700 in 2026/27. How far away is he from moving up to the higher rate?

£37,700 - £34,700 = £3,000

Dividend income

When taxing dividends, the **dividend allowance** needs to be considered and, for SQE1, you need to appreciate how it operates.

Key term: dividend allowance (DA)

The DA provides that the first £500 of a taxpayer's dividend income will be free from tax (this applies to all taxpayers irrespective of their taxable income).

The available DA is added to the taxable NSNDI, the available PSA, and the remaining interest income and then taxed at 0%. The tax-free amount still counts towards the cumulative total in moving from one threshold to the next. Any dividend over the DA is taxed at the appropriate rate for dividend income (see **Table 8.3**), based on the cumulative income taxed so far (see **Practice example 8.7**).

Practice example 8.7

Sergey has taxable NSNDI of £5,000 and receives a gross dividend payment of £250. He has no other income in 2026/27. How much IT will he pay on the dividend?

Sergey is a BRT. The dividend falls within the ordinary rate band, but due to the DA, no IT is payable.

Emmelie has taxable NSNDI of £38,000 and receives a gross dividend payment of £3,000. She has no other income. How much IT will she pay on the dividend?

Emmelie is an HRT. Her basic rate band has already been used up (and exceeded) with her NSNDI. She will be entitled to a DA of £500 but will pay IT at 35.75% on the balance.

Full IT calculation

Practice example 8.8 sets out how a full IT calculation works in practice.

Practice example 8.8

In 2026/27, Lulu has total income of £40,000 from her salary. She also receives gross interest of £2,000 and a gross dividend payment of £10,000 in the same tax year. She pays £500 interest on a loan to buy a share in a partnership. What is her IT liability?

Step one **– Lulu's total income is £52,000**

Step two **– £500 can be deducted as an AR = £51,500**

Step three **– PA of £12,570 can be deducted. Her taxable income is £38,930, so she is an HRT**

Step four (a) **– Deduct savings and dividend income from taxable income to give £26,930. This is taxed at 20% = £5,386 (she has £10,770 of income left before she moves up to the higher rate)**

Step four (b) **– As an HRT, Lulu is entitled to a PSA of £500. The remaining £1,500 will be taxed at 20% = £300 (she has £8,770 of income left before she moves up to the higher rate)**

Step four (c) **– Lulu is entitled to a DA of £500. The remaining £9,500 falls into two tax rates. The first £8,270 is taxed at the ordinary rate of 10.75% and the remaining £1,230 is taxed at the upper rate of 35.75% = £889.03 + £439.73 = £1,328.76**

Step five **– Lulu's IT liability is £5,386 + £300 + £1,328.76 = £7,014.76. She can deduct any tax previously paid under PAYE to give her IT payable.**

The process for a full IT calculation is summarised in **Figure 8.2**.

STEP ONE – Calculate total income (ie gross income from each source)
Total income can include salary, trading profit (for sole traders and partners), rental income, interest received and dividends (salary is usually paid net)

STEP TWO – Deduct allowable reliefs to give net income
Remember, you are looking to deduct the interest paid on a loan to buy a share in a partnership or to invest in a close trading company

STEP THREE – Deduct personal allowance(s) to give taxable income

STEP FOUR – Calculate the tax
Separate taxable NSNDI from interest and dividend income and calculate tax at the applicable rate(s)

STEP FOUR (A) – Tax NSNDI first using the relevant rate(s)
Remember to keep a note of how much the client is away from moving on to the next succeeding rate increase

STEP FOUR (B) – Tax interest next:
Before doing so, add the total of any available PSA to the taxable NSNDI and tax at 0%
Tax any interest over and above the PSA using the relevant rate(s)
Remember to keep a note of how much the client is away from moving on to the next succeeding rate increase

STEP FOUR (C) – Finally, tax dividends:

Before doing so, add the total of any available dividend allowance to the taxable NSNDI, PSA and interest income and tax at 0%
Tax any dividend over and above the dividend allowance using the relevant rate(s)

STEP FIVE – Add the three figures from step four (a), (b) and (c) together to give the income tax liability and deduct tax already paid at source to give the Income Tax Payable

Figure 8.2: Taxable income calculation

Income tax in Wales

There is potential for NSNDI rates to vary in Wales as they are set by the Welsh Government. However, the rates are currently the same in England and Wales. For the most up-to-date rates, go to https://gov.wales.

CALCULATION OF IT: SOLE TRADERS

For SQE1, you need to have a good working knowledge of how IT is calculated for sole traders.

A sole trader will prepare accounts for the business for an 'accounting period' (usually 12 months) to show how much profit/loss has been made (see **Chapters 5 and 7**). The accounting period will not always match the IT year, so it is necessary to know the rules for assessment of trading profits.

If the business has made a profit, IT is payable on those income profits. If the business has made a loss, relief may be available (see **Chapter 7**).

Basis of assessment

The rules relating to the basis of assessment of the income profits of unincorporated business (ie sole traders and private individuals in partnerships) were simplified from the tax year 2023/24.

Where an accounting period does not correspond with a tax year, profits or losses will be apportioned between the relevant tax years, generally on a daily basis (ie the number of days of the accounting period that fall within the relevant tax year).

CALCULATION OF IT: PARTNERS

For SQE1, you need to have an appreciation of the way in which the income profits of partnerships are determined and assessed. The rules relating to the basis of assessment of the income profits of unincorporated business (ie sole traders and private individuals in partnerships) were simplified from the tax year 2023/24. Allocation and appropriation of profits between the partners is considered further in **Chapter 5**.

Partnerships generally

A partnership will be charged IT on the income profits the business makes in the same way as sole traders (see **Chapter 7**).

The basis of assessing the taxable profit of the business for any given tax year is the same basis as applies to sole traders.

The taxable profit is apportioned between the partners as agreed between them for the relevant accounting period (see **Chapter 5**). This could be under the default provisions of the PA, a formal partnership agreement, or some other express or implied agreement between them.

Partners are separately taxed on their own share of the partnership's profits and each partner is liable to pay their own tax. It is not a partnership liability as the partnership is not a separate legal entity.

If the partnership has made a loss, each partner may choose what type of relief to claim in respect of their share of the loss (see **Chapter 7**).

Change of partners

When the composition of a partnership changes (eg a partner leaves or a new partner joins), profits or losses will be apportioned between the relevant tax years. This is because for each individual partner, the business begins when they become a partner and ends when they cease to be a partner.

COLLECTION OF IT

Some IT is deducted at source (eg employment income). If a taxpayer receives other income, they must complete a **tax return** under the self-assessment scheme.

Key term: tax return

A form submitted to HMRC annually, in circumstances where not all of an individual's IT has been deducted at source. The form sets out the income the individual has received and a self-assessment of the amount of tax payable.

If an individual is liable for self-assessment, HMRC must be notified within six months of the relevant tax year, or the individual will be fined.

Tax returns must be submitted by 31 January (online) or 31 October (paper) following the end of the relevant tax year.

Payment is made by way of two **payments on account**.

Key term: payments on account

Two payments, generally representing half of the individual's tax bill from the previous tax year and made by 31 January in the tax year and

31 July after the tax year. A final balancing payment (the amount of the remaining tax liability) must be made by the following 31 January (see **Practice example 8.9**).

Those who have already paid more than 80% of their tax bill through deduction at source or with a small self-assessment liability in the previous tax year (less than £1,000) do not need to make payments on account.

Penalties include interest on late payments and fixed penalties if tax is not paid, or paid late. There are also penalties for not keeping accurate records. Appeals are made to the First-Tier Tribunal (see ***Revise SQE: The Legal System and Services of England and Wales***).

Practice example 8.9

Albert had self-assessment tax liability of £20,000 in the tax year 2025/26. In the following tax year, 2026/27, he has self-assessment tax liability of £30,000. When will he pay his tax liability for 2026/27?

He must make two payments on account of £10,000 by 31 January 2026 and 31 July 2026. The balancing payment of £10,000 will be payable by 31 January 2027.

Exam warning

April 2026 saw the start of 'Making Tax Digital' for IT. From 2026/27, sole traders, landlords and individuals with gross self-employment and/or property income over £50,000 will need to maintain digital records using HMRC-compliant software. From April 2027, the threshold is set to reduce to £30,000.

ANTI-AVOIDANCE PROVISIONS

For SQE1, it is important to appreciate the difference between **tax avoidance** and **tax evasion**.

Key term: tax avoidance

Working, usually within the law, to minimise tax liability.

Key term: tax evasion

Deliberately misinterpreting or misapplying the law to minimise tax liability. Tax evasion is illegal.

The **general anti-avoidance rule (GAAR)** applies to IT.

Key term: general anti-abuse rule (GAAR)

A rule that applies to certain taxes (including IT) to combat **abusive tax avoidance arrangements** that go beyond lawful tax avoidance.

Key term: abusive tax avoidance arrangement (ATAA)

A tax arrangement is abusive if it 'cannot reasonably be regarded as a reasonable course of action ... having regard to all the circumstances' (s 207 Finance Act 2013).

Under the GAAR procedure, the taxpayer will be notified if an ATAA is uncovered and a request for tax adjustments will be made.

The GAAR advisory panel deals with any representations made by the taxpayer.

Any person who enabled the scheme as part of their business may be fined. Taxpayers have a right of appeal to a tax tribunal.

Revision tip

HMRC issues guidance on GAAR, the detail of which is beyond the scope of this book. For the purposes of SQE1, you simply need to be aware of the scope of the provisions and the potential liability that can arise.

KEY POINT CHECKLIST

This chapter has covered the following key knowledge points. You can use these to structure your revision, ensuring you recall the key details for each point, as covered in this chapter.

- IT is a tax on income and is paid by individuals (including partners), trustees and personal representatives. The IT year runs from 6 April to 5 April in the following year.
- A key characteristic of income is that it is usually recurring. It includes salary, trading profit, rent, interest and dividends.
- It is important to be able to calculate an individual's IT liability, using a five-step process (see **Figure 8.2**).
- As the accounting period of a business may not correspond with the IT year, profits or losses will be apportioned between the relevant tax years, generally on a daily basis. This applies to sole traders as well as partnerships. Each partner has their own liability for IT, based on their share of the profits for the period during which they are a partner.
- Interest and penalties are payable for late payment or non-payment of IT and the GAAR applies to ATAAs. Adjustments may apply when ATAAs are uncovered.

KEY TERMS AND CONCEPTS

- chargeable persons (**page 161**)
- income tax (**page 161**)
- income (**page 161**)
- income tax year (**page 162**)
- taxable income (**page 163**)
- basic rate taxpayer (**page 163**)
- higher rate taxpayer (**page 163**)
- additional rate taxpayer (**page 163**)
- NSNDI (**page 164**)
- total income (**page 165**)
- allowable reliefs (**page 166**)
- net income (**page 166**)
- personal allowance (**page 167**)
- personal savings allowance (**page 168**)
- dividend allowance (**page 169**)
- tax return (**page 173**)
- payments on account (**page 173**)
- tax avoidance (**page 174**)
- tax evasion (**page 174**)
- general anti-abuse rule (**page 175**)
- abusive tax avoidance arrangement (**page 175**)

SQE1-STYLE QUESTIONS

QUESTION 1

A client has a taxable salary of £41,000 and receives a gross dividend of £5,000 on shares that they own in a limited company. They have no other income.

How much income tax, if any, should the client pay on the dividend?

A. The client will have to pay tax at the additional rate on the proportion of the dividend that exceeds their dividend allowance.

B. The client will have to pay tax at the ordinary rate as the dividend does not exceed the basic rate threshold.

C. The client will have to pay tax at the ordinary rate as the dividend does not exceed the basic rate threshold. However, the first £500 will be taxed at 0%.

D. The client will have to pay tax at the ordinary rate on the entire dividend because it exceeds their dividend allowance.

E. The client will have to pay tax at the upper rate on £4,500 of the dividend. The first £500 will be taxed at 0%.

QUESTION 2

A client has a total salary of £65,000 and pays interest of £100 on a loan to buy a share in a partnership. The client receives a gross dividend of £3,000 and gross interest of £1,000 on their savings.

The personal allowance is £12,570 and the higher rate threshold for taxable income is £37,700.

Which of the following best describes the client's liability for income tax?

A. The client is a higher rate taxpayer (HRT) and their basic rate band has been fully used up by their taxable salary. They will pay tax on the interest received and dividend at the higher/upper rates.

B. The client is an HRT with taxable income of £56,330 and their basic rate band has been fully used up by their taxable salary. They will pay tax on the interest received and dividend at the higher/upper rates, but the first £500 of the interest will be taxed at 0% and the first £500 of the dividend will be taxed at 0%.

C. The client is an HRT with taxable income of £56,330 and their basic rate band has been fully used up by their taxable salary. They will pay tax on the dividend at the higher/upper rates, but the interest received will be taxed at 0% as it falls within the personal savings allowance and the first £500 of the dividend will be taxed at 0%.

D. The client is an HRT with taxable income of £56,430 and their basic rate band has been fully used up by their taxable salary. They will pay tax on the interest and dividend at the higher/upper rates, but the first £500 of the interest will be taxed at 0% and the first £500 of the dividend will be taxed at 0%.

E. The client will not be liable to tax on the interest as it does not exceed £5,000. They will pay tax at a rate of 10.75% on £1,000 of the dividend as it does not exceed £37,700, but the first £500 of the dividend will be taxed at 0%.

QUESTION 3

A client has taxable non-savings/non-dividend income of £35,000 and receives gross interest of £6,000 on their savings. They have no other income.

What rate(s) of tax will they be required to pay on the interest?

A. 20%.

B. 40%.

C. 0% on £500, 20% and 40%.

D. 0% on £1,000 and 20%.

E. 0% and 20%.

QUESTION 4

A client has taxable non-savings/non-dividend income of £38,000 and no savings income. They receive a gross dividend of £2,000.

How much tax will they be required to pay on the dividend?

A. £536.25.

B. £357.50.

C. £161.25.

D. £215.

E. £715.

QUESTION 5

A client is concerned about potential liability under the general anti-abuse rule (GAAR) and penalties for late payment of income tax.

Which of the following best describes the position?

A. Under the GAAR procedure, a taxpayer will be notified if an abusive tax avoidance arrangement (ATAA) is uncovered and a fine may be payable. Penalties for late payment include interest and fixed penalties.

B. Under the GAAR procedure, a taxpayer will be notified if an ATAA is uncovered and a request for tax adjustments will be made. Penalties for late payment include interest and fixed penalties.

C. Under the GAAR procedure, a taxpayer will be notified if an ATAA is uncovered, a fine may be payable and a request for tax adjustments will be made. Penalties for late payment include interest and fixed penalties.

D. Under the GAAR, HMRC must notify a taxpayer before imposing a fine. The GAAR advisory panel deals with any representations made by the taxpayer. Penalties for late payment are limited to payment of interest.

E. Any breach of GAAR will automatically be referred to a tax tribunal, which will consider any representations made by a taxpayer. Penalties for late payment include interest and fixed penalties.

■ ANSWERS TO QUESTIONS

Answers to 'What do you know already?' questions at the start of the chapter

1) Individuals, individual partners, trustees and personal representatives pay IT. Companies pay corporation tax on their income profits. IT is charged on income, which includes salary, dividends, interest received,

trading profit and rent received. The fundamental hallmark of income is that it is usually recurring in nature.

2) The IT year runs from 6 April in one year to 5 April in the next year. It is named after the two years that it straddles (eg 2025/26 for the tax year that started on 6 April 2025 and ended on 5 April 2026).
3) Taxable income is total gross income *after* deduction of allowable reliefs and personal allowances. From this figure, we can tell whether someone will pay tax at the higher rate(s).
4) False. IT is a progressive tax, which means that the rate increases as income increases. Individuals may make use of the lower rate(s) first, but pay IT at the higher rate(s) as their income increases.
5) False. What were previously known as the opening year rule, closing year rule and current year basis no longer apply and instead profits are apportioned between the relevant tax years.

Answers to end-of-chapter SQE1-style questions

Question 1

The correct answer was E. This is because their taxable salary already exceeds the basic rate band. The client is into the upper rate for the dividend (not the additional rate as suggested in option A, or the ordinary rate as suggested in options B, C and D). Option B is also incorrect, because it does not mention the dividend allowance and option D does not explain it correctly.

Question 2

The correct answer was B. The taxable income figure in option D is incorrect, as it does not take into account the allowable relief. As a higher rate taxpayer, the dividend allowance (DA) will be £500 and the personal savings allowance (PSA) will be £500, not £1,000, as suggested in option C. Option A is incorrect as it ignores the PSA and DA. Option E is incorrect, as it does not take into account the progressive nature of income tax.

Question 3

The correct answer was C. Taxable non-savings/non-dividend income (NSNDI) means that the personal allowance and any allowable reliefs have already been deducted. Taxable NSNDI of £35,000 and taxable savings income of £6,000 means that the client is a higher rate taxpayer, so they will be entitled to a personal savings allowance of £500, taxable at 0% (not £1,000 as suggested in option D). They will be taxed on the balance of £2,200 at 20% and the balance of £3,300 at 40%. All of the other options state the incorrect rate(s) and/or ignore the crossover between rates.

Question 4

The correct answer was A. Taxable non-savings/non-dividend income (NSNDI) means that the personal allowance and any allowable reliefs have already been deducted. Taxable NSNDI of £38,000 and taxable dividend income of £2,000 means that the client is a higher rate taxpayer, so they will be entitled to a dividend allowance of £500, taxable at 0%. They will be taxed on the balance of £1,500 at 35.75%. Option B is incorrect as it suggests the dividend allowance is £1,000. Option C is incorrect as it calculates the tax at 10.75%. Options D and E are incorrect as they both ignore the dividend allowance and charge the whole amount to tax at 10.75% and 35.75% respectively.

Question 5

The correct answer was B. Fines are not payable under the GAAR (as suggested in options A, C and D), but a request for tax adjustments may be made. Penalties for late payment include interest and fixed penalties, which also makes option D incorrect. Breaches of the GAAR are not automatically referred to a tax tribunal, as suggested in option E.

■ KEY CASES, RULES, STATUTES AND INSTRUMENTS

The SQE1 Assessment Specification does not require you to know statutory authorities or recall specific case names for this topic. However, you should be able to apply the key provisions relating to IT from a practical perspective. Remember that IT is renewed annually, so you should be aware of the prevailing rates, thresholds, reliefs and exemptions at the time you sit SQE1.

9

Capital gains tax and inheritance tax

■ MAKE SURE YOU KNOW

This chapter provides an overview of capital gains tax (CGT) and the business property relief (BPR) aspect of inheritance tax (IHT). For the SQE1 assessments, you will need to understand who is liable to pay CGT (chargeable persons/entities) and the basis of the charge for CGT (for individuals and unincorporated businesses). You will also need to know how CGT is calculated and collected, and have knowledge of the scope of the anti-avoidance provisions. Finally, you will need to understand BPR in the context of IHT. Your understanding of these subjects will enable you to identify and apply the relevant legal rules and principles to SQE1-style single best answer MCQs. For the latest tax rates, please check https://www.gov.uk/browse/tax.

■ SQE ASSESSMENT ADVICE

For SQE1, you are required to understand CGT and BPR from a practical perspective. It is likely that you will be required to identify whether someone will be liable for CGT or eligible for BPR, how their tax will be calculated, and apply the rules to problem-based, single best answer MCQs. You may also be required to advise on liability under the anti-avoidance provisions.

As you work through this chapter, remember to pay particular attention in your revision to:

- who is liable to pay CGT (chargeable persons/entities)
- what CGT is charged on (the basis of the charge)
- how CGT is calculated (including the main reliefs and exemptions)
- collection of CGT
- liability under the anti-avoidance provisions
- the requirements and operation of BPR.

■ WHAT DO YOU KNOW ALREADY?

Attempt these questions before reading this chapter. If you find some difficult or cannot remember the answers, remember to look more closely at that area during your revision.

1) Who pays CGT and what is it charged on?
   [Chargeable persons/entities, page 182, and Basis of charge to CGT, page 182]
2) What can be deducted from the disposal value to calculate a basic gain?
   [Calculation of a basic gain: individuals and sole traders, page 184]
3) True or false? The annual exemption can only be used when tax is paid. It cannot be used when a gain is being held over, rolled over or deferred.
   [Annual exemption, page 190]
4) True or false? A higher rate taxpayer will pay CGT at the higher rate on all of their chargeable gains.
   [Calculation of CGT charge: rates, page 187]
5) True or false? Shares are not qualifying assets for the purpose of business asset disposal relief and an individual will not usually pay CGT on the gain in value of their main home.
   [Basis of charge to CGT, page 182, and Business asset disposal relief, page 188]

CHARGEABLE PERSONS/ENTITIES

The starting point is to know who are **chargeable persons** for CGT purposes.

> **Key term: chargeable persons**
>
> Chargeable persons for CGT are:
> - individuals (including sole traders) (see **Chapter 1**)
> - individual partners (see **Chapter 2**)
> - trustees (see ***Revise SQE: Trusts Law***)
> - personal representatives (see ***Revise SQE: Trusts Law***).

Companies and corporate partners pay corporation tax on their income profits and capital gains (see **Chapter 10**).

BASIS OF CHARGE TO CGT

For the purposes of SQE1, you need to know the basis of the charge to **capital gains tax (CGT)**.

> **Key term: capital gains tax (CGT)**
>
> CGT is a tax on an increase in an asset's value during a period of ownership. It is charged on a **chargeable gain (CG)**, made by a chargeable person, on **disposal** of a **chargeable asset**. These terms are explored further in this section.

Key term: chargeable asset

Most forms of property are chargeable assets, with the exception of sterling. They can include tangible and intangible property, such as land and shares. They will not usually include plant/machinery and motor vehicles, as they are wasting assets (ie they usually depreciate over time).

Key term: disposal

Disposal is construed widely for CGT purposes and includes a sale (whether at full value or undervalue) or a gift. Death will usually give rise to a charge for IHT and not a charge to CGT.

Procedural link: IHT

For SQE1, IHT is dealt with more generally in the context of wills and administration of estates (see ***Revise SQE: Wills and the Administration of Estates***). However, BPR will be dealt with in this volume (see **page 198**).

Key term: chargeable gain (CG)

The part of the gain that is liable to tax (after deduction of any reliefs or exemptions).

Procedural link: principal private residence exemption (PPRE)

An individual's main home, subject to limitations, is usually exempt from CGT, under the PPRE (see ***Revise SQE: Property Practice***). However, CGT is always payable on second homes and investment properties.

The main charging statute is the Taxation of Chargeable Gains Act 1992 (TOCGA).

For CGT purposes, the tax year is the same as the income tax (IT) year (see **Chapter 8**).

Unlike income, which is usually recurring, capital gain builds up over a period, as an asset appreciates in value. CGT is paid on the genuine increase in an asset's value and not, for example, because of capital improvements (see **Practice example 9.1**).

Practice example 9.1

Miki buys an investment property for £100,000 and sells it for £200,000. What is his basic gain?

Miki's basic gain is £100,000.

Michela buys an investment property for £100,000 and builds an extension, costing £50,000. She sells it for £200,000. What is her basic gain?

Michela's basic gain is £50,000. She can deduct the cost of the extension from the acquisition cost, as it should be reflected in the sale price.

CALCULATION OF A BASIC GAIN: INDIVIDUALS AND SOLE TRADERS

The basic calculation for CGT is as follows:

Disposal value

LESS
- Acquisition cost/value
- **Allowable expenditure**

EQUALS
- **Basic gain (BG)**

Apply reliefs/exemptions (see **Principal CGT reliefs/exemptions**, below)

GIVES
Chargeable gain (CG)

CGT is charged at the appropriate rate(s) (see **Calculation of CGT charge: rates**).

Key term: disposal value

This is usually the sale price, but can be the market value in the following circumstances:

- a gift
- a sale at undervalue with a gift element (ie a deliberate undervalue to benefit the recipient). Conversely, the actual sale price will be used for a sale at an undervalue as a result of a bad bargain (eg due to ineptitude or a lack of information) (see **Practice example 9.2**)
- disposal to a **connected person**.

Practice example 9.2

Mel sells a property worth £200,000 to her friend for £150,000. She knows that the true market value is £200,000, but sells it for £150,000 as an act of generosity. What will the disposal value be for CGT purposes?

The disposal value will be £200,000.

Graham sells a property worth £200,000 to his friend for £150,000. He is under the impression that the market value is £150,000 and that £150,000 is a fair price. He has not had the property valued for several years. What will the disposal value be for CGT purposes?

The disposal value will be £150,000.

Key term: connected person

This term is defined in s 286 of TOCGA and includes:

- spouses and civil partners
- close relatives - ie parents, children, grandparents, grandchildren and siblings, but not uncles and aunts and nieces and nephews
- close relatives of one's spouse or civil partner.

Exam warning

It is important to have a good general appreciation of the definition of connected person for the purposes of SQE1.

Key term: allowable expenditure

As CGT is charged on a genuine increase in an asset's value, the following three categories of allowable expenditure may be deducted:

- incidental costs of acquisition (eg solicitors' and surveyors' fees)
- subsequent expenditure - the cost of capital improvements that increase the size of the property (eg extensions). It does not generally include the cost of repair, redecoration or replacement of items (even though these may make the property more saleable, desirable and valuable)
- incidental costs of disposal (eg estate agents' and solicitors' fees).

Key term: basic gain (BG)

The gain that has been made after the acquisition cost and allowable expenditure have been deducted from the disposal value, but before application of reliefs and exemptions (see **Practice example 9.3**).

Practice example 9.3

Alexander runs a shop as a sole trader from freehold premises.

He bought the business (including the premises) in 2020 for £100,000.

Alexander spent a total of £3,000 on professional fees in buying the business and, in 2022, spent £50,000 adding an extension to the property.

He subsequently sold the business for £300,000 in May 2026.

Legal costs of £2,000 (including VAT) were incurred in the sale.

What is Alexander's BG?

Alexander's BG is as follows:

Sale price	**£300,000**
<u>Less</u>	
Acquisition cost	**£100,000**
Allowable expenditure	**£3,000 + £50,000 + £2,000 = £55,000**
BG	**£145,000**

If a capital loss is made, the loss may be deducted from gains in the tax year or carried forward to future tax years to reduce the tax payable.

CALCULATION OF A BASIC GAIN: PARTNERS

Partnerships are transparent for CGT purposes and each partner is treated as owning a fractional share of each of the chargeable assets of the firm. On a disposal by the partnership, each partner is considered to be making a disposal of their fractional share in an asset.

There are two steps to calculating the BG of individual partners:

Step one: Identify the fractional share of capital gain for the partner. Remember, capital gains are shared equally (s 24(1) Partnership Act 1890 - see **Chapter 2**), unless there is an express or implied agreement to the contrary (eg in a partnership agreement).

Step two: Calculate the gain by apportioning the relevant fractional share of the acquisition cost, disposal proceeds and allowable expenditure to the partner.

The same principles of apportionment apply when part of an asset is disposed of.

See **Practice example 9.4** for a demonstration of how this works in practice.

Practice example 9.4

Alexander and Sergiu run a shop in partnership, from freehold premises that the partnership owns. The purchase price, sale price and allowable expenditure remain as in **Practice example 9.3**.

Alexander and Sergiu have agreed to share the partnership's profits/losses in the following percentages:
Alexander - 60%
Sergiu - 40%
What is Alexander's BG?

Alexander's BG is as follows:	
Sale price	**£180,000 (60% of £300,000)**
Less	
Acquisition cost	**£60,000 (60% of £100,000)**
Allowable expenditure	**£33,000 (60% of £55,000)**
BG	**£87,000**

When paying CGT, reliefs and rates apply to the individual partners.

When a partner leaves, they are treated as disposing of their proportionate share to the other partners.

When a new partner joins, each partner is treated as disposing of part of their existing share to accommodate the new partner.

CALCULATION OF CGT CHARGE: RATES

In the tax year 2026/27, CGT is charged at the following main rates, which are set out in **Table 9.1**.

Table 9.1: CGT rates

Where business asset disposal relief or investors' relief applies	**18%**
Where total taxable income and gains do not exceed the IT basic rate band (£37,700 in 2026/27) (BRT)	**18%**
On the amount over the threshold, where total taxable income and gains exceed the IT basic rate band (HRT)	**24%**

Gains realised by trustees and personal representatives are taxed at a flat rate of 24%.

Exam warning

CGT is renewed annually, so rates, thresholds, exemptions and reliefs can change from year to year. For the purposes of SQE1, it is important that you know the annual exemption for the current tax year (see **Principal**

CGT reliefs/exemptions, below), the basic and higher rate thresholds and the key rates of CGT. These can be found on www.gov.uk.

Like IT, CGT is a progressive tax, which means that the rate increases as the CG increases. Individuals may make use of the lower rate(s) first, but pay CGT at the higher rate(s) as their CG increases (see **Practice example 9.5**).

Practice example 9.5

In 2026/27:

- Zena makes a CG of £10,000 and has total taxable income of £20,000
- Chingiz makes a CG of £10,000 and has total taxable income of £30,000
- Bilal makes a CG of £20,000 and has total taxable income of £40,000.

What rate(s) of CGT will Zena, Chingiz and Bilal pay on their respective CGs? You can assume that business asset disposal relief and investors' relief do not apply (see **Principal CGT reliefs/exemptions**, below).

Zena will pay CGT at 18%. Remember that 'CG' means that reliefs and exemptions have already been taken into account.
Chingiz will pay CGT at 18% on the first £7,700 and 24% on the balance.
Bilal will pay CGT at 24%. Her basic rate has already been used up by her taxable income.

PRINCIPAL CGT RELIEFS/EXEMPTIONS

For SQE1, you need to have a good working knowledge of the principal CGT reliefs and exemptions and these are set out below:

- **business asset disposal relief (BADR)**
- **annual exemption (AE)**
- **hold-over relief (HOR)**
- **roll-over relief (ROR)** on replacement of business assets
- **deferral relief (DR)** on reinvestment in **Enterprise Investment Scheme (EIS)** shares
- **investors' relief (IR)**
- **roll-over relief on incorporation of a business (RORIB)**
- transfers between spouses
- buyback of shares.

Business asset disposal relief (BADR)

BADR was introduced with effect from 6 April 2008 and was originally known as 'Entrepreneurs' relief'.

Key term: business asset disposal relief (BADR)

BADR applies where there is a **qualifying business disposal (QBD)**.

Key term: qualifying business disposal (QBD)

A QBD includes three types of transactions:

ONE: The sale or gift of *the whole or part of* a business carried on as a sole trader or in partnership (ie *an unincorporated business* - see **Chapter 1**), provided that the business has been owned for at least the *two years* prior to the disposal.

TWO: The sale or gift of *shares in a company* provided that:

1) The company is a *trading company.*
2) The shareholding represents at least *5% of the company's ordinary voting shares* with the right to at least 5% of the profits/assets or sale proceeds of the company.
3) The individual is an *employee or officer* of the company.
4) These conditions have been satisfied for at least the *two years* prior to the disposal.

THREE: The sale or gift of assets used by such a trading company or partnership business, but owned individually by the partner or shareholder. Such disposals qualify if they are associated with another qualifying disposal and involve reducing their share in the company/business by at least 5%. The assets must have been owned for at least three years and used by the business throughout the previous two years.

Gains qualifying for BADR are usually taxed first.

For qualifying gains, an allowable lifetime limit of £1m is taxed at the flat rate of 18%.

Qualifying gains made above this allowable lifetime limit of £1m will be taxed at the appropriate rate (see **Calculation of CGT charge: rates**, above).

If applicable, the annual exemption (see **Annual exemption**, below) can be used against qualifying gains, as tax is being paid.

The time limit for making a claim is on or before the first anniversary of 31 January following the tax year of the disposal.

See **Practice examples 9.6 and 9.7** below for demonstration of how BADR works in practice.

Practice example 9.6

Leonora is a sole trader. She bought her business in 2015 for £300,000 and sells it in July 2026 for £800,000. There is no allowable expenditure. What is Leonora's BG, and will she qualify for BADR?

Leonora has made a BG of £500,000. Assuming she has not used up her lifetime limit, she will be entitled to BADR as this is a QBD of the first type. She is selling her sole trader business that she has owned for at least the two years prior to the sale.

Practice example 9.7

Serhat is a director of and 20% shareholder in a trading company. He bought the shares (which are ordinary voting shares) in 2020 for £200,000. He then sold the shares for £3m in September 2026. There is no relevant allowable expenditure and Serhat is an HRT, based on taxable income alone. What is Serhat's BG, and will he qualify for BADR?

Serhat has made a BG of £2.8m. Assuming he has not already used up his lifetime limit, he is entitled to BADR as this is a QBD of the second type. He is selling at least a 5% ordinary shareholding in a trading company and he is an officer of the company. He has satisfied these conditions for at least the two years prior to the sale.

The chargeable gain (up to £1m of the unused lifetime limit) qualifies for BADR. The remaining amount will be taxed at the higher rate of 24%.

Annual exemption (AE)

Each individual has an annual exemption (AE) for CGT purposes.

Key term: annual exemption (AE)

The amount of capital gain that an individual can make each year without being subject to CGT (£3,000 for the tax year 2026/27).

Like the personal allowance for IT, it is not possible to carry forward the whole or any part of an unused AE. The AE can only be used when tax is paid (not when liability to tax is being held over, rolled over or deferred).

The AE can be used first against CGs where the rate of tax would be higher, in order to save tax.

Exam warning

The AE is available to anyone who has *not made any previous capital disposals* in the relevant tax year. To give you confidence in making calculations, look out for this, or similar wording in a question, or confirmation that the AE has already been used in whole or in part (see **Practice examples 9.8 and 9.9**).

Practice example 9.8

Assi runs a shop as a sole trader from freehold premises that he owns.

He bought the business, including the premises, in 2021 for £100,000 and subsequently sold them for £300,000 in June 2026. There is no allowable expenditure and *Assi has not made any previous capital disposals in the relevant tax year*. What is Assi's CG and how much CGT will be payable?

Sale price	**£300,000**
Less	
Acquisition cost	**£100,000**
BG	**£200,000**
Less	
AE	**£3,000**
CG	**£197,000**

£197,000 x 18% = CGT of £35,460 (as BADR applies)

Practice example 9.9

Nikkie is a director of and 25% shareholder in a trading company.
She bought the shares (which are ordinary voting shares) in 2022 for £500,000. She then sells the shares for £3.5m in August 2026. There is no relevant allowable expenditure and Nikkie is already an HRT, based on income alone. *Nikkie has made a previous BG of £1,000 in the relevant tax year* and has not made any previous claim for BADR. What is Nikkie's CG and how much CGT will be payable?

Nikkie has made a BG of £3m. She is entitled to BADR as this is a QBD of the second type. She is selling at least a 5% shareholding in a trading company, and she is an officer of the company. She has satisfied these conditions for at least the two years prior to the sale.

After deduction of the unused part of the AE, the gain (up to £1m) qualifies for BADR and will be taxed at a flat rate of 18%. The remaining amount will be taxed at 24%, as Nikkie is an HRT for CGT purposes.
BG = £3m

Less remaining AE - £2,000
CG = £2,998,000
£1,000,000 x 18% = £180,000
£1,998,000 x 24% = £479,520
Total CGT = £659,520

Hold-over relief (HOR)

The effect of hold-over relief (HOR) is to postpone the potential payment of CGT until the eventual disposal by the transferee of the business asset concerned.

Key term: hold-over relief (HOR)

HOR is available to an individual who disposes of a **business asset** by way of gift (or at an undervalue, if there is a gift element) provided both parties (transferor and transferee) elect for it to apply.

The election is very important as the transferee agrees to take on the transferor's tax liability. It must be made within four years from the end of the tax year in which the disposal was made.

Key term: business asset

Business assets for the purposes of this relief include those used in the transferor's trade, shares in a trading company not listed on a recognised stock exchange, shares in a trading company where the transferor owns at least 5% of the voting shares (a 'personal company') and assets owned by a shareholder and used in his 'personal company'.

Neither the AE nor BADR can be used in conjunction with HOR, because the gain is being held over, so tax is not being paid. However, if available, both can be applied on the subsequent disposal of the asset.

See **Practice example 9.10** for a demonstration of how HOR works in practice.

Practice example 9.10

Eleni gifted a commercial investment property, worth £400,000, to John in 2025. She had bought the property three years earlier for £200,000.

There was no relevant allowable expenditure and Eleni and John both elected to claim HOR.

John, who is an HRT, then sells the same property in June 2026 for £500,000.

There is no relevant allowable expenditure and neither Eleni nor John have made any other capital disposals during these years. What is John's CGT liability?

Eleni's gain of £200,000 is held over

John	
Sale price	**£500,000**
Less	
Acquisition cost	
(£400,000 less £200,000*)	**£200,000**
BG	**£300,000**
Less	
AE	**£3,000**
CG	**= £297,000**
CGT at 24% = £71,280	

BADR could not apply, as John has not owned the property for at least two years.

***** ***The held-over gain is deducted here to reduce the amount deducted as part of the acquisition cost, which in turn increases the tax payable.***

Roll-over relief on replacement of qualifying business assets (ROR)

The effect of roll-over relief (ROR) is to postpone the potential payment of CGT until the replacement asset is sold.

Key term: roll-over relief (ROR)

ROR is available if a **qualifying business asset (QBA)** is sold and the proceeds of sale are then used to buy another qualifying business asset, usually within one year before or three years after the sale of the original asset.

Key term: qualifying business asset (QBA)

QBAs include most business assets used in the trade (eg land and buildings). The term also includes assets owned by a shareholder, but used by a company (provided that the shareholder has at least 5% of the voting shares). *Company shares are not QBAs for the purposes of ROR.* It is not a requirement for the assets disposed of and replaced to be of the same type (eg business premises may be sold and the proceeds used to buy a share in a partnership).

Exam warning

The fact that company shares are not qualifying assets for the purpose of ROR is crucially important, but often overlooked by candidates. If a scenario deals with what looks like a situation of ROR, because assets are being replaced, make sure that shares are not involved.

Neither the AE nor BADR can be used in conjunction with ROR, because the gain is being rolled over, so tax is not being paid. However, if available, both can be applied on the subsequent disposal of the asset.

ROR must normally be claimed within four years from the end of the tax year in which the replacement asset was acquired.

See **Practice example 9.11** for a demonstration of how ROR works in practice.

Practice example 9.11

Lill is in business as a sole trader and owns the freehold business premises.

She bought the premises in 2005 for £100,000.

She sold the premises in 2007 for £160,000 and, using the sale proceeds, immediately bought another business property ('the second property') for £240,000, claiming ROR.

There was no relevant allowable expenditure.

She sold the second property in June 2026 for £300,000 and moved her business into rented premises.

There is no relevant allowable expenditure and Lill has not made any other capital disposals during the relevant tax years. She is an HRT and has already used up her lifetime threshold for BADR, following an earlier disposal in the previous tax year. What is Lill's CGT liability on the sale of the second property?

Rolled-over gain	**£60,000**
Replacement asset	**£300,000**
Less acquisition cost	
(£240,000 less £60,000*)	**£180,000**
BG	**= £120,000**
Less AE	**£3,000**
CG	**= £117,000**

CGT at 24% = £28,080 (as HRT and lifetime limit for BADR exceeded)

*** The rolled-over gain is deducted here to reduce the amount deducted as part of the acquisition cost, which in turn increases the tax payable.***

Deferral relief (DR) on reinvestment in Enterprise Investment Scheme (EIS) shares

The effect of deferral relief (DR) is to postpone the potential payment of CGT until Enterprise Investment Scheme (EIS) shares are sold.

Key term: deferral relief (DR)

DR is available following a disposal of *any asset* by an individual (not just business assets), who then reinvests the proceeds of sale in buying EIS shares within one year before or within three years after the sale of the original asset.

Key term: Enterprise Investment Scheme (EIS)

The EIS offers tax reliefs to individual investors who buy new shares in a company whose shares are part of the scheme. The detail of the scheme is beyond the scope of this book, and a question will usually specify whether shares are EIS shares.

Neither the AE nor BADR can be used in conjunction with DR, because the gain is being deferred, so tax is not being paid. However, if available, both can be applied on the subsequent disposal of the asset.

See **Practice example 9.12** for a demonstration of how DR works in practice.

Practice example 9.12

Fredi sells his sole trader business, which he has run for 10 years, in January 2026.

He had bought the business for £100,000 and sells it for £1,360,000. There is no relevant allowable expenditure.

In December 2026, Fredi invests the gain he makes in selling the business in buying EIS shares.

He has not made any other relevant capital disposals and would like to claim DR. What is Fredi's deferred gain?

Fredi's deferred gain is as follows:

Sale price	**£1,360,000**
Less	
Acquisition cost	**£100,000**

Deferred gain = £1,260,000

Investors' relief (IR)

Investors' relief (IR) works in a similar way to BADR.

Key term: investors' relief (IR)

IR can be used for gains made on the disposal of **qualifying shares** in unlisted trading companies.

Key term: qualifying shares

Shares must be fully paid ordinary shares that were issued to the investor in return for cash on or after 17 March 2016. The shares must have been held by the investor for at least three years from 6 April 2016.

Because of the time restrictions, the impact of IR will become more important over time.

A special rate of 18% (for gains made on or after 6 April 2026) applies to the gain (subject to a lifetime cap of £1m).

Roll-over relief on incorporation of a business (RORIB)

Roll-over relief on incorporation of a business (RORIB) applies in order to postpone the potential payment of CGT when an unincorporated business is incorporated. The rationale is to encourage businesses to expand.

Key term: roll-over relief on incorporation of a business (RORIB)

RORIB applies where there is a transfer of a business as a going concern (ie a business which is operating and making a profit), with all of its assets (cash is ignored). It only applies to the extent that the business is transferred in consideration of shares.

RORIB works in the same way as ROR, so the AE and BADR cannot be used in conjunction with it, for the same reasons. However, if available, both can be applied on the subsequent disposal of the asset.

Transfers between spouses

Transfers between spouses are deemed to be made with no gain or loss. However, any liability to tax is deferred until the eventual disposal of the item.

Buyback of shares

Buyback of shares (see **Chapter 5**) usually involves the payment of IT by the shareholder, as the consideration is taxed as a dividend. However, in some circumstances, CGT will be payable instead. This is where (a) the company is an unlisted trading company, (b) the buyback is to benefit the trade, (c) the shares have been owned for at least five years and (d) the shareholding must be reduced by at least 25% to a maximum of 30% of the company's shares.

Summary

The essential information on how to approach a CGT calculation is summarised in **Figure 9.1**.

STEP ONE - Consider whether the annual exemption, business asset disposal relief or investors' relief apply

STEP TWO - Consider other reliefs - what is the nature of the transaction/what is being done with the proceeds of disposal?

STEP THREE - Make your calculation

Market value/Sale price

Less:

- Acquisition cost
- Allowable expenditure - incidental costs of acquisition, subsequent (capital) expenditure and incidental costs of disposal

Apply:

- Annual exemption (if tax is being paid now)

Consider:
Other reliefs/exemptions

Figure 9.1: CGT calculation

COLLECTION OF CGT

CGT is part of the self-assessment scheme (see **Chapter 8**), and it is usually payable by 31 January following the end of the tax year. However, a provisional calculation must be made, and tax paid, within 60 days of completion of the sale of a residential property, where CGT is payable. Instalment options are available in some circumstances, but the detail is outside the scope of this book.

ANTI-AVOIDANCE PROVISIONS

The general anti-abuse rule (GAAR, see **Chapter 8**) applies to CGT, and HMRC may make adjustments to liability where required.

INHERITANCE TAX AND BPR

For the purposes of SQE1, you need to be able to recognise the circumstances where **business property relief (BPR)** (now formally known as business relief) will provide relief from **inheritance tax (IHT)**.

Key term: inheritance tax (IHT)

Death will usually give rise to a charge for IHT and not a charge to CGT. The personal representatives acquire property at its market value on the death of the original owner (s 62 TOCGA) (see more generally, ***Revise SQE: Wills and the Administration of Estates***).

Key term: business property relief (BPR)

BPR provides that on death there is no charge to IHT in respect of the following business assets:

- an interest in an unincorporated business
- the value of unlisted/unquoted company shares not trading on a recognised stock exchange relevant to trading activities.

Note that assets qualifying for 100% relief are subject to the cap referred to below.

BPR also provides that there is a reduction of 50% of the value transferred for IHT purposes for the following:

- qualifying property above the cap referred to below
- unlisted/unquoted company shares trading but not listed on a recognised stock exchange relevant to trading activities (eg shares trading on the Alternative Investment Market (AIM shares))
- listed company shares where the transferor had voting control *immediately prior to the transfer*. Therefore, if part of a controlling shareholding is disposed of, this may give rise to BPR, but if the remaining part is subsequently disposed of, where the transferor no longer has control, that will not qualify
- land, buildings, plant and machinery owned by the transferor but used either (a) in the business in which they were a partner or (b) a company (listed or unlisted) in which they had voting control. Control, in this context, means more than 50% voting power on all resolutions and takes into account the shares of spouses/civil partners.

For the relief to apply, the assets must have been owned for at least two years or be a replacement for assets with a combined period of ownership of more than two years.

Except in the case of lifetime transfers, any spouse or civil partner is deemed to have owned the property from the original acquisition date. Therefore, if they subsequently transfer relevant property, BPR may apply even if they have not themselves owned the assets for the relevant period. Spouses or civil partners may also transfer any unused cap (see below) on death.

If the transferor dies within seven years of a lifetime transfer, BPR will be withdrawn unless the business property or substituted business property is still owned by the transferee. Therefore, if the business property is sold and the proceeds are, for example, used to pay off debts and make home improvements, BPR will be withdrawn.

BPR will not apply if there is a binding contract for the sale of the relevant property, for example an *obligation* in a partnership agreement to sell a partnership share on death, rather than an *option* for the continuing partners to buy. In these circumstances, the interest will be in the proceeds of sale, rather than relevant business property.

Exam warning

Note that assets qualifying for 100% BPR and Agricultural Property Relief (see ***Revise SQE: Wills and the Administration of Estates***) are now subject to a cap. Only the first £2.5m of qualifying assets will be exempt and the excess will attract 50% relief.

See **Practice example 9.13** for an illustration of BPR in practice.

Practice example 9.13

Charlotte, who for 10 years owned a 30% shareholding in an unlisted trading company not trading on a recognised stock exchange and a 25% share of the business premises, dies suddenly. There is no binding contract to sell the assets, and you can assume that the relevant cap will not be exceeded. Will BPR apply?

Charlotte's shareholding qualifies for 100% BPR, although her interest in the premises does not qualify for 50% BPR as she did not have voting control. Had the shareholding been in a listed company, BPR would not have applied. Had the shares been trading but not listed on a recognised stock exchange, Charlotte would have qualified for 50% rather than 100% BPR. Had Charlotte instead owned 30% of a partnership business and a 25% share of the business premises, she would have been entitled to 100% BPR for the business interest and 50% BPR for the property interest.

KEY POINT CHECKLIST

This chapter has covered the following key knowledge points. You can use these to structure your revision, ensuring you recall the key details for each point, as covered in this chapter.

- CGT is payable on chargeable gains, made by a chargeable person, on disposal of a chargeable asset.
- Chargeable persons include individuals, individual partners, trustees and personal representatives.
- Disposal is construed widely and includes gifts.
- Most assets are chargeable assets for CGT purposes, save for sterling and wasting assets.
- The acquisition cost and allowable expenditure may be deducted from the disposal value to calculate the basic gain.
- Partnerships are treated transparently for CGT purposes, so the disposal value, acquisition cost and allowable expenditure need to be apportioned between the partners.
- The main reliefs and exemptions are the AE, BADR, ROR, HOR and DR.
- On death, there is usually no charge to CGT but instead a charge to IHT. The assets are deemed to be acquired by the personal representatives at their market value. BPR can be used to eliminate or reduce the charge to IHT by 50% for relevant assets.

KEY TERMS AND CONCEPTS

- chargeable persons (**page 182**)
- capital gains tax (**page 182**)
- chargeable asset (**page 183**)
- disposal (**page 183**)
- chargeable gain (**page 183**)
- disposal value (**page 184**)
- connected person (**page 185**)
- allowable expenditure (**page 185**)
- basic gain (**page 185**)
- business asset disposal relief (**page 189**)
- qualifying business disposal (**page 189**)
- annual exemption (**page 190**)
- hold-over relief (**page 192**)
- business asset (**page 192**)
- roll-over relief (**page 193**)
- qualifying business asset (**page 193**)
- deferral relief (**page 195**)
- Enterprise Investment Scheme (**page 195**)
- investors' relief (**page 196**)
- qualifying shares (**page 196**)
- roll-over relief on incorporation of a business (**page 196**)

- inheritance tax (**page 198**)
- business property relief (**page 198**)

SQE1-STYLE QUESTIONS

QUESTION 1

A client, who is a sole trader, purchased their business (which included a freehold commercial property) 10 years ago for £100,000. The client has now retired and has sold the business for £200,000. They have not made any previous capital disposals.

Which of the following will the client be able to deduct from the sale price in order to calculate their basic gain?

A. The purchase price, estate agents' fees of £3,750 incurred in the sale, £2,500 spent repairing the roof, £3,000 in legal fees on the sale, £2,000 in legal fees on the purchase and £4,000 in installing a replacement kitchen and windows.

B. Estate agents' fees of £3,750 incurred in the sale, £3,000 in legal fees on the sale and £2,000 in legal fees on the purchase.

C. The purchase price, estate agents' fees of £3,750 incurred in the sale, £3,000 in legal fees on the sale and £2,000 in legal fees on the purchase.

D. The purchase price, estate agents' fees of £3,750 incurred in the sale, £3,000 in legal fees on the sale, £2,000 in legal fees on the purchase and £4,000 in installing a replacement kitchen and windows.

E. Estate agents' fees of £3,750 incurred in the sale, £3,000 in legal fees on the sale, £2,000 in legal fees on the purchase and £4,000 in installing a replacement kitchen and windows.

QUESTION 2

A client is selling their 25% ordinary shareholding in a trading company for £2m. They bought the shares 20 years ago for £500,000 and they carry 25% of the voting rights in the company. You can assume that there is no allowable expenditure. The client was a director of the company, until they retired five years ago. The client is a higher rate taxpayer (HRT) and has only made one other capital disposal, three years ago, where they claimed business asset disposal relief (BADR) on a chargeable gain of £200,000.

Which of the following best describes the client's liability for capital gains tax (CGT)?

A. The client will be entitled to the full annual exemption (AE) and to BADR on the chargeable gain. CGT will be charged at 24%, as the client is an HRT.

B. The client will be entitled to the full AE and to BADR on the chargeable gain, up to £1m. CGT will be charged at 24% on the balance, as the client is an HRT.

C. The client will be entitled to the full AE and to BADR on the chargeable gain up to £800,000. CGT will be charged at 24% on the balance, as the client is an HRT.

D. The client will be entitled to the full AE and to BADR on the chargeable gain. CGT will be payable at a rate of 18%.

E. The client will be entitled to the full AE, but not to BADR. CGT will be payable at a rate of 24% as the client is an HRT.

QUESTION 3

A trading partnership has three partners (a man, a woman and a client) who have been in partnership for five years. They share income profits equally and capital profits in accordance with their capital contributions, which are as follows:

Man: 50%
Woman: 30%
Client: 20%

Four years ago, the firm purchased office premises for £100,000, and they have just been sold for £200,000. None of the partners have made any previous capital disposals and they are all higher rate taxpayers.

Which of the following best describes the partners' liability to capital gains tax (CGT) on the sale?

A. Each partner will pay CGT on the percentage of the basic gain that corresponds with the proportion in which they share capital profits. They will be entitled to deduct any allowable expenditure and the annual exemption first and it is likely they will qualify for BADR, paying tax at 18%.

B. Each partner will pay CGT on the percentage of the basic gain that corresponds with the proportion in which they share capital profits. They will be entitled to deduct the annual exemption first, but it is unlikely that they will qualify for BADR.

C. Each partner will be liable to pay CGT on one-third of the basic gain. They will be entitled to deduct any allowable expenditure and the annual exemption first and it is likely they will qualify for BADR, paying tax at 18%.

D. Each partner will be liable to pay CGT on one-third of the basic gain. They will be entitled to deduct any allowable expenditure and the annual exemption first, but it is unlikely they will qualify for BADR, so they will pay tax at 24%.

E. Each partner will pay CGT on the percentage of the basic gain that corresponds with the proportion in which they share in capital profits. They will be entitled to deduct any allowable expenditure and the annual exemption first and it is likely they will qualify for BADR, paying tax at 24%, as higher rate taxpayers.

QUESTION 4

A client sold their holiday home in England two weeks ago. The client is a higher rate taxpayer and the property has never been let commercially. The property was bought for £400,000 five years ago and is now being sold for £700,000. Legal fees of £1,500 were paid on the acquisition, and solicitors' and estate agents' fees together totalling £3,500 have been incurred on the sale. Three years ago, the client built a substantial extension costing £100,000. The current annual exemption is £3,000 and the client has made no previous capital disposals.

Which of the following best identifies the client's capital gains tax liability?

A. £58,400.

B. £38,400.

C. £19,200.

D. £70,080.

E. £46,080.

QUESTION 5

A client who was a 50% partner in an accountancy business dies. He purchased his share in the business 10 years ago for £200,000 and it is now worth £350,000. He also owned, for eight years, business premises that were occupied by the business. There is no binding contract for sale of these assets in the partnership agreement.

Which of the following best describes the tax position in respect of the business interest and the premises?

A. The personal representatives will pay capital gains tax (CGT) on the market value of the business interest and the chargeable gain on the premises.

B. The personal representatives will pay CGT on the chargeable gain of the business interest and the premises.

C. No CGT will be payable, but the personal representatives will acquire the business interest and the premises at their market value as at the date of the client's death. Inheritance tax will be payable.

D. No CGT will be payable, but the personal representatives will acquire the business interest and the premises at their market value as at the date of the client's death. It is likely that business property relief (BPR) of 100% will apply to the business interest and BPR of 50% will apply to the premises.

E. No CGT will be payable, but the personal representatives will acquire the business interest and the premises at their market value as at the date of the client's death. It is likely that BPR of 100% will apply to the business interest and the premises.

ANSWERS TO QUESTIONS

Answers to 'What do you know already?' questions at the start of the chapter

1) CGT is payable by individuals (including sole traders), individual partners, trustees and personal representatives. It is a tax on an increase in an asset's value during a period of ownership. It is charged on chargeable gains made by a chargeable person on disposal of a chargeable asset.
2) The acquisition cost and allowable expenditure are deducted from the sale price to give the basic gain. Exemptions and reliefs are then applied to give the chargeable gain and this is taxed at the appropriate rate(s).
3) True. The annual exemption can only be used when tax is paid. It cannot be used when a gain is being held over, rolled over or deferred.
4) False. A higher rate taxpayer will be entitled to use up the basic rate first, to the extent that taxable income does not exceed the basic rate band. Sometimes, higher rate taxpayers pay CGT at a flat rate of 18% (eg business asset disposal relief and investors' relief).
5) True. Shares are not qualifying assets for the purpose of business asset disposal relief and an individual will not usually pay CGT on the gain in value of their main home (due to the principal private residence exemption).

Answers to end-of-chapter SQE1-style questions

Question 1

The correct answer was C. This is because the purchase price must be deducted (which is why option B is incorrect and partially why option E is incorrect). The other items listed are allowable expenditure. Options A, D and E are incorrect, as repair/replacement/renewal of existing items does not usually qualify as allowable expenditure.

Question 2

The correct answer was E. The AE applies as the client has not made any previous capital disposals in the current tax year. However, BADR does not apply (as assumed in options A–D) as they fail to satisfy the condition of being an employee or officer of the company for the last two years. Options A, B and D are also incorrect, as if BADR had been available, they would have been taxed at a flat rate of 18% for the first £800,000 (bearing in mind the lifetime limit of £1m) and 24% on the balance. Option C would have been correct if all conditions for BADR had been satisfied.

Question 3

The correct answer was A. The express agreement sets the share of capital profits, which displaces the presumption of equal shares. Therefore, options C and D are incorrect. The allowable expenditure and annual exemption can be deducted. Option B is incorrect as it fails to mention the allowable expenditure and suggests BADR will not apply (as does option D). BADR applies as they have owned the business for at least two years and it gives a flat rate of 18% (not 24%, as suggested in option E). They are clearly within their lifetime limit, having not made any previous capital disposals.

Question 4

The correct answer was E. £700,000 - £400,000 - £1,500 - £3,500 - £100,000 - £3,000 = £192,000 chargeable gain. This is taxed at 24% as the client is a higher rate taxpayer. Option A is incorrect, as the cost of the extension was not deducted, and tax was charged at 20%. Option B is incorrect as tax was charged at 20%. Option C is incorrect as tax was charged at 10%. Option D is incorrect, as the cost of the extension was not deducted. The transaction does not qualify for business asset disposal relief as it is not business property.

Question 5

The correct answer was D. There is no liability to CGT on death, so options A and B are incorrect. Option C is partially correct, but does not acknowledge BPR. BPR is correctly applied in option D, but incorrectly applied in option E.

■ KEY CASES, RULES, STATUTES AND INSTRUMENTS

The SQE1 Assessment Specification does not require you to know statutory authorities or recall specific case names for this topic. However, you should be able to apply the key provisions relating to CGT from a practical perspective. Remember that CGT is renewed annually, so you should be aware of the prevailing rates, thresholds, reliefs and exemptions at the time you sit SQE1.

10

Corporation tax

MAKE SURE YOU KNOW

This chapter provides an overview of corporation tax (CT). For the SQE1 assessments, you will need to understand the basis of the charge, how CT is calculated, and the tax treatment of different distributions. You will also need to have knowledge of how CT is paid and collected and an outline of the anti-avoidance legislation. Your understanding of these subjects will enable you to identify and apply the relevant legal rules and principles to SQE1-style single best answer MCQs. For the latest corporation tax rates, please check https://www.gov.uk/corporation-tax.

SQE ASSESSMENT ADVICE

For SQE1, you are required to understand CT from a practical perspective. It is likely that you will be required to identify how CT will be calculated, the tax consequences of different distributions and apply the rules to problem-based, single best answer MCQs. You may also be required to advise on payment and collection, as well as liability under the anti-avoidance provisions.

As you work through this chapter, remember to pay particular attention in your revision to:

- what CT is charged on (the basis of the charge)
- how CT is calculated
- the CT consequences of different distributions
- collection of CT
- liability under the anti-avoidance provisions.

WHAT DO YOU KNOW ALREADY?

Attempt these questions before reading this chapter. If you find some difficult or cannot remember the answers, remember to look more closely at that area during your revision.

1) Who pays CT and what is it charged on?
   [Basis of charge to CT, page 207]
2) When does the CT year begin and end?
   [Basis of charge to CT, page 207]

3) Explain what the term 'close company' means.
   [Close companies, page 214]
4) True or false? Dividends are deductible expenses for the purposes of CT.
   [Calculation of income profits, page 209, and Tax treatment of distributions, page 213]
5) True or false? A deposit must be paid to HMRC whenever a close company makes a loan to a shareholder.
   [Close companies, page 214]

BASIS OF CHARGE TO CT

Companies pay **corporation tax (CT)** on both their income profits and capital gains.

Key term: corporation tax (CT)

A tax chargeable on a company's income profits and capital gains.

Income profits of companies are calculated according to income tax (IT) principles (see **Calculation of income profits**, below) and capital gains of companies are calculated according to capital gains tax (CGT) principles (see **Calculation of chargeable gains**, below).

The key charging statutes are as follows:
- Corporation Tax Act 2009 (CTA 2009)
- Corporation Tax Act 2010 (CTA 2010).

Companies are assessed for CT on their income profits and capital gains during the **corporation tax financial year (CTFY)**.

Key term: corporation tax financial year (CTFY)

The period from 1 April in one year to 31 March in the next. It is named after the year in which it commenced (eg the CTFY 2026 started in April 2026).

If the company's accounting period differs from the CTFY and the rate changes, the company's profits will have to be apportioned.

CT rates

As at CTFY 2026 there are three rates of CT, and CT is calculated by applying the appropriate rate to the profits made (see **Practice example 10.1**) in each of the company's accounting periods (see **Chapter 7**). The 2026 rates are shown in **Table 10.1**.

Table 10.1: CT tax rates

Rate	When applicable	Percentage rate
Small profits rate	Companies with taxable profits of up to **£50,000**	**19%** on total taxable profits
Main rate	Companies with taxable profits of more than **£250,000**	**25%** on total taxable profits
Marginal rate	Companies with taxable profits above **£50,000** but not exceeding **£250,000**	Tax the first £50,000 at **19%** and the balance at **26.5%**

The effect of the relief given by the marginal rate is that it reduces as the profits get closer to the main rate.

Practice example 10.1

Seebach Limited makes up its accounts to 31 March in each year and has income profits of £90,000 and capital gains of £60,000. How much CT will the company pay?

Ignoring any reliefs that may be available, the company will pay CT on the total income profits and capital gains, at the marginal rate.
£90,000 + £60,000 = £150,000
£50,000 x 19% = £9,500
£100,000 x 26.5% = £26,500
£9,500 + £26,500 = £36,000

Revision tip

CT is renewed annually, so rates, thresholds, exemptions and reliefs may change from year to year. For the purposes of SQE1, it is important that you know the key information for the current CTFY. This can be found on www.gov.uk. It is also important to appreciate that CT is not progressive in the same way as income tax and capital gains tax. The rate payable is governed by the total taxable profits.

CALCULATION OF CT

The basic calculation for CT is as follows:

Step one: Calculate income profits
Step two: Calculate chargeable gains

Step three: Add together the income profits and chargeable gains to give *total profits*
Step four: Apply reliefs
Step five: Calculate the tax.

Calculation of income profits

Step one is to calculate **income profits**.

> **Key term: income profits**
>
> Income profits are calculated according to the usual principles of chargeable receipts, less deductible expenses and capital allowances (see **Chapter 7**).

> **Revision tip**
>
> Please note that dividends and payment for the buyback of shares (see **Chapter 5**) are *not* deductible expenses for CT purposes (see **Tax treatment of distributions**, below). This can have a real impact on the CT the company pays (see **Withdrawal of profits**, below).

Calculation of chargeable gains

Step two is to calculate **chargeable gains**.

> **Key term: chargeable gains**
>
> These are calculated according to the usual principles of calculating a basic gain from the disposal of a chargeable asset (see **Chapter 9**) and applying any available reliefs.

> **Revision tip**
>
> Please note that for CT, there are special rules that apply to goodwill and intellectual property (eg copyrights, patents and trademarks). Although these are assets, any gains from these are treated as income, rather than capital gain, and expenditure on them is treated as a deductible expense.

The same CGT rules on the value of undervalue disposals apply (usually the market value is used), as do the rules on connected persons (see **Chapter 9**).

For CT purposes, people who control a company (see **Chapter 4**) (either alone or with other connected persons) are treated as connected. Companies are connected if the same person (either alone or with other connected persons) controls both.

Capital losses may be deducted from chargeable gains in the same accounting period or carried forward to later accounting periods.

Indexation allowance

Once the basic gain has been calculated, the **indexation allowance** may be applied, but only to certain allowable expenditure (see **Chapter 9**).

Key term: indexation allowance

Adjustment(s) to account for any increase in value that is simply a result of inflation between 31 March 1982 (the date the allowance was introduced) and 31 December 2017 (the date the allowance was stopped). In addition to *acquisition cost*, it applies to *incidental costs of acquisition* (eg solicitors' fees) and *subsequent expenditure* (eg capital improvements/extensions), but *not* the *disposal value* or *incidental costs of disposal* (eg agents' fees).

Exam warning

The adjustments involve multiplying the relevant expenditure against the multiplier for the relevant year and deducting it from the basic gain. The multipliers are published by HMRC on www.gov.uk. For SQE1, it is not necessary to know the multipliers, as they would usually be provided as part of the question. However, you should be aware of the principle of the indexation allowance and the categories of allowable expenditure it relates to so you can make basic calculations (see **Practice example 10.2**).

Practice example 10.2

Annie Cotton Limited bought land in 2004 and paid a total of £500,000 (including solicitors' and site investigation costs). The company also spent £200,000 in 2007 on doubling the size of the property and is now selling for £2m. The relevant multiplier for 2004 is 0.519, the relevant multiplier for 2007 is 0.379 and the incidental costs of disposal are £5,000. What is the gain after indexation?

Sale price **£2m**
LESS
Acquisition cost and incidental costs of acquisition
£500,000
Incidental costs of disposal **£5,000**
Subsequent expenditure **£200,000**
= £1,295,000 Gain before indexation
LESS
£500,000 x 0.519 **= £259,500 (ie acquisition cost and**

incidental costs of acquisition x relevant multiplier)	
£200,000 x 0.379	**= £75,800 (ie subsequent expenditure x relevant multiplier)**
= £959,700 Gain after indexation	

Roll-over relief on replacement of qualifying business assets

One of the main reliefs for a company's chargeable gains is **roll-over relief on replacement of qualifying business assets (RORRQBA)**.

Key term: roll-over relief on replacement of qualifying business assets (RORRQBA)

RORRQBA works in the same way to the equivalent CGT relief for individuals (see **Chapter 9**). However, there are different rules for goodwill and intellectual property. Although receipts from these assets are treated as income (see **Calculation of chargeable gains**, above), roll-over relief will usually be available if such assets are sold and replaced with other goodwill or intellectual property.

Calculate total profits and apply reliefs

Step three is to add together the income profits and chargeable gains to give *total profits*.

Step four is to apply reliefs that apply to total profits.

There are a number of reliefs that may apply, and although the company may choose whichever relief(s) work(s) best for them, the same loss cannot be claimed for twice. The key reliefs and points are set out below:

- **carry-across/carry-back relief for trading losses**
- **terminal carry-back relief for trading losses**
- **carry-forward relief for trading losses.**

Revision tip

It is important to appreciate that the reliefs referred to in this section apply to companies when calculating CT. The reliefs referred to in **Chapter 7** apply to unincorporated businesses (see **Chapter 1**) when calculating liability for income tax (see **Chapter 8**).

Key term: carry-across/carry-back relief for trading losses

Carry-across – set trading loss against *total profits* for the *same accounting period*.

Carry-back – if the full loss is not absorbed with carry-across, set trading loss against *total profits of the same trade* during the *accounting period(s) in the previous 12 months*.

Time limit for claim - within two years from the end of the loss-making accounting period.

A temporary extension to carry-back relief was introduced as a result of the Covid-19 pandemic. This has now come to an end.

Key term: terminal carry-back relief for trading losses

For losses in the final year of trade.

Set trading losses against *total profits* from the *loss-making accounting period* and the *previous three accounting periods* before the start of the *final 12 months of trade* (taking later periods first).

Time limit for claim - within two years from the end of the loss-making accounting period.

Key term: carry-forward relief for trading losses

Set trading loss against subsequent *total profits* (or profits of the same trade if the *conditions* are not met) in the *next accounting period* and *subsequent accounting periods*, until the loss is absorbed.

The conditions include that the company must continue to trade and certain trades are excluded (eg farming). The full detail of the exclusions is outside the scope of this book as you only need to know the general rules.

Time limit for claim - within two years from the end of the accounting period where losses will be applied.

Cap - £5m, plus 50% of remaining total profits after deduction of the allowance.

Revision tip

It is important to know the basic rules for these reliefs so that you can apply them to practical scenarios (see **SQE1-style questions**, below). **Table 10.2** provides a summary of the key points to help you.

Table 10.2: Reliefs for trading losses

	Accounting periods	Set against total profits	Final year losses only
Carry across	Loss-making	Yes	No
Carry back	Previous one if carry across does not absorb loss	Yes	No
Terminal carry back	Loss-making and three previous years (later first)	Yes	Yes
Carry forward	Subsequent periods	Yes, although same trade if conditions not met	No

Calculate the tax

Step five is to calculate the tax. Remember that as at CTFY 2026 there are three rates of CT (see CT rates in **Table 10.1**).

As previously indicated, if the company's accounting period differs from the CTFY and the rate changes, the company's profits will have to be apportioned.

TAX TREATMENT OF DISTRIBUTIONS

A company may deal with its profits in five main ways:

- retain them in the business
- pay them as dividends to its shareholders (see **Chapter 5**) – dividends paid by a company are *not* deductible expenses in calculating the company's liability to CT
- use them to pay loan/debenture interest (see **Chapter 5**) – debenture interest paid by a company *is* a deductible expense in calculating the company's liability to CT
- pay directors' fees – remuneration paid to directors (and other employees) by a company *is* a deductible expense in calculating the company's liability to CT
- making loans to directors/shareholders – see the rules on **close companies**, below. These are *not* deductible expenses in calculating the company's liability to CT.

Because dividends are not deductible expenses, generally, the most tax-efficient ways of distributing profits from the company's point of view are by the payment of directors' fees and/or debenture interest.

Withdrawal of profits

The rules on withdrawal of profits are illustrated in **Practice example 10.3**.

Practice example 10.3

Sandy is the sole director and shareholder of Shaw Products (Harrogate) Limited. The company is in its first year of trading and has made a profit of £500,000. Sandy wishes to receive £100,000 from the company before tax. What is the most tax-efficient way for the company to do this?

The most tax-efficient way for the company to deal with the distribution will be by way of directors' fees or debenture interest, as these are deductible expenses for CT purposes. Paying dividends instead would increase the company's CT liability.

Close companies

For SQE1, it is important to know the provisions on **close companies** (ie how to identify them and whether the special rules relating to loans will apply). The rules are designed to stop people involved in certain companies receiving loans which are untaxed. Without the rules, this would give the recipient a tax advantage over other distributions, such as directors' fees or dividends, particularly if the loan is not repaid.

Key term: close company

A close company is a company **controlled** by five or fewer **participators** or any number of participators who are also directors (s 439 CTA 2010).

Key term: participators

Participators are essentially shareholders and debenture holders.

Key term: controlled

Such participators control a company if they own, or have the right to acquire, a majority of the voting shares, or have the majority of voting power (see **Chapter 4**). In determining control, the rights of the participators' associates (these include a spouse, parents, children, siblings and business partners) are taken into account.

Practice example 10.4 provides an illustration of the rules on the definition of close companies.

Practice example 10.4

Wogan Limited has 20 shareholders and all of the shareholders are also directors. *Ignoring the question of 'control'*, is it potentially a 'close' company for tax purposes?

Yes, it is. It passes on the 'all the shareholders are directors' point, which applies irrespective of the number of shareholders. If the company instead had five or fewer shareholders, even if none of the shareholders were directors, it would pass on the 'five or fewer' point. If the company had 15 shareholders and none of them were directors, it would not pass on either point (subject to the question of control).

If a close company makes a loan to a participator or a participator's associate, the company must (subject to limited exceptions, see below) pay a levy to HMRC equivalent to 35.75% of the loan (there are no tax consequences for the recipient at this stage).

If the loan is repaid, the levy will be refunded and there are no tax consequences for the recipient.

If the loan is written off, the levy is again refunded to the company, but in the hands of the recipient, it is taxed in the same way as a dividend (see **Chapter 8**).

There are two main exceptions that apply:
- where the company is in the business of money lending and the loan is made as part of that business
- (1) where the loan (together with any other outstanding loan balance) does not exceed £15,000, (2) the borrower works full-time for the company and (3) owns 5% or less of the company's shares. *All three conditions must be satisfied.*

The rules on close companies are illustrated in **Practice example 10.5**.

Practice example 10.5

Ding-dong Doorbells Limited, a trading company, has an issued share capital of 100,000 £1 ordinary shares, held as follows:

Jessica	-	30,000 shares
Samantha	-	30,000 shares
Donatan	-	30,000 shares
Imaani	-	7,000 shares
Cleo	-	3,000 shares

All the shareholders are also full-time working directors. During the current accounting period, the company made loans of £20,000 and £10,000 to Imaani and Cleo respectively. What are the tax implications of the loans?

This is a close company as five or fewer participators control it. Imaani is a 'participator' and therefore the company must pay a levy of 35.75% of the loan to HMRC. The loan is not a deductible expense. Although

Cleo is also a participator, no levy is necessary as the loan does not exceed £15,000 and she owns 5% or less of the company's shares.

Group companies

Companies have a separate legal personality, so each company within a group of companies is taxed separately.

Group relief

Group relief for income losses and expenses and chargeable gains may apply to **group companies**. The full detail is beyond the scope of this book, but the main points are set out below.

Key term: group companies

For the purposes of **group relief for income profits and expenses**, a group company is one that owns 75% or more of the other's ordinary shares or both companies own 75% or more of the ordinary shares in another company.

For the purposes of **group relief for chargeable gains**, a group includes companies that directly own 75% or more of another's ordinary shares. All of the companies must be entitled to more than 50% of the profits and assets of each company within the group.

Key term: group relief for income profits and expenses

This allows certain income losses and expenses (not capital losses) to be transferred from one group company to another, to reduce the transferee's income profits, in an accounting year which overlaps between the two companies.

Key term: group relief for chargeable gains

This allows group companies to transfer chargeable assets between them without a loss or gain occurring. Roll-over relief can also be used to roll over a gain made from selling property into the acquisition of assets by another company in the same group (rather than into the acquisition of assets by the same company).

COLLECTION AND PAYMENT OF CT

CT is a self-assessment tax and HMRC must be notified within three months of the start of the first accounting period.

CT is usually payable nine months and one day from the end of the accounting period and the tax return must be made by 12 months from the end of the accounting period.

Larger companies with taxable profits of £1.5m or more may pay CT by four instalments and these dates are set by HMRC. There are different dates for companies with annual taxable profits over £20m.

ANTI-AVOIDANCE LEGISLATION

The general anti-abuse rule (GAAR) (see **Chapter 8**) applies to CT, and HMRC may require adjustments to be made.

■ KEY POINT CHECKLIST

This chapter has covered the following key knowledge points. You can use these to structure your revision, ensuring you recall the key details for each point, as covered in this chapter.

- Companies pay CT on their income profits and capital gains during the CTFY.
- CT is paid on income, according to IT principles, and chargeable gains, according to CGT principles. The indexation allowance may be applied to chargeable gains and RORRQBA may be available.
- Various reliefs for trading losses may apply, although the company cannot claim for the same loss twice.
- Generally, the most tax-efficient ways of distributing profits from the company's point of view are by the payment of directors' fees and/or debenture interest.
- When a close company makes a loan to a participator, a deposit equivalent to 35.75% of the loan must be paid to HMRC (subject to exceptions).
- Although group companies are taxed separately, group relief for income losses and expenses and capital gains may be available, and roll-over relief may be applied between the companies.

■ KEY TERMS AND CONCEPTS

- corporation tax (**page 207**)
- corporation tax financial year (**page 207**)
- income profits (**page 209**)
- chargeable gains (**page 209**)
- indexation allowance (**page 210**)
- roll-over relief on replacement of qualifying business assets (**page 211**)
- carry-across/carry-back relief for trading losses (**page 212**)
- terminal carry-back relief for trading losses (**page 212**)
- carry-forward relief for trading losses (**page 212**)

- close company (**page 214**)
- participators (**page 214**)
- controlled (**page 214**)
- group companies (**page 216**)
- group relief for income profits and expenses (**page 216**)
- group relief for chargeable gains (**page 216**)

■ SQE1-STYLE QUESTIONS

QUESTION 1

A man has a 40% shareholding in a trading company with four shareholders. Two of the other shareholders each own 28% of the shares and the remaining shareholder holds 4%. All shareholders are full-time working directors of the company. In the current financial year, the company makes trading profits and chargeable gains (after indexation) totalling £1.7m. The company pays directors' fees of £300,000, dividends of £700,000 and debenture interest of £100,000. It also makes a loan of £10,000 to the remaining shareholder.

Which of the following best describes the company's corporation tax liability and the position with the loan?

A. The directors' fees, dividends and debenture interest are deductible expenses. A deposit must be paid to HMRC in respect of the loan, as this is a close company.

B. The directors' fees and debenture interest are deductible expenses. A deposit must be paid to HMRC in respect of the loan, as this is a close company.

C. The directors' fees, debenture interest and loan are deductible expenses. No deposit must be paid to HMRC in respect of the loan as it falls within one of the exceptions under the close company rules.

D. The directors' fees, dividends, debenture interest and loan are deductible expenses. No deposit must be paid to HMRC in respect of the loan as it falls within one of the exceptions under the close company rules.

E. The directors' fees and debenture interest are deductible expenses. No deposit must be paid to HMRC in respect of the loan as it falls within one of the exceptions under the close company rules.

QUESTION 2

In its first 12-month accounting period of trade, a company makes neither a trading profit nor a trading loss, but did make a chargeable gain (and no overall capital loss) from the sale of a freehold property. In the second

12-month accounting period, a trading loss was made and there was no capital gain or capital loss. In the third (but not final) accounting period, a trading profit was made and there was no capital gain or capital loss.

Which of the following best describes the corporation tax relief(s) that may be available to the company?

A. Carry-across, carry-back and carry-forward.
B. Carry-across and carry-forward.
C. Carry-back and carry-forward.
D. Carry-back, carry-forward and terminal carry-back.
E. Carry-forward and terminal carry-back.

QUESTION 3

A company makes income profits of £800,000 and a chargeable gain (after indexation) of £900,000 in the same tax year. The directors are considering whether to pay dividends of £500,000 or directors' fees of £500,000.

Which of the following best describes the tax position?

A. The company will pay income tax on the income profits and capital gains tax on the chargeable gain.
B. The company will pay corporation tax on the income profits and chargeable gain. The dividends and directors' fees are deductible expenses.
C. The company will pay income tax on the income profits and capital gains tax on the chargeable gain. The dividends and directors' fees are deductible expenses.
D. The company will pay corporation tax on the income profits and chargeable gain. The directors' fees are deductible expenses.
E. The shareholders and directors will pay income tax on their dividends and directors' fees respectively, and the company will pay corporation tax on the income profits.

QUESTION 4

A company makes income profits of £600,000 and a chargeable gain (after indexation) of £1m in the same tax year. The company pays directors' fees of £400,000 and pays debenture interest of £50,000.

Which of the following accurately states the company's corporation tax liability?

A. £287,500.
B. £400,000.
C. £300,000.
D. £387,500.
E. £218,500.

QUESTION 5

In its third 12-month accounting period of trade, a company makes a trading profit from manufacturing, but a trading loss from its property portfolio (which made a profit in the second accounting period). It made no chargeable gain or loss in the same periods. In the fourth and final 12-month accounting period, trading profits were made for both parts of the business and there were no capital gains or capital losses.

Which of the following best describes the potential corporation tax relief(s) that may be available to the company?

A. Carry-across, terminal carry-back and carry-forward.
B. Carry-forward and terminal carry-back.
C. Carry-across and carry-forward.
D. Carry-back, carry-forward and terminal carry-back.
E. Carry-across, carry-back and carry-forward.

■ ANSWERS TO QUESTIONS

Answers to 'What do you know already?' questions at the start of the chapter

1) Companies pay CT on both their income profits and capital gains.
2) The CT year begins on 1 April in one year and ends on 31 March in the next. It is named after the year in which it commenced.
3) A close company is a company controlled by five or fewer participators or any number of participators who are also directors.
4) False. Dividends paid by a company are *not* deductible expenses in calculating the company's liability to CT.
5) False. There are two exceptions to this rule, (1) for money lending businesses and (2) for small loans (subject to conditions).

Answers to end-of-chapter SQE1-style questions

Question 1

The correct answer was E. The dividends (options A and D) and loan (options C and D) are not deductible expenses. No deposit is payable, as although this is a close company, one of the exceptions applies. Therefore, options A and B are incorrect in this respect.

Question 2

The correct answer was C. Carry-across does not apply (as suggested in options A and B) as the company made no other profits in the loss-making year. Terminal carry-back does not apply (as suggested in options D and E) as the company has not ceased to trade.

Question 3

The correct answer was D. Companies do not pay income tax or capital gains tax (as suggested in options A and C). Dividends are not deductible expenses for corporation tax purposes, so options B and C are incorrect. Although income tax is payable by individuals on dividends and directors' fees, corporation tax is payable on both a company's income profits *and* chargeable gains, so option E is incorrect.

Question 4

The correct answer was A (£600,000 + £1,000,000 - £400,000 - £50,000 x 25%). Option B is incorrect as it does not deduct the directors' fees and debenture interest. Option C is incorrect as it does not deduct the debenture interest. Option D is incorrect as it does not deduct the directors' fees. Option E is incorrect because it applies corporation tax at 19%.

Question 5

The correct answer was E. On the facts, all three reliefs may be an option and all other options omit one or more of them. Carry-across could be used for the trading loss in the third year, even though it relates to a different part of the business. Carry-back could be used against the trading profit in year two. Carry-forward could be used against the trading profit in year four. Terminal carry-back relief could not be used (as suggested in options A, B and D) as although the company is ceasing to trade, it did not make a loss in the final 12 months of trade.

■ KEY CASES, RULES, STATUTES AND INSTRUMENTS

The SQE1 Assessment Specification does not require you to know any statutory authorities or specific case names for this topic. However, you should be able to apply the key provisions relating to CT from a practical perspective. Remember that CT is renewed annually, so you should be aware of the prevailing rates, thresholds, reliefs and exemptions at the time you sit SQE1.

Index

AA01 form 48
absences, partnerships 24
abusive tax avoidance arrangement (ATAA), income tax (IT) 174–6, 178, 180
accounting periods 48, 56–7, 110, 145–6, 148–52, 158, 172–7, 179, 207, 211–13, 218–21
accounting reference dates 48, 56, 57
accounts 26–7, 48, 56–7, 79, 89–90, 94–8, 108–20, 144–59, 167, 172–7, 213–15
accruals 109–10, 115
acquisition costs 183–97, 200, 201, 204, 210–11
actual authority, partnerships 19, 24, 27–9, 32–3, 35, 37
actual notice to third parties 30–1, 33, 35, 37
AD01 form 56
additional rate taxpayers (ARTs) 163, 165, 168, 176
administration 121–2, 132, 136–8, 139–40
administrative receivers 124–5, 136–9
agendas 50
agents 8, 11, 18, 27–33, 37
Agricultural Property Relief 199
allotment of shares 48, 91–2, 95
allowable expenditure 184–97, 200, 201–3, 204–5, 210–11
allowable reliefs (ARs) 163–78, 179–80
allowances 144–5, 146–52, 155–9, 160–70, 176–7, 179–80, 209–18
alternate directors 71
alternatives to bankruptcy 121–2, 131–2, 139
alternatives to liquidation 136–9
annual exemption (AE), capital gains tax (CGT) 182, 188, 189–97, 200, 202–3, 204–5
annual general meetings (AGMs) 38–9, 45, 52–3, 58
annual investment allowance (AIA) 147–9, 155, 158–9
anti-avoidance provisions 160–1, 174–6, 178, 180, 181–2, 198, 206, 217
AP01/AP02/AP03/AP04 forms 66, 77, 81, 83
apparent/ostensible authority, partnerships 19, 24, 27–9, 32, 33, 35, 36–7
appointments of limited company officers 39, 43–5, 63–4, 65–7, 72, 77, 81, 83–4, 87
appropriation accounts 112–13, 116, 172
articles of association 38–9, 40, 43, 47–58, 59–60, 61–2, 65–88, 91–119
assets 7, 10, 12, 104, 108–9, 110–11, 115, 121–57, 162, 181–218, 220–2; types 108–9, 146–7, 183; wasting assets 183, 200
associates 126–9, 131, 139, 143, 214
audit exemptions 57
auditors 48, 57, 100–1
authorised share capital 91–4
authority to borrow 102–3
authority to issue shares 91–6

bad debts 109–10, 111–12, 115
balance sheets 57, 90, 94–5, 98–9, 108–15, 118–19
bank accounts 47–8
bankruptcy 4, 7, 22, 24, 33, 65, 70–1, 75, 95, 121–32, 134, 138–9, 140–3
bankruptcy orders 124–5, 130, 139–40, 142–3
bankruptcy restriction orders (BROs) 124–5, 130, 140
bankruptcy restriction undertakings (BRUs) 130, 140
bankrupt's property 123–4, 125–6, 138–9
base/nominal/par values of shares 94–5, 101–2, 113
basic gains (BGs) 182, 184–7, 190–4, 200, 201–2, 204–5
basic rate taxpayers (BRTs) 162–70, 176–80, 187–8, 204
basis of charge to CGT 181–7
basis of charge to CT 206–8
basis of charge to IT 161–2, 172–3, 175–6
best interests and success of the company, directors 67–8, 99
bipartite arrangements 30
blind person's allowance 167
board of directors 45
board meetings (BMs) 38–9, 41, 47–62, 66–9, 71–2, 77, 81–7, 96, 103
board resolutions (BRs) 41, 48–9, 50–62, 66–9, 77, 83, 85–7, 91–2, 102–3
'born' aspects, limited companies 8, 47, 58
breaches of director's duties 67–9, 71, 76–7, 81, 86, 87–8
bribery and benefits from third parties to directors 69
Bushell v Faith clauses xvi, 76, 82, 84
business accounts 26–7, 48, 56–7, 79, 89–90, 94–8, 108–20, 144–59, 167, 172–7, 213–15
business asset disposal relief (entrepreneurs' relief) (BADR) 182, 188–90, 193–7, 200–2, 204–5
business assets, taxation 182, 188–90, 192, 193–7, 198–9, 200–2, 204–5, 211, 217–18
business medium types xvi, 1–17, 39
business names 20–2, 40–1, 47–8, 56, 61
business organisations, characteristics viii, 1–2, 12–14
business property relief (BPR) 181–2, 198–201, 204–5
buyback of shares 89–90, 99–102, 115, 117–18, 119, 188, 197, 209
buyback of shares from capital 99–102, 115, 119
buyback of shares from profits 99–102, 115, 117–18, 119, 209

cap on reliefs, trading losses 150–2
capital, definition 23, 108–9, 113–15
capital account for partnerships 23, 25–6, 113, 116
capital allowances 144–5, 146–52, 155–9, 209–18
capital expenditure 145–7, 158–9, 197
capital gains 7, 10, 12, 162, 181–205, 207–17, 219–21
capital gains tax (CGT) 7, 10, 12, 181–205, 208–21
capital improvements, capital gains tax (CGT) 183–4, 185, 203, 204–5, 210–11
capital reserves 114–16
carry-across/-back one year relief/ trade loss relief against general income (CA/CB) 150–1, 152–3, 155, 157, 158–9, 211–13, 217, 219–21
carry-forward relief (CF) 150, 151, 152–3, 155, 157, 158–9, 211–13, 217, 219–21
carry-forward relief on incorporation of business (CFIB) 150–1, 152–3, 155, 188, 196–7

central/public registers held at Companies House 46, 58, 61–2, 78
Certificate of Incorporation (COI) 10, 47, 58, 59, 62
certificates, shares 48, 97
CH01/CH02/CH03/CH04 forms 71, 77
chairperson, limited companies 47–8, 50, 53–4, 56, 61, 62
chargeable assets 181–3, 200–1
chargeable gains (CGs) 182–3, 184–5, 188–95, 200–1, 204, 208–21
chargeable persons/entities 160–1, 175, 178–9, 181–2, 200–1, 204
chargeable receipts 144–52, 155, 157–8, 209–18
charges 10, 12, 47, 90, 103–7, 115–20, 134–45
child benefit IT exemption 165
CIGA 2020 restructuring plans 138
civil litigation 3
civil partners 125–7, 129–30, 143, 185
classes of shares 54–5, 78, 91–3, 104, 119
clawback of bankruptcy assets 121
close companies 166, 207, 213–21
closing stock/work in progress 109–10, 115
closing year rule (CYR) 179
commencement date of partnership 21
companies, definition 1–2, 7–11, 12–13, 38–58, 61–2, 78
Companies House 2–3, 8–11, 16–17, 36–48, 54–62, 66, 71–2, 76–8, 90–2, 95, 105–7, 115–18
company seals 47–8
company secretaries 44–5, 46, 58, 61, 63–4, 77, 83–4
company voluntary arrangements (CVAs) 121, 132, 136, 138–40
competing businesses ('secret profit') 26–7
compulsory liquidation 132–3, 140
computer code, company names 40–1
confirmation statements (CS01 form) 57, 97
conflicts of interest 50–2, 56, 60–1, 62, 68–9, 72, 84–8, 96, 103
connected persons 73–4, 84, 87, 134–5, 184–5, 200, 209–10
consent to act statement 46
constructive notice to third parties 30–1, 33, 35, 37
contract law 29, 62, 107
corporate insolvency 17, 25, 71, 76, 79–81, 103, 106, 121–5, 132–9, 142–3
corporation tax (CT) 10, 48, 107, 114–15, 144, 178, 182, 206–21
corporation tax financial year (CTFY) (1 April to 31 March) 206, 207–8, 217–18, 220–1
costs/expenses 5, 7, 10–14, 48, 108–15, 129, 144–52, 155, 158–9, 215–17
county court, insolvency 124, 133, 136
creditors 25, 29–33, 36–7, 101, 105, 107, 121–43
creditor's petition 107, 123–4, 128–9, 133, 139, 140, 143
creditors' voluntary liquidation (CVL) 132–3, 140
criminal offences 40, 51, 57, 69–71, 76–8, 100, 174–5
crystallisation 104–5, 115, 117, 118–19
CS01 form 57
current accounts for partnerships 113, 116
current assets 108–10, 118, 119, 146
current liabilities 108–9, 110, 118, 119
current year basis (CYB) 161, 179

damages for personal injuries or death 165
de facto directors 64–5, 84
death 19, 22–4, 33, 95, 161, 175, 178, 181–2, 183, 187, 198–200, 203–5
debentures 10, 89–90, 103, 104–7, 115, 116, 118, 213–14, 217–21

debt (loan) finance 89–91, 102–7, 109–10, 115–20
debt relief orders (DROs) 121, 131, 140
debt respite scheme (DRS) 132
debtor's bankruptcy application 123–5, 133, 139
decision-making division between directors/members 48–9, 54–6, 58, 61, 63–4, 81–3
declaration of dividends 98–9
declarations of personal interest (DOIs) 51, 56, 60–1, 62, 69, 81–3, 85, 88, 96, 103
deductible expenses 144–52, 154–9, 209–18, 219, 220–1
deed of priority 105
deed of release 22, 30, 32, 33, 35, 37
default provisions in partnerships 6–7, 11, 18–19, 20, 21, 32–3, 173
deferral relief (DR) 182, 188, 190, 195–6, 200, 204
delegation of directors' powers 50, 71
depreciation 109–10, 111, 115, 147, 183
derivative actions 69, 81, 86, 88
directors 2–3, 8–9, 13, 16, 38–9, 42–52, 58, 61–88, 91–2, 97–8, 102–3, 113–14, 133, 137–8, 151, 213–21; definition 64; first directors 39, 44–9, 58, 61, 65–6, 83; loans 75, 82, 213–15; powers 9, 48–52, 58, 63–4, 66–9, 71, 83, 91–2, 97–8, 102–3, 133, 137–8; removal 45, 63–4, 75–7, 80, 82–3, 87–8, 166; remuneration 65–6, 72, 75–6, 81, 113–14, 151, 213, 217–21
directors' service (employment) contracts 47–8, 51, 64, 65–6, 72, 75–6, 79, 82, 83, 85, 87–8
discharge, bankruptcy 123, 130–1, 139
disclaiming onerous property 125–6, 139
disclosure requirements 5, 7, 10–11, 12, 20–1, 38–9, 63–4, 71–2, 144–5
dishonesty/deception, company names 40
disposal values 181–3, 184–97, 200–5, 209–10
dispute resolution 3, 123
disqualification of directors 65, 76–7, 83, 130
dissolution of partnerships 19, 22, 24–6, 34, 36–7, 121, 186–7
distributable profits 99–102, 114–15, 117–18, 119, 206–7, 209, 213–18
distributions, corporation tax (CT) 206–7, 209, 213–21
dividend allowance (DA) 169–71, 176, 179–80
dividends 45, 78–83, 86, 89–90, 95–9, 107, 114–15, 161–71, 176–80, 207, 213–21
double-entry accounting system 108
doubtful debts 109–10, 111–12, 115
drawings 23, 36, 109, 113, 115
due diligence 103, 115
duration of partnerships 22, 26, 33, 36
duty of good faith, partnerships 26–7

earnings, income tax (IT) 162, 166
Economic Crime and Corporate Transparency Act 2023 (ECCTA) 38, 41–6, 57, 63, 66, 71, 76–8, 89, 95
email addresses 42, 53
employees 23, 47–8, 66, 112–13, 125, 130, 143, 151, 160–2, 165–80, 219–21
Enterprise Investment Scheme (EIS) 188, 195–6, 200
equity finance 89–102, 107, 114–15, 117–20
ex-partner restrictive covenants 26
executive directors 65–6, 72, 83–4, 113–14, 151, 166
exemptions 57, 125, 142, 153–60, 165, 180–5, 187–97, 200–5, 210–11
existing partnership debt liabilities 29–33, 35, 37

expenses 5, 7, 10–14, 48, 108–15, 129, 144–52, 154–9, 215–17
expulsion of a partner 22, 25, 33, 34, 37
extortionate credit transactions 125–6, 129, 135, 140
extraordinary general meetings ((E) GMs) 45, 52–3, 58

fees 40, 56, 57, 65, 106, 151, 217–18
fiduciary duties 26–7, 51, 63–4, 65–6, 67–9, 71, 83, 99–101
filing requirements 5, 7–12, 38–48, 53–64, 66, 71–2, 76–7, 81–3, 91–6, 114
financial reports 57, 79, 114
financing businesses 5, 10, 12–13, 14, 16–17, 89–107, 114–20
first directors 39, 44–9, 58, 61, 65–6, 83
first members 44–7, 78
first year allowance 147–9, 155, 159
five-step taxation calculation process 163–71, 175, 208–12
First-Tier Tribunal income tax appeals 174
fixed assets 108–9, 146–7
fixed charges 10–12, 90, 103, 104–6, 115–17, 118–19, 135–6, 138–9, 141–2
floating charges 10–12, 17, 90, 103, 104–5, 115–17, 118–19, 134–7
formal partnership agreements 6, 11, 18–19, 20, 21–7, 32–3, 36–7, 173, 186
formation, limited companies 7, 8–10, 12, 16, 38–48, 57–8, 61–2, 65–6, 77, 83–4, 91, 130, 188; limited liability partnerships (LLPs) 11–12; partnerships 6–7, 11, 18–26, 32–3, 36–7; sole traders 5, 12
former partner liabilities 18, 26, 29–33, 35–7
fraud 8, 70–1, 76–7, 83–4, 88, 125–6, 129, 135, 140
FRS102 compliance, accounts 114
full expensing (FE) 148–9, 155
full IT calculation example 170–1
fully-paid shares 10, 11, 15, 17, 94–5, 100, 101–2
future partnership debt liabilities 30–1, 32–3, 35, 37

general anti-abuse rule (GAAR) 175–6, 178, 180, 198, 217
general meetings (GMs) 38–9, 45, 48–9, 52–60, 61–2, 66, 69–76, 79–87, 91–2, 95–101
gifts 183, 184, 189, 192, 200
going-concern sales 26, 136, 137–8, 196
goodwill value 26, 209–11
gross income, income tax (IT) 165–71, 179
group companies 114, 216–18
guarantees 8, 9, 10, 41, 45, 70, 78, 83, 105–6

higher rate taxpayers (HRTs) 161, 162–70, 176–80, 187–94, 201–5
HMRC 5, 7, 47–8, 61, 140, 143, 151, 153, 158, 173–5, 198, 215, 217–18
hold-over relief (HOR) 182, 188, 190, 192–3, 200, 204
holding out, partnerships 31–3
homes 122, 125, 142–3, 183

identity verification 44
IN01 form 40–6, 57, 58, 61, 65, 77
inability to pay, insolvency 122–7, 132–9, 142
income 23–6, 33–7, 108–15, 144–55, 160–2, 167–80, 183, 204–22; recurring aspects 108, 146, 162, 175, 179, 183; types 145, 160–2, 167–71, 175
income expenditure 145–7, 158–9
income payment agreements, bankruptcy 125
income profits, corporation tax (CT) 207–17, 219–21
income tax (IT) 7, 10, 12, 47, 144–5, 160–80, 187–8, 208–11

income tax year (6 April to 5 April) 161, 162, 175, 179, 183
incorporate/form a new business ix, 1–17, 39–40, 200
incorporated businesses, definition 1–14, 16, 39–40, 65–6, 89–91, 196–7, 200, *see also* limited companies
indemnity uses, partnerships 29, 30, 32, 33, 37
independent judgement, directors 68
indexation allowance 210–11, 217–19
individual (personal) insolvency 121–32, 134, 135, 139, 142–3
individual savings accounts (ISAs) 165
individual voluntary arrangements (IVAs) 121, 131, 140
individuals, capital gains tax (CGT) 181–2, 184–6, 189–90, 200; income tax (IT) 160–71, 175–6
inflation rates 210
inheritance tax (IHT) 181–2, 183, 198–200, 203, 205
input tax, VAT 145, 153–4, 157–9
insolvency, definition 4–5, 104, 121–32, 135–6, 139, 142–3
insurance 7, 47–8
intellectual property 209–11
interest payments 23, 27, 34–5, 37, 108–9, 112–13, 166, 175
interest received 145, 161, 165–6, 167–8, 170–1, 175, 176–7
International Accounting Standards Board 114
investigating past transactions, insolvency 122, 125–6, 132–5, 139
investment properties 183–4, 192
investors' relief (IR) 188, 196–7, 200
invoices, VAT 144–5, 154
issues of shares 43, 54–5, 58, 61–2, 67, 78, 89–102, 114–15, 117–20
IVA Protocol 131
joint creditors' petition 124
joint and several liabilities of partners 29–30
judgment debt 123, 132–3, 139
just and equitable grounds, winding-up 81

Land Registry 106
lawful purpose statement 46
leaving a partnership 18–19, 24–6, 29–33, 35, 37, 173, 175, 187
legal identity 3, 4
legal personality ix, xvi, 2, 3–4, 7–14, 38, 39, 79, 113–14
legal title, land 103–4, 115, 125, 142
liabilities 7, 12–13, 18–33, 35–7, 108–9, 115, 160, 164, 170–5, 177–8
lifetime transfers, taxation 199
limited by guarantee 8, 9, 10, 41, 45
limited by shares 8, 9, 10–11, 15, 17, 41, 43
limited companies 1–3, 5, 7–11, 12–13, 14, 16–17, 38–58, 61–6, 78, 89–120, 189–90; advantages/disadvantages 5, 7, 8, 9–11, 12–13, 14, 16–17; decision-making division between directors/members 48–9, 55–6, 58, 61, 63–4, 81–3; formation and constitution 7, 8–10, 12, 16, 38–48, 57–8, 61–6, 77, 83–4, 91, 130, 151, 188; termination 17, 25, 71, 76, 79–81, 103, 106, 107, 121–5, 132–9, 142–3; types 7–14, 41
limited liability ix, xvi, 1–2, 7, 9–10, 12–14, 15, 16, 17
limited liability partnerships (LLPs) 1–3, 6, 7, 11–14, 17, 20, 104–7, 118
liquidated and unsecured sums 122–3, 139
liquidation 121–2, 132–9
listed public companies 8, 11, 13, 198
LLIN01 form 11–12
loans 27, 75, 82, 102–9, 115–18, 166, 170–1, 176–7, 179, 207, 213–21

London Gazette 31, 101
longer-term liabilities 109, 119
LPA (Law of Property Act 1925)
receivers 136, 138–40

main CT rate 208
maintenance of capital 89–90, 98–102, 114–16
majority shareholders 79–80, 84
management 3–9, 11–12, 16, 24–7, 34, 37–9, 57–8, 61–4, 71–3, 130, 137–8
marginal CT rate 208
marriage allowance 167
meetings of limited companies 38–9, 41–62, 65, 66, 69–76, 79–87, 91–2, 95–101, 103
members of companies 7–11, 38–58, 61–4, 69, 75–84, 91–6, 107, 117–20, 122, 132–42, 213–21
members' voluntary liquidation (MVL) 122, 132–3, 140, 142–3
memorandum of association 40, 46–7, 57–8, 91–2, 102–3
minimum capital requirements 11
minority shareholders 64, 69, 78–80, 84, 87–8, 98
minutes of meetings 41, 47, 52, 54, 56, 62, 79, 81–3, 96
misfeasance, directors 70, 71, 83–4
model articles (MAs) 39, 42–3, 47–57, 58, 61–2, 65–88, 91–7
mortgages 103–5, 115
MR01/MR04 forms 106–7

names of businesses 20–1, 40–1, 47–8, 54–5, 56, 58, 61–2
National Insurance 47–8
national savings certificates 165
natural (human) person requirements, directors 44, 65
nature of partnership business 21–2, 24, 35, 37
negative pledge clauses 105, 115, 118
negligence claims, insurance 7
net assets 87, 102, 108–9, 110, 117–18, 119
net current assets 108–9, 117–18, 119
net income 163, 165–6, 176
net profits 98, 108
new partner admissions 21, 161, 173, 175, 187
new partner liabilities 21, 29–33, 161, 173, 175, 187
non-cash benefits, income tax (IT) 166
non-executive directors 65–6, 84, 151
non-savings/non-dividend income (NSNDI) 163–71, 176, 177, 179–80
notice/calling requirements for meetings 39, 50, 53–5, 60, 61–2, 75–6, 80–1, 82–3, 84
novation agreements 30, 32, 33, 35, 37

objects of the limited company 47
onerous property 125–6, 139
opening stock/work in progress 109–10, 115
opening year rule (OYR) 161, 179
order of distribution 121–2, 123, 127, 129–30, 132, 135–6, 142–3
orders of payment under the IA 139
ordinary resolutions (ORs) 39, 48–58, 61, 66, 69, 72–6, 80–7, 91–9, 102, 117–20
ordinary shares 54–5, 78–9, 94, 189–90, 193–6, 215–16
output tax 145, 153–4
overdrafts 103–4, 115
overlap profits 161
owners, managers 3–9, 11–12, 16, 38–9, 58, 63–4

paid-up shares 11
participators, corporation tax (CT) 214–16, 217–18
partly paid shares 2, 9, 11, 17, 94–5
partnership agreements 6, 11, 18–19, 20, 21–7, 32–3, 36–7, 172–3, 186

partnership at will 19, 22, 33, 36
partnerships xvi, 1–3, 6–37, 90, 102, 112–13, 160–80, 181–2, 186–7, 199–205
passing off action in tort law 41
past transactions, insolvency 122, 125–6, 132–5, 138–9
PAYE 47–8, 165–6, 170–1
payments of tax 154–5, 173–4, 178–80, 198, 206, 216–17
penalties, taxation 155, 174, 175, 178–80
pensions 162, 165
people with significant control (PSC) 38–9, 44–6, 58, 95–6, 101, 127, 198, 209, 214–18, 220
personal allowances (PAs) 162, 163, 166–9, 176–7, 179–80, 190
personal liabilities of directors 51, 63–4, 70–1, 83, 86, 87–8, 105, 133
personal representatives on death (PRs) 95, 161, 175, 178, 182, 187, 198–200, 203–5
personal savings allowance (PSA) 168–9, 170–1, 176, 179
persons connected to directors 73–4, 84, 87, 134–5
place of partnership business 21–2, 26
plant and machinery 145, 146–9, 155, 156, 158–9, 183, 198
poll votes 53, 80
pooling of assets 147–9, 155, 156, 158–9
post-incorporation steps/ considerations, limited companies 39, 42, 47–8, 58
postponed creditors 129–30
pre-emption rights 90, 91, 92–6, 114–15, 117–19
pre-pack (pre-packaged) administration 137–8, 140
preferences, insolvency 125–6, 127–9, 135, 140, 142–3
preferential creditors 122, 129–30, 136, 140, 142–3
preferential debts 122, 129–30, 136, 140, 142–3
preferential shares 78, 94
prepayments 109–10, 115
previously paid/deducted IT at source 164, 170, 173–4
prices, shares 94–5
principal private residence exemption (PPRE), capital gains tax (CGT) 183, 204
priority of security 89, 105, 124, 129–30, 135–6, 142–3
private limited companies 1–3, 8–17, 38–62, 63–88, 91–119
privity of contract 29, 62
profit and loss accounts 90, 108–15, 118–19, 145–6, 172–80
profits 6–7, 10, 12, 19, 23–7, 33–7, 78–90, 98–102, 108, 113–19, 144–89, 196, 202–21; calculation method 144–52, 155–6, 158–9, 172–6, 208–11
property 24, 123–6, 138–9, 145, 162, 165–7, 181–2, 183, 198–200, 203–5
proxy notice, general meetings (GMs) 53, 79
public limited companies (plcs) 1–2, 8, 10–13, 40–1, 44, 77, 196–8

qualifying business assets (QBAs) 193–4, 200
qualifying business disposals (QBDs) 182, 189–91, 200
qualifying floating charge (QFC) 136–7, 140
qualifying loans 166, 170–1, 176–7, 179, 207, 214–17, 219, 220–1
qualifying shares 182, 189, 191, 193–5, 196, 200, 204
quorum at meetings 50, 51, 53–4, 58, 61, 62, 65, 72, 103

rates of tax 151–2, 158–9, 162–78, 180, 187–8, 196, 202–5, 207–13

reasonable care/skill/diligence duty of directors 68, 71, 76–7
receivers 107, 124–5, 133, 136–9
record-keeping requirements 38–9, 44–6, 47, 52, 62–4, 77, 144–5, 154–5, 174
recurring aspects of income 108, 146, 162, 175, 179, 183
registered number, limited companies 71–2
registered office address, limited companies 41–2, 47, 56, 71–2
registers 41–6, 66, 71–2, 76–9, 81–3, 91–7, 101, 105–6
registration requirements 40–7, 65–6, 78–9, 90, 105–6, 115–18, 144–5, 153–7, 158–9
remuneration of directors 65–6, 72, 75–6, 81, 113–14, 151, 213, 217–21
rent received, income tax (IT) 145, 162, 165–6, 175
reserves, limited companies 98–9, 114–16
restrictive covenants 26
retained profits 113–14, 213–14
retirement/resignation 22, 24, 30–2, 33, 34, 37, 75, 76, 166
revenue reserves 114, 115, 116
revolving credit facilities 103–4, 115
ring fencing for unsecured creditors 136
roll-over relief on incorporation of a business (RORIB) 182, 188, 196–7, 200, 204, 217
roll-over relief on replacement of qualifying business assets (ROR) 188, 193–6, 200, 204, 211, 217–18

salaries 23, 66, 112–13, 125, 146, 151, 160–2, 166–80
sale of goods and services 146, 153
savings 163–71, 176
secret profits 26–7, 67–8
security 89–90, 91, 102–7, 115, 124–5, 129–30, 133–4, 136–7, 142–3
self-assessment scheme 173–4, 198, 216
separate legal personality ix, xvi, 2, 3–4, 7–14, 38, 39, 79, 113–14
SH01/SH03/SH06 forms 95, 96, 100–1
shadow directors 64–5, 84
share capital account 113–16
share premiums 94–5, 113–16
shareholders 2, 8–17, 38–40, 42–58, 61–88, 107, 161–71, 176, 179, 183, 189–98, 213–21
shares 2, 9–17, 44–8, 54–5, 73, 78–84, 89–107, 113–19, 161–2, 182–3, 189–95, 200, 213–16
shelf companies 39–40, 58
'sleeping partners' 24
slices of income, income tax (IT) 164–5, 167–71
small companies 44, 57, 58
small profits CT rate 208
sole practitioners 4, 180–2
sole traders 1–8, 12–17, 90, 160–2, 172–3, 175–6, 179–86, 189–90, 194–5, 199–200, 204
special notice 75–6, 83, 84
special resolutions (SRs) 41–9, 52–60, 61–2, 71, 92–7, 101–2, 117–20, 133–4
spouses 125–7, 129–30, 142–3, 185, 188, 197, 214
stamp duty 82, 97
start-up loss relief/early trade losses relief (SULR) 150, 152–3, 155, 157, 158–9
starting new businesses 1–17, 39–40, 150, 155, 162, 176–7
statement of capital and initial shareholdings 44–5
statement of solvency (SOS) 100
stationery requirements 20–1, 31, 47, 56, 71–2
statutory books 42, 47, 54, 58, 61–2, 71–2, 76–8, 81–3, 105–6

statutory demand for payment 122–3, 132–3, 139
statutory duties of directors 51, 63–4, 65–6, 67–9, 76–7, 80–1, 83–8, 91–2, 99–101
sterling 183, 200
stock exchanges 8, 11
stock transfer forms (STFs) 97
student loans, bankruptcy 130
subscribers 10, 45–7, 78
substantial property transactions (SPTs) 62, 64, 69, 72, 73–4, 82–4, 87, 94, 96

Table A basis, articles of association 43
tailor-made companies 39–48
tax avoidance 160–1, 174–5, 176, 178, 180, 198, 206, 217
tax evasion 174–5, 176
tax reliefs 144–58, 160–1, 163–78, 179–83, 187–99, 200–5, 208–20
tax returns 145, 154–5, 173–4, 176, 217
tax year (6 April to 5 April) 161, 162, 172–3, 175, 179, 183
taxable income 161, 163–80, 187–8
taxable persons 145, 153–5
taxable supplies 145, 153–5, 158–9
taxation 5, 7, 10–12, 47, 82, 107, 114–15, 144–59, 160–80, 181–205, 206–21, *see also* capital gains tax; corporation tax; income tax; inheritance tax; VAT
terminal carry-back relief for trading losses 211–13, 217, 219, 220–1
terminal loss relief (TLR) 150, 151–3, 155, 157, 158, 211–13, 217, 219, 220–1
termination 9, 15, 17, 22, 24–6, 34, 36–7, 72, 75–7, 107, 121–43, *see also* bankruptcy; dissolution; insolvency; liquidation; winding-up
TM01/TM02 forms 76–7, 82, 83
total income 163–78, 179
trademarks 41
trading losses 25, 144–5, 149–52, 155, 157, 158, 172–5, 211–21
trading profits 6–7, 10–12, 19, 23–7, 33–7, 108, 144–55, 158–9, 160–80, 206–21; calculation method 144–52, 155–6, 158–9, 172–6, 208–11
trading/business names 20–2, 41, 47–8, 56, 61
transactions, at an undervalue 122, 125–9, 135, 139, 143, 184, 192, 209; defrauding creditors 125–6, 129, 135, 140
transfers of shares 43, 78–9, 89–90, 95–7, 107, 114–15
transmission of shares 95–7, 115
trial balance 108, 109
trustee in bankruptcy (TIB) 95, 123–32, 139, 142–3
trustees 95, 123–32, 139, 142–3, 161, 175, 178, 182, 187, 200, 204
trusts 26, 95, 97–8, 123–32, 139, 142–3, 161, 175, 178, 182, 187, 200

unanimous-decision scenarios, directors 52, 71
undervalue transactions 122, 125–9, 135, 139, 143, 184, 192, 209
unfairly prejudicial conduct court petition 80–1, 86, 88, 98–9
unincorporated businesses, definition 1–7, 12–13, 16, 17, 19–20, 89–91, 108–9, 172, 211, *see also* partnerships; sole traders; unlimited liability
unlimited liability 1–2, 4, 13, 15, 16, 17, 33
unlisted public companies 1–2, 8, 13–14, 196–9
unsecured creditors 103, 106, 122–5, 129–30, 135–6, 138–9, 141, 142–3

VAT 5, 7, 47–8, 144–5, 153–6, 157–9, 186
verification of identity 44

votes 24–5, 34–7, 45–62, 68–9, 73–83, 92–8, 100–3, 189–90, 192, 198, 214

Wales, income tax (IT) 172
wasting assets 183, 200
winding-up 17, 25, 71, 76, 79, 81, 103, 107, 121–2, 125, 132–9, 140–3
work in progress 109–10, 115
writing-down capital allowance (WDA) 147–9, 155, 159
written resolutions 54, 76, 79–80, 99–100
wrongful trading 70–1, 77, 83–4, 86, 88

zero-rated supplies, VAT 154, 159